The Complete Book of
HERBS
and Herb Growing

D1511230

The Complete Book of
HERBS
and Herb Growing

Roy Genders

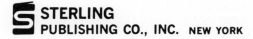

STERLING PUBLISHING CO., INC. NEW YORK

DEDICATED
to the memory of
Stephen Willoughby
of Arlington, Texas, USA
1953–1977

First published in the United States of America in 1980 by
Sterling Publishing Co., Inc., Two Park Avenue, New York,
N.Y. 10016

First published in Great Britain in 1980 by Ward Lock
Limited, London, a Pentos Company

© Roy Genders 1980

Reprinted 1982, 1984

Line drawings by Rosemary Wise

ISBN 0-8069-3928-1 Trade
      0-8069-3929-X Library
      0-8069-3930-3 Paper

Text filmset in Monophoto Plantin Light
by Asco Trade Typesetting Ltd, Hong Kong.

Printed and bound in Hong Kong
by Everbest Printing Co. Ltd.

Contents

CONTENTS

PART II Herbs A–Z: their culture and uses 77

Preface

During the last hundred years, much of the art of using herbs in cooking, as medicine or for cosmetics has been lost, especially in the industrialized societies. Few people in the crowded cities had space to grow anything and gardens were a luxury to be enjoyed by few. In the country, the knowledge lingered longer, but with the advent of refrigeration, which meant that the strong taste of old meat no longer had to be disguised, of full time work for women outside the home and the advent of readily prepared, 'packaged' food, not to mention medicines and beauty preparations, the growing of herbs declined rapidly.

Today, whether we will admit it or not, most people have far more leisure and few do not have a small patch of ground, or a window sill or balcony large enough for a pot or two of herbs. These facts, coupled with the beginnings of a revolt against standardized foods and perhaps also a mistrust of the 'side effects' of some of today's medicines, herbs have taken on a new popularity.

The culinary uses of herbs are endless and they can be used both dried and fresh all the year round. When lettuce is in short supply and expensive, lamb's lettuce, blanched dandelion leaves and salad burnet may be included in salads instead, and will provide essential vitamins. For simple medicinal remedies and aids to beauty there are many herbs to use, as there are to make teas to enjoy ice-cold in summer and hot in winter. Herbs are multi-purpose plants, for all occasions and for all seasons. They provide skin tonics and relaxing baths, hair restorers and blood purifiers. Sauces and soups can be improved with the delicious flavour of herbs, and meats can be improved out of all recognition. Sweet bags and scented waters, pomanders and pot-pourris can be made from them to use about the home, and to place amongst clothes and linen. What is more, their ease of culture and beauty of form are a bonus in the garden. The colour and variation in their leaves is enormous, from the deep metallic blue of rue, to the silver-grey of lavender and the artemisias, and the sombre green of rosemary and bay. Most herbs are plants of considerable hardiness, although many are natives of the warm climate of the Mediterranean regions, and they grow best in a well-drained sandy soil, over chalk or limestone, where few other plants grow well. They are also able to survive long periods during the heat of summer without artificial watering and so they are among the most labour-saving of plants. They are the epitome of the cottage garden and a more leisurely age, and in addition to their beauty and many uses one may obtain much enjoyment from a walk among them, pressing the leaves as one passes, and inhaling the many delicious scents of pine and eucalyptus, lemon and mint, apple and pine-apple and others too subtle to describe. The plants are also an attraction for bees and butterflies when in bloom; rosemary in spring when there are few other flowers to attract bees; lavender in late summer to satisfy the last of the butterflies.

The dictionary defines the word 'herb' as 'a plant with leaves that are used for seasoning, medicine and food'. To this could be added 'for beauty and pleasure'. They are, in fact, the most useful plants of the garden and they are as valuable today as they were in mediaeval times although we are only just beginning to appreciate them again.

R. G.

Acknowledgements

The publishers gratefully acknowledge the following persons and agencies for granting permission for reproduction of the colour photographs:

A–Z Collection (pp. 70 (lower), 105, 106, 123 (top), 124, 142 (lower), 159 (both), and 160); Pat Brindley (p. 51); Eric Crichton (pp. 87, 123 (lower), 141 (both)); Harry Smith Horticultural Photographic Collection (pp. 33, 34, 52 (both), 69, 70 (top), 87 (lower), 88, 106 (lower), 142 (top).

All line drawings are by Rosemary Wise. All drawings of herb plants were drawn from life. The drawing on p. 56 is after the illustration on p. 35, *Herbs*, J. V. Crockett and O. Tanner, Time-Life Books, 1977.

PART I

General horticulture and uses

1
An introduction to herbs

A great many of the herbs used in the western world today have their origins in the countries around the Mediterranean. There they were tried and tested by the ancient civilizations and then taken further afield by the all-conquering Romans. The two most popular of herbs, lavender and rosemary, abound along the shores of the Mediterranean and were made into bunches to bring indoors to mask unpleasant smells, while the housewives of the Roman world no doubt hung their washing upon the bushes to dry as the housewives of southern Italy do to this day. Every part of a lavender bush can be made use of, even the stems which, when burnt over a low fire, fill the room with an incense-like scent.

To this knowledge brought from the south was added the lore of the wise woman or witch of the northern countries of Europe, and by the Middle Ages, herbalism in all its senses was a vital part of life. In the ninth century, St. Boniface, an English monk travelling in continental Europe, received word asking him to send back to England herbs to make simples that no longer grew there, although their value for medicinal purposes had been known from early writings. In a book of the tenth century there is mention of a number of herbal simples sent north to Britain by the Patriarch of Jerusalem. In this book there is also a prescription for relieving sunburn by boiling ivy twigs in butter, while for tired eyes, there are several made from chamomile and wild lettuce, and the reader is advised upon rising to 'look into cold water', which is sound advice, much to be recommended.

The monasteries and their use of herbs

It was the monasteries however that were probably the first to make greater use of medicinal and culinary herbs. Monastic foundations were set up throughout Europe in the centuries following the fall of the Roman Empire. The monks became widely skilled in their use of herbs, using them to cure ailments and, before the advent of the medical profession, were the only practising 'doctors', though herbalist would be a more suitable word. People went to them to cure all manner of illnesses and injuries incurred during their daily life. Days when a man was unable to work meant days with no food coming in and for some, the real fear of starvation.

Every monastery had its herbarium which was under the care of the sacristan who administered potions to the monks. They in turn administered to the people of the surrounding countryside who came to seek their help. Only the monks seemed to have any real knowledge of herbs and their properties, for some plants are dangerous if not used properly and wisely. Even so it was sometimes a case of trial and error. Herbs were also grown near most churches to provide health giving recipes for the village community, and to provide the plants for use on the church floors where they counteracted the often unpleasant smells of those who attended the church services, for washing was then considered less important than now and dry cleaning was unknown!

The monks with their classical upbringing and love of nature imparted their knowledge of plants to the population, and many people began to understand the reason for the medicinal and culinary uses of a large number of the plants which grew about the countryside. Those with specialized knowledge set up as herbalists and would walk about the countryside gathering all those plants that had a use, selling them to those who had not the same knowledge. They were known as Green men because they carried their wares about with them and today their name is perpetuated on the signs of village inns (the Green Man) where they would call and sell their wares.

One of the first important books on the growing and use of herbs appeared towards the end of the 13th century. It was written by a Franciscan monk, Bartholomaeus Anglicus, who was probably a son of one of the Earls of Suffolk in England, but who received his education at the University of Paris. This work which was written in French, was made up of seventeen volumes of accurate descriptions of flowers and trees, while one volume is devoted entirely to herbs and their properties. By this date large quantities of herbs were being imported into northern Europe from the Mediterranean countries where they grew wild. Accounts of the monasteries during the 14th and 15th centuries give some idea of the importance of herbs both in the diet of the population and for medicine. The most important ones were also being grown wherever the climate permitted for in 1427 the accounts of the abbey of Norwich in eastern England record payments for 'medicines of the gardener' and to the 'cellerer' including one for 'knives for cutting herbs', which would be needed for cutting the hard stems of the shrubby herbs such as rosemary and lavender. There are also numerous items paid for herbs for strewing the floors of the abbey and monastic apartments.

In 1440 there appeared the first practical work on gardening in the English language. It was written by one John the Gardener and a copy of the original manuscript is in the library of Trinity College, Cambridge, England. By then flowers as well as herbs were often used to flavour food and drink. The flowers of the clove-scented pink, *Dianthus caryophyllus*, were placed in wine and ale to impart its unique clove perfume, the plant being known as sops-in-wine. Violet flowers were also used in spring salads and from cowslips a delicious drink was made. The red rose was also known as the apothecary's rose as their retention of their perfume for many years after drying caused it to be included in many apothecary's concoctions. From its petals a syrup called melrosette was made, the petals being simmered in honey.

Herbs in a more enlightened age

In the more settled days of the 16th century, herbs and flowers came to be planted more widely in cottage gardens and the distillation of them was one of the accepted chores in manor house and cottage alike. Herbs were by this time used not only for medicine and cooking but in personal hygiene, their perfumes being used to scent the ladies' toilet waters much as we use bath salts or lavender water today. Almost all large houses had their herb gardens as well as those still maintained by the monasteries. The herbs were usually planted in small beds surrounded by low hedges also made from herbs. These were kept in trim by regular clipping and remained green the year through. Gardeners were employed to tend these small gardens, one of their chief tasks being to keep the 'knots' clipped. These were the small beds which were surrounded and joined together by low, neat hedges in the form of lovers' knots and usually made of marjoram, germander, hyssop, thyme or cotton lavender, the best of all herbs for a knot garden hedge. Herbs too were in great demand for cooking, both to serve with the fish and to counteract the often strong smell of the meat as there was no method of keeping it fresh for any length of time. They were also used to strew over the stone floors, to make into toiletwaters and as aids to beauty, for by this time the standards of living were higher especially in the great courts of Europe. Large quantities of herbs were sold too in the streets and markets of the great cities and this rhyme from the Roxburgh Ballads gives an idea of what was being sold.

> Here's fine rosemary, sage and thyme,
> Come buy my ground ivy.
> Here's featherfew, gillyflowers and rue,
> Come buy my knotted marjoram too! . . .
> Let none despise the merry, merry cries
> Of famous London town.

Herbs have so many uses which accounts for the interest taken in them through the ages. Rosemary for example will impart its delicious aromatic flavour to roast meat if a few sprigs are stuck into the meat as it is placed into the oven. From the simmering of its leaves a valuable hair tonic is obtained and if a small amount of rosemary water is drunk upon rising, it will keep the breath sweet all day. Oil of rosemary is also an excellent embrocation when gently massaged into rheumatic joints, and 30 g (1 oz) infused in half a litre (1 pint) of boiling water makes an admirable tonic to firm the flesh and soothe tired nerves. Rosemary was Queen Anne of England's favourite perfume to fumigate a room and Mary Eales, her confectioner, gives a delighful recipe for this. It is to take three small spoonsful of dried and powdered rosemary and as much powdered sugar as will fill half a walnut. Place them in a perfume pan over hot embers and in a few minutes the room will be filled with a delicious scent. This was especially when the bedrooms of wayside inns, and of all large houses, had a low open fire burning in winter time and the bedclothes as indeed one's personal attire, would be permeated with the aroma.

Angelica seeds were also used for fumigating apartments while another practice of the time was to rub the juice of sweet cicely over oak panelling and oak furniture to which it would impart an excellent gloss and a delicious myrrh-like perfume. It was also used to rub church pews and choir stalls and gave the gloss and unmistakeable smell to the oak floors of large houses. The juice of lemon scented balm (*Melissa officinalis*) was also used in a similar way. Today we use atomisers of synthetic scents which are more expensive and the scent they leave is not nearly so long lasting.

Through the 16th, 17th and 18th centuries, perfumes for personal pleasure and cleanliness came to be more and more appreciated. Scented talcum powders, made from the root of the Florence iris (orris powder), and the dried leaves of rosemary and lavender were popular with dressmakers to rub on to clothes and gloves which the men as well as the ladies wore by day and in the evening. A special perfumed powder of Queen Elizabeth I of England was made up for her use from orris root, dried rose petals, calamus (sweet flag) and powdered cloves, a rich and lasting concoction.

The inventor of that perfume, Sir Hugh Platt, also had a recipe for scented water 'a little of which will sweeten a basin of fair water for your table'. In the homes of the wealthy, silver bowls were kept in bedrooms and parlours, filled with scented waters to sprinkle about the room and wash the hands and face. By now the rushes on the floor had given way in the homes of the wealthy to carpets imported from the east. Silver bowls filled with rose water were also provided at table, one for each person, for washing hands before and during meals as meats were usually eaten from a platter with the fingers.

Scented waters were also kept in small bottles of chased silver which were carried from room to room, suspended on the arm or shoulder on a silver chain or cord. The first scent bottles were recorded in the 16th century. They held waters made from lavender, rosemary, roses and rose-root (the root of *Sedum rosea*). Pomanders were also hung up in every room and were also carried around, usually suspended from the waist on a cord. The name pomander takes its name from a corruption of pomme d'ambre, an apple-sized ball of musk carried in this way. Because amber was always very expensive it was later replaced by a dried orange filled with herbs and stuck with cloves. The early pomanders were fashioned with as much care as a piece of jewellery while today, pretty glazed porcelain pomanders are available from perfume shops, filled with long-lasting, sweet-smelling herbs, and will perfume a large room if suspended from the ceiling.

A glazed porcelain pomander, such as can be bought today. Traditionally these were filled with musk and either hung up in a room or carried around, suspended from the waist on a cord.

By the early 19th century, pomanders were being replaced in the fashionable world by vinaigrettes, small flat boxes of silver which would fit in a pocket or small handbag. They were filled with a sponge soaked with an otto of lavender or rosemary. The lid was raised and the scent inhaled to clear the head in poorly ventilated rooms, or outdoors where there was no proper sanitation. Dried herbs were commonly placed in bowls and kept in the rooms of houses for they were still built with small windows for winter warmth and without a damp course, which gave rise to musty conditions. These mixtures of herbs and flowers, which had been carefully dried and prepared, were known as pot-pourris and are still to be found in old country houses with their low ceilings and stone floors. A well made pot-pourri will retain its fragrance for many years.

The uses of herbs were governed by the Doctrine of Signatures by which every plant (leaf or flower) was identified by a particular character, such as its colour or where it grew. Thus the marigold with its yellow flowers was thought to be a cure for jaundice, and those plants which grew in damp places were used to treat rheumatism. The theory was first formulated by the Italian inventor Della Porta who published his work, *Phytognomonica*, in 1588. For a hundred years after, physicians and herbalists (those who treated simple disorders by the use of herbs) used the Doctrine of Signatures in treating illnesses and disease until Culpeper, an English astrologer and herbalist, put forward the theory that the planets should be given priority in determining the remedy for any particular illness. His book, *The English Physician* (better known as *The Complete Herbal*), which first appeared in 1653 had, by the end of the century, gone into five editions and it remained the poor man's medical directory until the beginning of the 19th century. Much of his advice was sound and has been borne out by modern scientific research.

From the 19th century onwards, many thousands of families left overcrowded Europe for the new lands of America, S. Africa, New Zealand and Australia. They took their herb lore with them and roots or slips of the plants they considered essential to their health and well-being. With no doctors in their early settlements, this knowledge of herbs was to prove very important, though the plants they brought with them did not always thrive in their new homes. Conversely, some thrived too well and have since become weeds which have spread throughout the new lands. To the knowledge brought with them from the old world, the new settlers, particularly in North America, added information about local plants learned from the indigenous populations, these plants later making the return journey to Europe and being added to the herb gardens there. One of the first of these was *Monarda didyma*, bergamot, which is now widely grown.

Many of the suggestions put forward by the herbalists of old have in recent years been proved scientifically correct. Borage always had a reputation for stimulating the nerves; 'I borage always bring courage' went the old adage, and ploughmen, with a long day to get through, would place borage leaves with the cheese in their sandwiches and would be completely revived after lunch to continue working for the rest of the day. The plant is rich in potassium salts, the juice containing 30% nitrate of potash. Today, the leaves are used in Pimm's No. 1 and in cider drinks to give them a coolness in summer, but if the stems are also included, the saline mucilage has greater stimulating properties.

In the same way, Gerard, a British apothecary, who published his herbal in 1597 and who was a member of the Barber Surgeons' Company, thus having considerable knowledge of the properties of plants, advised including the little prostrate herb brooklime in salads. He said 'It is good against scurvy, being used in the manner of watercress'. Modern science has shown that both of these plants are rich in vitamin C, the antiscorbutic vitamin that supplies one of the body's most important needs.

Borneol acetate, present in pine needles (leaves), is also present in rosemary as an essential oil, and in lavender and thyme as eucalyptol. In lavender it combines with the bergamot-scented linalyl acetate, and with a trace of geraniol, to produce the familiar and pleasing perfume. It is geraniol, with its rose scent, which gives the bay leaf its delicious smell and adds to the enjoyable scent of many other plants of the herb garden.

In the leaves of herbs, the essential oil is stored in several ways. In St John's Wort it is stored as tiny capsules, visible as transparent dots when a leaf is held against the light; in rosemary as goblet-like cells, the scent being released by the slightest pressure or a light breeze, hence the smell of rosemary can be detected far out to sea when approaching the island of Corsica. Napoleon, a native of the island, used large quantities of Eau de Cologne, the chief constituent of which is rosemary, when on the battlefield.

The essential oils, the scented substances, are the waste products of the plant's metabolism; really a plant's excreta. Working in Paris during the last century, Professor Eugene Charabot described the development of the essential oil of lavender, showing how the slightly scented linalol of the unopened or unripe bud combines with acetic acid to produce the richly scented linalyl acetate of the mature inflorescence. This, by the evaporation of moisture in sunlight, becomes geraniol, an alcohol which is the principal substance of attar of roses.

Today, growers in Europe, America and in several African countries, such as in the Shire Valley of southern Malawi and in Tanzania, are producing herbs in ever increasing quantities for the manufacture of aerosol sprays and men's toilet preparations which now rival women's perfumes in popularity. Marjoram, lavender, rosemary and thyme are the most popular herbs, but others are being used in women's natural beauty preparations which are now enjoying an unprecedented popularity. As long ago as 1652 it was suggested that cucumber juice rubbed on the skin soothed and cleansed it. The healing powers of this juice have now been confirmed by modern beauticians and the juice is included in most face creams. Watercress was also recommended for spotty skins, the remedy being taken internally. It is rich in vitamin C as is the herb parsley which the American dietician, Mr Gaylord Hauser, extols above all other plants for its health giving properties.

The use of herbs declined in all industrialized countries from the eighteenth century onwards, but has happily never been completely forgotten, even in these days when their substitutes are so easily available from shops.

2
Making a herb garden

The use of herbs in the garden

Provided they can be given a position in the garden where they will receive plenty of sunlight, herbs can be grown almost anywhere. They associate admirably with old shrub roses and enjoy similar conditions—a sunny border and a well-drained soil. The shrubby herbs such as cotton lavender, rosemary and lad's love which are hardy in all but severe continental climates are perfectly at home in a shrub border, provided it does not become overcrowded and so deprive the plants of their share of sunlight. Herbs may also be grown in the herbaceous border where the unique shades of their foliage act as a striking foil for the brilliant scarlet, yellow and blue flowers of the border plants. Many of the herbs too, such as cotton lavender with its multitudes of tiny, yellow, ball-like flowers, and the sages which bear purple-blue flowers, make their own contribution to a colourful border. They are also trouble-free plants and labour-saving in that they need little or no staking. The culinary herbs are often found growing in the vegetable garden together with other food crops, but nowhere do herbs seem more attractive than when they are growing in a garden by themselves. Some have flowers which are quite as colourful as any plant in the garden, while no other plants are their equal for diversity of hue and form of foliage. There are low-growing herbs and those which can grow 1.5–1.8 m (5–6 ft) tall, and others which grow to many different heights between the two extremes.

Making the herb garden

If there is a small part of the garden that can be used for making a herb garden it will be decorative and useful all the year round. Perhaps a herb garden could be made at one end of the garden, where vegetables are also grown. It may be possible to segregate a small part of the vegetable garden by erecting a screen of rustic or interwoven fencing, or hurdles used for penning sheep which would associate well with herbs because they are always a reminder of a country cottage garden where sheep hurdles are used to protect the plants from wind. The herb garden need be no larger than 3.6 m (12 ft) square, perhaps with a wooden garden seat let into one side to take up the minimum amount of room.

A pleasing effect will be obtained if a path is made 30 cm (12 in) wide of stone or old bricks, surrounding a central bed made about 1.2 m (4 ft) square, at the middle of which is a stone sundial, or a bird bath kept filled with clean water. Such a garden would give hours of pleasure to those who sit out in summer enjoying the wild life and insects (bees and butterflies) that visit the herbs. In the central bed low-growing herbs such as thyme and marjoram can be grown, and the more prostrate thymes can be planted in gaps

Layout for a small herb garden. A 30 cm (12 in) wide path surrounds a centre bed about 1.2 m (4 ft) square, in which low-growing herbs such as thyme and marjoram could be planted. Around the outer edge of the path is a 90 cm (3 ft) wide and 3.6 m (12 ft) long border in which a wide variety of herbs can be grown.

made between the bricks or stones. Around the outer edge of the path will be a border 90 cm (3 ft) wide and 3.6 m (12 ft) in length along each side of the garden, and this will enable a wide variety of herbs to be grown.

The herb garden will be enhanced if the rustic work is clothed with plants of the lovely thornless climbing rose, 'Zéphirine Drouhin', which is one of the first roses to bloom in June and the last to finish, remaining in flower until well into autumn. The glorious clear pink of its flowers, which are as large as many a hybrid tea rose, is enhanced by a unique silvery sheen, while it will fill the herb garden with its delicious scent on a warm sunny day. This rose will make rapid growth and needs little pruning. It may be trained along galvanized wires held in place by strong stakes driven into the ground at 1.8 m (6 ft) intervals.

Not only do herbs require plenty of sunlight to produce the maximum amount of essential oil in the leaves, which gives them their unique fragrance and flavour, but it is also needed for their successful ripening and drying which should be partly completed before the herbs are cut and taken indoors. For this reason herbs are more satisfactory when grown in areas with long summers and a high average of sunshine. This will have the value of ripening and drying the herbs, and making strong firm growth which will withstand a hard winter better. Where summers are cool and rainfall high they will be less successful. This will also be the case where winters regularly have temperatures below −20° C (0° F). In such extreme climates many of the perennial herbs will need over-wintering under glass.

A light dry soil is the best for herb growing. One which is well drained in winter and in summer, and which dries out rapidly after heavy rain. These light soils are often those which lie over chalk or limestone, where the top soil is shallow and quickly heats up in dry sunny weather. This makes it difficult to grow good crops of fruit and vegetables but under such conditions herbs grow admirably, for many are native of the barren sea coast of the Mediterranean regions. There the plants achieve the maximum of essential oil and have a high commercial value. The essential oil in the leaves protects the plants from pests and diseases, and the oxidizing oil provides an invisible cloud about the plants which prevents undue loss of moisture from the leaves during hot weather. The hotter the weather, the more essential oil the plant makes. For this reason it is rarely necessary to water herbs by artificial means or spray them for pests and diseases. Truly, they are the most labour-saving of plants.

However, herbs do require protection from cold winds which may cause browning of the foliage on occasions. In the home garden this protection is provided by hurdles or interwoven fencing, or by climbing roses or cultivated blackberries growing against rustic poles or along wire fencing.

Among the hardier of the shrubby herbs are lavender, rosemary and cotton lavender (*Santolina*), which quickly grow into dense shrub-like bushes 90 cm–1.2 m (3–4 ft) tall and make an efficient hedge for a herb garden. Planted 90 cm (3 ft) apart, they will have grown into each other in less than two years to form a dense hedge 60–90 cm (2–3 ft) thick. To give protection, and its tiny glossy leaves are almost immune to gale-force winds and sea spray, rosemary can be grown against a wire fence or a screen made of trellis when, within two years, it will reach a height of 1.5 m (5 ft). It needs a minimum of pruning and where it is happy it will remain healthy and vigorous for at least fifty years.

If herbs are grown commercially, and this is a healthy and rewarding occupation, hedges of rosemary or cotton lavender should be planted on the side of the prevailing winds. Each of the hedge herbs will withstand regular clipping to maintain the shape and will give privacy and protection to a herb garden, at the same time encouraging bees and butterflies.

If the garden faces north make the herb garden in a position where the plants will receive as much sunlight as possible, so that it is not obscured by the house or outbuildings, nor by tall trees. A fairly open situation will best suit herbs and, as artificial watering is rarely necessary, they can be grown in fields or on an allotment, possibly situated well away from a water supply. This is important if one is looking for a suitable crop as a source of income from badly situated land.

Preparation of the ground

Herbs require no manure but the soil should be friable and well drained. Most of all it should be free of perennial weeds and be well limed and should have an alkaline reaction. Unlike some fruits, for example strawberries and blueberries, which crop well in acid soils and rarely do well on chalk or limestone, and potatoes which enjoy similar conditions, few herbs do well in an acid soil.

As the ground is being prepared, and the soil should be dug to a depth of at least a spit (spade), remove all perennial weeds such as docks and nettles and incorporate some lime rubble (mortar), obtainable from old buildings being demolished, or give a dressing (1 oz per sq yd or 35 g per sq m) of hydrated lime and work in drainage materials such as shingle or clearings from ditches. This is especially important if the soil is heavy and not too well drained, for herbs will not grow well in waterlogged ground.

There are also several chemical compounds which will improve the condition of heavy soil. They will break up a heavy soil, but will bind together the particles of a sandy soil and so help it to retain moisture. They are usually obtainable from builders' merchants or garden shops.

To improve the depth of a shallow soil, often found over chalk or limestone land, and to help it to retain moisture there is nothing better than 'green manuring.' If done late in summer it can be dug into the soil early in autumn. The method is to cover thickly the surface of the ground with rape seed or with a specially prepared mixture of seeds obtainable from an agricultural seedsman. Rake the seed into the surface and water it in. In about six–seven weeks it will have grown several inches tall and have formed a dense mat, both below and above ground, which, when dug in, will provide the soil with valuable humus.

If any manure is used this should be well-decayed cow manure or old mushroom bed compost. Fresh manure and artificial fertilizers should be avoided for herbs.

Most herbs are best planted early in spring, in March or early April, or as soon as the ground has recovered to a fine tilth after the winter. Do not plant if the soil is wet and sticky or if there is frost in the soil. By planting in early spring the herbs will get away to a good start as the soil warms up in spring and summer. Planting distances and heights are given with each herb.

Making the beds

The beds will be most attractive if edged or surrounded by one or more of the low-growing shrubby herbs, as in the herb gardens of old. Francis Bacon said 'the herb garden is best square, encompassed on all sides with a stately hedge'. In the herb gardens of his time (his life time spanned the end of the 16th and start of the 17th centuries) the beds were usually square, divided from one another by low hedges of herbs which were usually clipped in spring. Sometimes the beds were heart-shaped, or arranged round a circular centre bed, but they were always surrounded by low hedges of herbs, knotted together. Some beds were also filled with flowering plants which were used to flavour drinks and to include in salads; plants such as the clove-scented pink and the violet, the primrose and cowslip, for both the flowers and the leaves of these plants were in daily use in springtime, and their habit made them admirable for small beds.

When herbs are used for a low hedge plant them 30 cm (12 in) apart, and while they are spreading clip them on top and on the sides bordering the paths and beds. This will encourage the plants to grow into each other all the sooner. For small hedges use germander and the upright thymes, or one of the dwarf lavenders, such as 'Hidcote' or 'Twickle Purple', which are the deepest blue of all the lavenders and which are handsome all the year in their silver-grey foliage. If planting a border of herbs this could be edged with chives which can be cut and used in the kitchen all the year. They are most attractive in bloom with their purple-pink, ball-shaped flowers. Or use the knotted marjoram, so called because it was once widely used to edge beds of herbs, joined together as lover's knots. Parkinson, an English botanist of the 1600's, said that it was used by the ladies 'to put in nosegays ... and to make sweet washing waters'. It grows 30 cm (12 in) tall and its rose-red flowers are visited by bees and butterflies in late summer. A low hedge will help to keep cold winds from the other herbs and give the beds a tidy appearance.

Although much of the charm of a herb garden lies in its informality, the planting of herbs too close to one another should be avoided. The plants must receive air and sunlight to all parts, otherwise they will not be in a suitable condition for harvesting in late summer nor will they be rich in essential oils. It will also be necessary to work between the plants, to cut them and hoe the soil, and also to remove any weeds. If they are too close together working between them may cause damage to the plants. It may be necessary to stake the taller growing herbs, such as fennel and angelica, to prevent them falling over less vigorous plants growing nearby.

If space allows, grow herbs in small groups of two, three or four plants. This will give worthwhile cuttings of the herbs for whatever purpose is required, and their foliage will also give a generous splash of colour to the border. Some herbs, however, may be less useful than others and only one or two plants may be required. As when planting a flower border, set the taller varieties at the back of the bed facing the sun, with the less tall ones in front of them, and the dwarf varieties at the front, arranging them in tiers. In this way the plants will be seen to advantage and all will receive their share of sunshine. Each one will also hide any bareness at the base of those growing behind.

To add a splash of rich coloration to the herb border plant a few groups of those flowering perennials that associate well with herbs on account of their antiquity, and the fact that they remain long in bloom. These flowers often have a brilliant hue; plants such as *Lychnis chalcedonica*, the cross of Jerusalem, with its scarlet flower heads borne on 1.2 m (4 ft) stems. *Achillea filipendulina* is another, with its flat heads of brightest yellow, and there are many others such as the monardas, 'Cambridge Scarlet' and 'Croftway Pink' are fine examples, which have bergamot-scented foliage so much used in pot-pourris, and which are more often classed as herbs. The michaelmas daisies, too, should be planted to give autumn colour, and the hardy spray chrysanthemums whose foliage is pungently scented. Indeed any perennials such as nepeta (catmint), and *Rhodiola rosea* (rose root), which will contribute in any way to the making of pot-pourris, scent bags and scented waters should be included in the herb border, as they always used to be. The herbaceous border takes its name from the herbs that grew therein; plants such as elecampane and alkanet, betony and St. John's wort.

With the perennials may be planted those herbs raised from seed, both annuals and biennials, which may be set out each year in spaces between the established perennials. Alternatively they may be sown in circles of about 40 cm (16 in) diameter and the plants thinned to several inches apart, depending on their height and sturdiness. But first plant the perennials, and give some thought to height and habit, and to foliage coloration. Set out those with silver and grey foliage near to those with dark green or steel blue foliage, and those bearing blue flowers near those with yellow flowers, with here and there a few red-flowering plants.

Herbs for the back of a border (P = Perennial: A = Annual: B = Biennial)

Common name	Botanical name	Height
Alexanders (A)	*Smyrnium olusatrum*	1 m (3–4 ft)
Angelica (P)	*Angelica archangelica*	1.5 m (4–5 ft)
Bergamot (P)	*Monarda didyma*	1 m (3–4 ft)
Elecampane (P)	*Inula helenium*	1.5 m (4–5 ft)
Fennel (P)	*Foeniculum vulgare*	1.5 m (4–5 ft)
Liquorice (P)	*Glycyrrhiza glabra*	1 m (3–4 ft)
Meadowsweet (P)	*Filipendula ulmaria*	1 m (3–4 ft)
Mugwort (P)	*Artemisia vulgaris*	1 m (3–4 ft)
Mullein (B)	*Verbascum thapsus*	1.5 m (4–5 ft)
Red rose (P)	*Rosa gallica*	1 m (3–4 ft)
Rosemary (P)	*Rosmarinus officinalis*	1.5 m (4–5 ft)
Sea holly (P)	*Eryngium maritimum*	1 m (3–4 ft)
Sweet Cicely (P)	*Myrrhis odorata*	1 m (3–4 ft)

Herbs for the middle of a border (P = Perennial: B = Biennial: HH = Half-hardy)

Common name	Botanical name	Height
Agrimony, common (P)	*Agrimonia eupatoria*	60–90 cm (2–3 ft)
Agrimony, fragrant (P)	*Agrimonia odorata*	60–90 cm (2–3 ft)
Alkanet (B)	*Anchusa sempervirens*	60–90 cm (2–3 ft)
Balm (P)	*Melissa officinalis*	60–90 cm (2–3 ft)
Borage (B)	*Borago officinalis*	60–90 cm (2–3 ft)
Caraway (B)	*Carum carvi*	60–90 cm (2–3 ft)
Chicory (P)	*Cichorium intybus*	60–90 cm (2–3 ft)
Comfrey (P)	*Symphytum officinale*	60–90 cm (2–3 ft)
Costmary (P)	*Tanacetum balsamita*	60–90 cm (2–3 ft)
Cotton lavender (P)	*Santolina chamaecyparissus*	60–90 cm (2–3 ft)
Curry plant (HHP)	*Helichrysum angustifolium*	60–90 cm (2–3 ft)
Dill (A)	*Anethum graveolens*	60–90 cm (2–3 ft)
Lavender (P)	*Lavandula angustifolia*	60–90 cm (2–3 ft)
Lovage (P)	*Ligusticum scoticum*	60 cm (2 ft)
Rampion (P)	*Campanula rapunculus*	60 cm (2 ft)
Rue (P)	*Ruta graveolens*	60 cm (2 ft)
Sage (P)	*Salvia officinalis*	60 cm (2 ft)
Sea Holly (P)	*Eryngium maritimum*	30–60 cm (1–2 ft)
Southernwood (P)	*Artemisia abrotanum*	1 m (2 ft)
St. John's wort (P)	*Hypericum perforatum*	60 cm (2 ft)
Tansy (P)	*Tanacetum vulgare*	60–90 cm (2–3 ft)
Tarragon (P)	*Artemisia dracunculus*	60 cm (2 ft)
Valerian (P)	*Valeriana officinalis*	60–90 cm (2–3 ft)
White horehound (P)	*Marrubium vulgare*	60 cm (2 ft)

Herbs for the front of a border (P = Perennial: A = Annual:
HH = Half-hardy; B = Biennial)

Common name	Botanical name	Height
Anise (HHA)	*Pimpinella anisum*	45 cm (18 in)
Apple mint (P)	*Mentha × rotundifolia*	45 cm (18 in)
Basil (HHA)	*Ocimum basilicum*	38 cm (15 in)
Bistort (P)	*Polygonum bistorta*	45 cm (18 in)
Calamint (P)	*Calamintha ascendens*	30 cm (12 in)
Catmint (P)	*Nepeta cataria*	40 cm (16 in)
Chamomile (P)	*Anthemis nobilis*	15–20 cm (6–8 in)
Chervil (A)	*Anthriscus cerefolium*	38 cm (15 in)
Chives (P)	*Allium schoenoprasum*	20 cm (9 in)
Clary (P)	*Salvia sclarea*	30 cm (12 in)
Coriander (A)	*Coriandrum sativum*	15–20 cm (6–9 in)
Cumin (A)	*Cuminum cyminum*	45 cm (18 in)
Feverfew (P)	*Chrysanthemum parthenium*	45 cm (18 in)
Herb bennet (P)	*Geum urbanum*	45 cm (18 in)
Hyssop (P)	*Hyssopus officinalis*	45 cm (18 in)
Ladies smock (P)	*Cardamine pratensis*	38 cm (15 in)
Marigold (A or B)	*Calendula officinalis*	38 cm (15 in)
Marjoram (P)	*Origanum vulgare*	30 cm (12 in)
Parsley (A or B)	*Petroselinum crispum*	25 cm (9–10 in)
Peppermint (P)	*Mentha × piperita*	25 cm (9–10 in)
Rose root (P)	*Rhodiola rosea*	30 cm (12 in)
Sorrel (P)	*Rumex acetosa*	30 cm (12 in)
Spearmint (P)	*Mentha spicata*	38 cm (15 in)
Summer savory (HHA)	*Satureja hortensis*	20 cm (8 in)
Thyme (P)	*Thymus vulgaris*	30 cm (12 in)
Winter savory (P)	*Satureja montana*	30 cm (12 in)
Wormwood (P)	*Artemisia absinthium*	30 cm (12 in)
Yarrow (P)	*Achillea millefolium*	38 cm (15 in)

Before planning the border it is important to know the heights to which all the herbs grow so that planting can be done from back to front as they diminish in height. There are also a number of semi-prostrate herbs suitable for planting in a path.

Herbs in a border will remain healthy and vigorous if, in autumn each year after harvesting, the plants are given a mulch of decayed manure or old mushroom compost. (Material from the garden compost heap is equally useful.) Before mulching fork between the plants to aerate the soil and to suppress weeds, removing any annual plants after harvesting the seeds in early autumn, and then give a forkful of compost around the base of each remaining (perennial) plant. This will also give some protection from hard frost.

A number of herbs are omitted from the lists of plants because they are unsuitable for a herb garden or border. Plants such as nettle and burdock which, though they have considerable health-giving qualities, by their obnoxious powers of reproduction are not garden plants and are best left in the wild from where they may be harvested and used in many ways.

Herbs in a wheel

Where garden space is strictly limited a small herb garden can be made in an old cart wheel, with the rim and spokes let into the soil, after treating the wood with a preservative. But cart wheels, once obtainable at a low cost, are now scarce and as an alternative a cir-

Where garden space is strictly limited a small herb garden can be made in an old cart wheel, with the rim and spokes let into the soil, after treating the wood with a preservative.

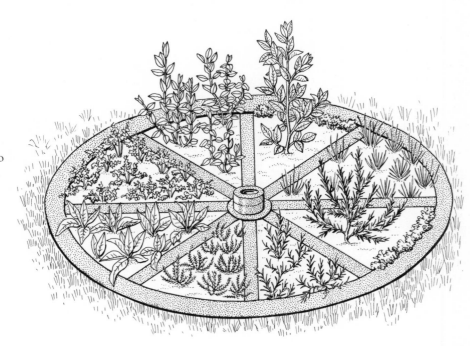

cular bed of about 1.8 m (6 ft) diameter can be cut in the middle of a lawn (or to one corner), removing turf for the whole area of the circle. For the 'spokes' low-growing plants of the upright thymes or chives can be planted, radiating from a central circular stone on which rests a sundial. The bed can be divided into eight sections, each of the same area, and planted with low-growing herbs of perennial habit. Each section will be separated from the next one by those plants used for the 'spokes' and the same plants may be used to form the outer perimeter. If chives are used for the purpose then the sections can be filled with eight other herbs. No plant has greater use in the kitchen than chives for adding to soups, to chop and include in salads, with cream cheese in sandwiches, and also to sprinkle over poached and scrambled eggs. One of the herbs to fill the centre section would be winter savory of

28

which Thomas Hyll, in his *Art of Gardening* (1563), wrote that the knot gardens of the time were 'set with winter savory and thyme, for these endure all the winter through greene'. It is used for stuffings, to make sauces to serve with fish and also to include in pot-pourris. It grows 25–30 cm (10–12 in) tall and has spreading branches. Another would be the emerald green and beautifully curled leaves of parsley, in daily use in the kitchen and garden, and lemon thyme, which has innumerable uses too. One of the marjorams should be included for they rarely exceed 30 cm (12 in) in height, and also have many uses in the kitchen and for making sweet waters. Salad burnet, with its cucumber-tasting leaves to use in salads and sandwiches, is also useful, as is also spearmint to make mint sauce to accompany lamb. Chamomile is a good choice to fill the last small bed for it, too, has considerable medicinal value and its dried leaves make a pleasing pipe smoke as an alternative to tobacco. Each of these plants is perennial and they can be kept in shape by their regular use. Set them 30 cm (12 in) apart.

A most pleasing effect can be obtained in spring by planting between the herbs all manner of small flowering bulbs such as crocuses, snowdrops, chionodoxa and dwarf scillas. Purchase 100 of each, mix them together in a bucket or box, and plant them in October, here and there, 5 cm (2 in) deep and about 10 cm (4 in) apart. They will need no further attention and will come into bloom year after year. In no way will they interfere with the herbs which will hide the foliage of the bulbs as it dies back in summer.

3
Herbs in tubs, hanging baskets and window boxes

The use of tubs

Those who have no garden can still grow a wide selection of herbs, in containers of various sizes and shapes, so long as the plants can be given the same amount of sunlight as they require when growing in the open ground. Those who live in a terraced town house which may be provided with a small walled courtyard, or a property with a sunny basement, can grow their herbs in tubs, the size of the tub depending on the area at one's disposal, but they must be sited where the maximum amount of sunlight can reach them.

Tubs vary in size from a diameter of about 38 cm (15 in) to 60 cm (24 in) and are often made from old cider or vinegar barrels cut in two. These will be of oak and though they may have been discarded for their original purpose, still have many years left in them for growing plants. Tubs may be placed on a terrace or verandah, and if the area is restricted, two or three of about 45 cm (18 in) diameter will present a more pleasing appearance than just one tub of larger size. In a large tub, however, several of the more vigorous herbs can be grown in the middle with those of less robust habit planted around them. Small tubs should be filled with herbs which are in keeping with the size of the tub, growing neat and compact, and if several tubs are used it is possible to plant each with herbs that have a special purpose. One tub could be planted with culinary herbs, another with herbs for making pot-pourris and sweet bags, another with herbs which provide aids to beauty, and so on, depending upon the number obtainable. When established the herbs will add to the enjoyment of the home, especially if they are sited where the various hues of the foliage can be seen from indoors. They will do much to add their beauty to what otherwise may be a drab town courtyard which will be additionally enhanced if small tubs or pots of climbing roses are placed at the foot of a wall against which they are allowed to grow. One suitable variety is 'Royal Gold' with its almost evergreen glossy foliage and hybrid tea-shaped blooms of deepest yellow. Another is the older shrub rose, 'Zéphirine Drouhin', which makes an excellent pot-pourri and will soon cover a 2.4 m (8 ft) wall with its beauty. From small tubs, at intervals of about 1.8 m (6 ft), rosemary can be trained to cover a wall to a height of 2 m (about 6 ft) and it will be green all the year. Its stems will be a mass of bright blue flowers in spring and early summer when they will be alive with honey bees, and rosemary honey is the most delicious of all. Tubs arranged a few feet away from the wall and planted with herbs will transform an otherwise dreary courtyard, and for an additional splash of colour in summer plant a few nasturtium seeds around the edge of the tubs; the leaves can be used in salads and the seeds make a delicious caper sauce to serve with fish. They will trail down the side of the tubs and will brighten a dull day with their flowers of scarlet and gold.

Preparing the tubs

Though the tubs will be well seasoned, and will be of durable oak, they will have a longer life if they are treated inside and out with a wood preservative. At the same time treat the iron rims or bands

A wide selection of herbs can be grown in containers of various sizes and shapes, such as this oak tub which would probably have been made from an old cider or vinegar barrel cut in two. It is advisable to rest the base of the tub on flat stones or bricks so that rain water can drain away as quickly as possible.

31

which hold the wooden staves in position with a rust protective paint, and afterwards paint them black. The tubs will then be well protected against wet weather and will present a pleasing appearance, more so in their natural state than if painted green or white.

It is advisable to rest the base of the tubs on flat stones or bricks, raising the base above ground to enable rain water to drain away as quickly as possible. Make sure that the base of the tubs is drilled with several holes of 2 cm ($\frac{3}{4}$ in) diameter to allow surplus moisture to drain away. Have the tubs in position before they are filled with soil for they will be too heavy to move once filled. Before filling them allow the tubs several days for the wood preservative to dry off and any fumes to escape. Then, in the bottom, place a layer of old crocks which will prevent the drainage holes from getting choked up with soil. Over the crocks or broken bricks place a layer of turf, grass side downwards, which will also assist drainage. Over it add a mixture of soil and shingle. By now the tubs will be about half-filled and will be ready for the growing compost. This should be of as good a quality as possible, preferably sterilized loam, which is obtainable from a garden shop or nurseryman who will usually deliver it for a small extra sum. Mix it first with some old mortar or hydrated lime to keep the soil sweet, which herbs love anyway, and with a little decayed manure. If this is not available mix into the soil prepared for each tub a generous handful of bone meal, or steamed bone flour, which will release its valuable plant foods over a long period. Use no artificial fertilizers for herbs, and do not use the soil of a town garden for tubs and window boxes for this is usually acid, due to deposits of soot and sulphur falling on it over the years, and it will also be full of weed seeds and perhaps disease spores. A well-prepared tub will last for years without renewing and so it is desirable to give detailed attention to its making up.

A friable, sweet and well-drained potting soil is all that is necessary and the tub should be filled to the top. After a week or so the mixture will have settled down to about 2.5 cm (1 in) below the rim of the tub and this will allow for watering or heavy rain falling without the soil splashing over the side. However, a well-made potting soil will need little artificial watering for herbs perform better when the soil is on the dry side. For this reason plants in tubs and window boxes can be left unattended at the height of summer for several weeks without coming to any harm. Whenever possible, however, the plants will respond by making plenty of new growth to a gentle syringing during hot, dry weather; this is best done in the evening.

Spring is the most suitable time to make up the tubs, but order them early in the year for delivery by March 1st. This will allow several weeks for the tubs to be treated with preservative and made ready for early April planting.

In the middle of a large tub plant tarragon, sage, hyssop and

Traditional 16th century knot garden at Hampton Court. Only three varieties of herbs are needed to create the effect of the intertwining strands of a knot.

Mixed herb border at the Royal Horticultural Gardens, Wisley showing angelica in the foreground.

balm, all of which have many culinary uses. One plant of each will be sufficient. Then around them set marjoram, salad burnet and winter savory, with chives and parsley (raised to planting out size first in pots) the upright thymes around the edge, and with a few nasturtium seeds planted between them. Except for the nasturtiums these are all perennial plants but for the first year there will be only a small amount of foliage to cut. First let them become established, then keep them in trim by removing the stems for kitchen use, always taking first any unduly long and overcrowded shoots. At the end of autumn carefully stir up the soil between the plants, and give a light top dressing of decayed manure and fresh soil, or use hop manure or mushroom bed compost. Do not forget to give the plants a light dressing with mortar or hydrated lime each year, preferably in spring. Looked after in this way the plants will remain vigorous and healthy for many years.

Herbs in pots and hanging baskets

The Elizabethan custom of planting evergreens in pots and hanging baskets, and suspending them from the low ceiling of a sunny room or in a window is a charming idea. In summer the plants will cool the room and make it pleasantly scented. Rosemary was preferred for this purpose for it is always green, and it is long-living in a pot. It should, however, be given several weeks outdoors in spring to become revitalized by fresh air and sunlight, and the warm April showers. Indeed, pots of rosemary can be grown outdoors hung from a strong iron stake driven into the wall of a courtyard, or suspended from strong hooks beneath the eaves of a bungalow. Hanging baskets may also be used in this way, and as herbs enjoy dry conditions they will need watering only about twice a week in summer, which is readily done from a step ladder.

Herbs from hanging baskets can be used in the kitchen the whole year round but they must have a sunny position to do well. Here again, seeds of the trailing nasturtiums can be pressed into the compost around the rim of a basket and they will provide a splash of vivid red and gold during the summer months. Pots or baskets can also be suspended from an arch made of rustic poles, possibly on one side of the herb garden, or they can be used to hide an unsightly corner. Grow climbing roses up the posts and over the top, and suspend the herbs between the posts to produce a most charming effect. A row of three or four baskets is extremely attractive. The same number of baskets around the sunny walls of a courtyard will provide herbs to use all the year round and brighten an ugly wall. Perhaps rosemary can be trained against the wall to a height of about 1.5 m (5 ft) with the pots or baskets suspended just above. Both rosemary and lavender can be planted at the base of a sunny wall.

Herbs may also be suspended from baskets in a sunny garden room or porch. The plants will flourish under such conditions and

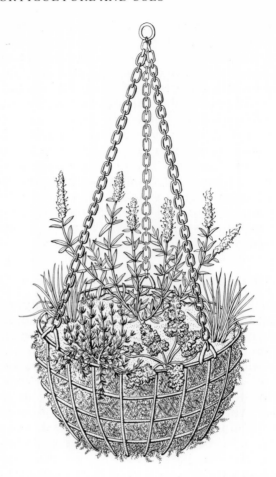

Herbs in a hanging basket. These can be hung either indoors or outdoors. A suitable size would be about 50 cm (20 in) in diameter and should be made of strong, galvanized wire. The basket should be lined with fresh moss which will absorb moisture and prevent the soil from falling through the wires.

will keep the air sweet and cool as well as providing the household with their foliage all the year round. All the attention they require is an occasional watering in winter, and perhaps twice-weekly in summer when they may be placed outdoors for several months to enjoy the warm, showery weather.

A basket of suitable size will be of 50 cm (20 in) diameter and made of strong galvanized wire so that it will have a long life and be impervious to the weather. Slightly smaller baskets made of plastic-coated steel wire may also be used, and this type is especially suitable for indoor use to hang in a garden room or porch, or in a sunny kitchen window.

To absorb moisture and prevent the soil falling through the wires it is advisable to line the basket with fresh moss. This can be obtained from deciduous woodlands or hedgerows and it should be used to completely cover the basket to a depth of about 5 cm (2 in). The weight of the soil filling will reduce its thickness to less than 2.5 cm (1 in). The moss should be nicely moist, and the best way of preparing a basket is to stand it on a table over a large plant pot or wooden box, or between two bricks, to prevent it rolling

36

over. If moss is unobtainable line the basket with turves, the grass to the outside. Then fill up the basket with soil. This should be a mixture of sterilized loam to which a handful of bone meal is worked in, together with a little coarse sand and a large handful of mortar. If mortar is not available work in a few pieces of charcoal to keep the mixture sweet. It should be in a friable condition, neither too dry nor too wet. After filling the basket allow the soil several days to settle down before planting the herbs.

Spring is the best time to make up the baskets, and after planting allow them to remain indoors for a week, in a greenhouse, shed or in the kitchen window, to allow the plants to become accustomed to the basket before placing outside.

The herbs should be of more compact habit than some of those used in tubs. Around the side plant the variegated form of ground ivy, which was much used in ancient inns to clarify ale before hops were found to do this better. The plants, with their neat heart-shaped leaves, will trail over the side of the basket for several feet. The leaves are marked with purple and white, and the small purple flowers are borne from the axils of the leaves. It is ever-green and has its uses in the kitchen.

In the middle of the basket plant hyssop which is also evergreen and intensely aromatic. The leaves have a pleasant, sharp taste in soups and stews. It has many uses and was mentioned in the Bible more than any other herb and came to be known as the Holy herb. Plant marjoram with it to use in stuffings and to season stews, while its leaves are included in pot-pourris. If the basket is small plant feverfew in place of hyssop. Two roots of chives should be included for their thin, pencil-like leaves can be used in soups and sprinkled over scrambled eggs. The thymes could also be grown, and include two or three plants of parsley, sown in pots so as not to disturb the roots. They will be in everyday use and they will add to the beauty of the basket with their emerald-green, fern-like leaves. Parsley will last two or three years in a basket if it is not allowed to seed.

If herbs are grown in pots use one of not less than 15 cm (6 in) diameter, made of either earthenware or plastic material. If wired round the rim it can be suspended from a large nail or iron stake about 15 cm (6 in) long, driven into a wall. Plant only one herb to each pot, but if a large size pot can be obtained, two or three plants of each herb can be grown. For pots parsley, chives, the marjorams and the thymes are most suitable. Grow them in a similar soil to that prepared for baskets, but in pots the plants will need more frequent watering.

Herbs in a window box

Most of those plants which can be grown in pots and baskets can also be grown in a window box. The variegated ground ivy (*Glechoma hederacea* 'Variegata') can be allowed to trail over the front of the box and with it plant parsley, thyme, marjoram and winter savory. They will grow no more than 15 cm (6 in) tall if the shoots are regularly pinched out for culinary use.

A window box may be used either inside or outside a window and a box of herbs growing in a sunny kitchen window is a delight to see and a pleasure to use. There is nothing new in the idea. In 1594 Sir Hugh Platt wrote: 'In every window you may make square frames either of lead or of boards, well pitched within. Fill them with some rich earth and plant such herbs therein as you like best'. In this way, a supply of herbs will be available when they cannot be grown by other methods. They can be tended from the kitchen and nothing could be easier. A wooden box can be made to the size of the window, which may be long and narrow or almost square. Drill holes in the bottom for drainage, line it with broken pottery, fill it with soil and set out the herbs 8–10 cm (3–4 in) apart. This is a convenient way of growing the half-hardy sweet basil, an eastern herb which gives its unique flavour to tomato dishes. A pot of basil is to be found in many a kitchen window from Beirut to Singapore.

Herbs can also be grown in an outside window box made of wood or simulated stone, the latter being more suitable for a terrace or verandah, while wooden boxes can be fixed with strong, angle-iron brackets to the sunny wall of a town courtyard. If several boxes are employed in this way quite a large number of herbs can be grown, but do remember that wherever herbs are to be grown, they must be given a sunny position to ripen and be rich in essential oils. In each box two or three geraniums, which enjoy the same conditions, can be grown with the herbs to give brilliant blooms in summer and autumn. Boxes made of concrete or wood may also be placed at the foot of a sunny courtyard wall which is covered with climbing roses. To preserve wooden boxes raise them on bricks, one at each end of the boxes. They should be made 15 cm (6 in) wide and the same depth, and no more than 75 cm (30 in) long or they will be too heavy to move. A box to fix outside a window must be made to the exact size of the window to which it is fixed by means of strong iron brackets. If the window opens inwards or is a sash window it will present no problems in fixing the box, which should be made in proportion to the size of the window. For the large window of a Georgian-style house make the box about 20 cm (8 in) deep, but for the long, narrow, mullioned window of an older property it should be no more than 15 cm (6 in) deep. A box not made in proportion will present an unbalanced effect to the house.

Making the box

As a window box will have to carry a considerable weight of soil it must be constructed of 2.5 cm (1 in) timber, cut to the correct measurements and planed. The end pieces will fit inside the back and front lengths, and they will be held in place by strong 5 cm (2

A sunny kitchen window sill is an ideal position for a window box full of herbs such as parsley, chives, rosemary, thyme and mint.

in) nails rather than large screws which tend to part the grain and split the wood. If any attempt is made to dovetail the corners remember that the strength of a dovetailed joint lies in the perfection of its construction, and a water-resistant glue must be used to make it secure. To give additional strength to the corners it will be advisable to screw a small angle bracket to each of the four top corners.

The base should be cut to the outer measurements of the four sides and must have 2 cm ($\frac{3}{4}$ in) holes drilled into it at regular intervals for drainage. For the timber use hardwood if possible, although this is now expensive. American red cedar is a useful alternative and remains impervious to moisture for many years. Remember that a window box is filled with soil which may remain wet with rain-water for weeks on end and poor quality timber would quickly disintegrate. To give the wood a longer life treat it with preservative before fixing. This is especially necessary if the box is made of deal, or of second-hand (but sound) timber. Soak the inside with preservative and allow the box to remain in the open for ten–twelve days for any fumes to escape. The outside of the box can be stained, if it is being fixed to an unpainted, mullioned window or it can be painted green or white to match the window frame. If the box is painted a different shade from the window the effect is rarely satisfactory.

Always fasten the box in place before filling it. When filled with soil a window box will be heavy and it is essential that it does not move. A window with a wood frame will present few difficulties; the base is allowed to rest on the sill to take the weight, while the box is made secure by fixing an angle-iron bracket to the top (at the ends) and to the window frame. The box can be watered and the herbs picked from inside the house; boxes fixed to a basement or low window can also be tended from outside.

If a box is to be fixed to the brick or stone surrounds of a window first plug the wall (between the brick or stone) to a depth of at least 5 cm (2 in) before securing it with angle brackets. Screws, not nails, should be used for the fixing, and to give extra security it may be advisable to fix a piece of strong galvanized wire to the outer corners of the box and to a position higher up the window frame to take some of the strain, especially if the window is near a public right of way or the box is fixed to an upper window.

Filling the box

It is advisable first to place a piece of fine mesh wire netting across the bottom of the box, although this is not essential. Then place broken pottery over the drainage holes to prevent the soil falling through. As an alternative fresh moss can be used to cover the wire netting. It will eventually decay but not until the plant's roots have bound the soil particles together. Pieces of turf may also be used, placed grass-side downwards.

The soil mixture should then be added. This should be made up of sterilized loam obtainable from a nurseryman or garden shop, to which some coarse sand has been added and about 0.5 kg (1 lb) of ground limestone or mortar to each box. If sterilized loam cannot be obtained find some soil from pastureland nearby. A handful of bone meal added to each box will release its plant foods over a long period and maintain the herbs in a healthy condition. Or add a little decayed manure or mushroom bed compost. The soil should be in a friable condition and the boxes are best made up in spring.

After filling the boxes allow a week for the soil to settle down when the level will be just below the top of the box and will allow for watering, by rain or can, without the soil splashing over the sides. Then set out the plants 7.5 cm (3 in) apart. At the front use ground ivy and trailing nasturtiums for summer colour. If plants of the old double-red nasturtium can be obtained no plant is more showy, but it sets no seed and its leaves are bitter. It is grown from cuttings and planted from pots.

From now onwards the plants will need very little attention; an occasional watering in dry weather, and syringing to keep the foliage fresh. As soon as they make some growth begin using them, for the more they are used, the better they grow. Remove and use any unduly long shoots to keep the plants compact.

4
Herbs for a path and dry wall

Herbs to be walked on

Before the introduction of synthetic perfumes for personal use, and to clear the musty air of those houses which had no damp course, almost every plant of the garden had either sweet-smelling flowers or aromatic leaves. Even paths, made of brick or stone, had scented plants growing between the stones which not only released their fragrance when trodden upon, but their leaves were also dried and used in pot-pourris, or scattered over rush matting to release their scent when walked upon. There were others, too, which were planted alongside a path so that those who walked by would brush the plants with their clothes and the delicious smell would remain on them for several hours. It was Francis Bacon who wrote of those herbs used to plant on paths '... which perfume the air most delightfully when trodden upon and crushed are Burnet, Wild thyme and Water mint'. 'You are to set whole alleys with them', he said and together with chamomile, one of the most useful of all herbs, they were also used to make a scented 'lawn' to lie upon when the plants were warmed by the summer sun for there were no grass lawns, as we know them today, until nearly the end of the 17th century. In 16th century Europe, almost all 'lawns' were of these almost prostrate herbs which made mats of scented foliage. Of chamomile Falstaff said: 'the more it is trodden upon, the faster it grows or the better it wears', when commending it to his friend and master, Prince Hal, later Henry V, victor of Agincourt. And Falstaff was right for the more a chamomile 'lawn' is walked upon the more quickly does it spread.

Making a path

The prostrate herbs are most attractive when used to plant between bricks or stones. If possible make a path of old, weathered bricks in the herb garden, or along one side of a herb border. The plants will grow over the bricks to give a delightful informal effect and many will remain green all winter. Plant with them the matted pinks, with their scented flowers and silver foliage. There are other suitable plants grown for their flowers such as the campanulas, saxifrages, alpine phlox, aubrieta and candytuft, all of which will spread their foliage over the stones.

If you are making a brick path it may be possible to obtain material from an old barn or outbuilding which is being de-molished. The bricks will often have a rich terracotta hue and will be of much the same size so that, when placed on their side, the laying of the path will present few difficulties. Make the path about 45 cm (18 in) wide, and so that the top edge of the bricks will be level with the surrounding ground. Remove the soil to just below the depth of the bricks and to the width of the path. Then beat down or roll the ground to make it firm and bed the bricks on a 2.5 cm (1 in) layer of sand, pressing the bricks firmly into it and setting them as close together as possible. As an alternative mix concrete (1 part cement to 2 parts sand) and spread this along the path about 2.5 cm (1 in) deep, bedding the bricks into it before it dries. The cement should be made nicely moist but not sloppy.

If you are making a path of flag-stones they will arrive in all shapes and sizes, and it will be necessary to select those stones with a straight side to use for the edges of the path, and to fill in the middle of the path with stones of various shapes. They, too, are laid on a bed of sand or cement. If flagstones or concrete stones are used, these will be of the same thickness and shape though they may vary in size. Before ordering measure the area of the path which is to be made and order accordingly. A path will take some time to make but will add much charm to the garden, and will enable the herbs to be visited even when the rest of the garden is saturated with rain. This will be appreciated by the housewife

Another way of growing herbs is to plant them both alongside and between the stones of a crazy-paving path.

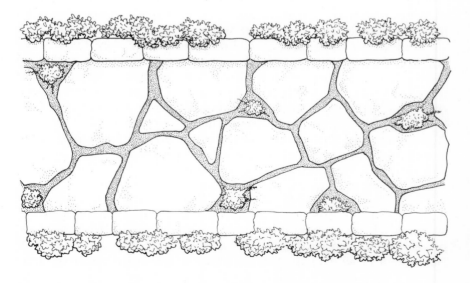

when looking for herbs to use in the kitchen. Remember to set the stones as close together as possible to prevent the appearance of weeds, but leave a space here and there for the carpeting herbs and other plants.

Apart from a good spade the only tool needed is a builder's spirit level which is about 60 cm (2 ft) long and can be placed across the path thus enabling the bricks or stones to be set at the same level. If stones are used these will be irregular in thickness as well as in shape, but keep the flat side to the top to make for easier walking or for wheeling a barrow when the path is made. There is no need to point the stones or bricks if they are placed close together.

If the ground is low-lying it may be advisable to make a 2.5 cm (1 in) base of small rubble or shingle, as an alternative to using sand or concrete, to provide additional drainage. If using concrete, remember to remove it, before it sets hard, from the spaces which are left between the stones in order to take the plants. These should be grown in small pots and are obtainable from specialist herb growers and alpine plant nurseries. They will either be sent in their plastic pots or removed from the pots with the soil ball intact and wrapped in sheet plastic. The path space should be large enough to take the soil ball intact.

Paths may be planted in this way at any time except when there is frost about, but spring is the best time when the plants will quickly become established in the warm showery weather. The plants should be set out in irregular fashion and not too near together. Allow 1 m (about 3 ft) between each for they will soon make spreading clumps, hiding many of the bricks or stones.

Plants to grow on a path

Among the plants of almost prostrate habit is *Thymus arcticus* (also known formerly as *T. drucei* and much confused in the trade with true *T. serpyllum*), one of the loveliest carpet formers making a dense mass. It has dark green, glossy leaves and bears a profusion of tiny flowers which are much loved by bees. It was mentioned in a 10th century manuscript and is of course Shakespeare's thyme of 'The bank whereon the wild thyme grows'. A tea made from its leaves is good for nervous disorders and it is an excellent restorative against tiredness. There are several lovely forms, 'Coccineus' bearing deep red flowers, and 'Bressingham Pink' with flowers of an attractive shade of strawberry pink. For contrast plant 'Albus' which has pure white flowers.

Wild thyme is also mat-forming and is present on downlands everywhere. It was highly valued by beekeepers for its honey, the only source of sweetening in medieval times. From its essential oil, thymol is obtained. The leaves, when placed in boiling water and inhaled, are effective for a sore throat.

Of other prostrate thymes, *T. doerfleri* has soft, woolly foliage and T. *fragrantissimus* has orange-scented leaves. *Mentha requienii*, known as the Corsican thyme, is really a mint. It will form a thick mat of green, peppermint-scented leaves and is studded with tiny mauve flowers for weeks on end.

Another little beauty is the plant grown in gardens as *Micromeria corsica* which is like a tiny heather although it grows only 7.5 cm (3 in) tall. It has tiny grey leaves which, like those of rosemary, guard it in hot weather against loss of moisture. It can be included in sachets and pot-pourris when dry and for its size no leaf is more highly aromatic. The scent is incense-like and is released when the plant is trodden upon. It is, however, much beloved by cats who will roll on and break it whenever they get a chance, unless the plant is protected by a chicken wire cage.

Another delightful plant for a path is *Calamintha acinos*, the basil thyme, which grows only 7.5 cm (3 in) tall and has leaves which, when crushed, emit a powerful minty scent. A sprig kept in the handbag all day will release its refreshing scent when the weather is hot and tiring, just as it will when it is walked upon. All of these plants will tolerate being walked upon and all of them retain their leaves throughout the year.

A fragrant lawn

To make a fragrant lawn select a piece of ground possibly on one side of a path, or in front of a terrace, but in an open, sunny situation. A dry bank where little else will grow is suitable, or a herb lawn may replace the grass lawn for it will need considerably less attention. The ground must always be well drained. Hence the herbs always do better in a well-drained sandy soil than in one of high clay content. When the soil is being prepared remove all weeds and large stones and incorporate some decayed manure; old mushroom compost is ideal. Also, work in some mortar, crushed limestone or chalk, or give a dressing of hydrated lime. Should the ground be low-lying it will be advisable to remove the soil to a depth of 15 cm (6 in) and to provide a 2.5 cm (1 in) layer of gravel or rubble to improve drainage before replacing the soil which is then prepared as previously described. Autumn is the best time to prepare the ground, before the winter rains, and if the surface is left rough the frost will bring it to a fine tilth. Do no planting until spring.

Chamomile is the best of all plants for a herb lawn for it may be walked over, rolled and clipped, although this is done only once a year, and so it provides a dense green lawn with the minimum of attention. Chamomile can be used in many ways: as a hair rinse, as a nerve tonic, to promote sleep, and, when dried, it makes a pleasant pipe smoke. John Evelyn, writing towards the end of the 17th century, said: 'it will now (October) be good to beat, roll and mow (clip) carpet walks of chamomile', and this is the best time to do so although planting is done in spring.

Perhaps the cheapest and best way is to purchase seed from a merchant—30 g (1 oz) will sow an area of 9 sq m (about 100 sq ft) —and to sow it in April. Sow the seed evenly and rake it into the surface, just covering the seed with soil. Keep comfortably moist during summer and where there is overcrowding thin the plants to 10 cm (4 in) apart. Use the thinnings to plant elsewhere, for chamomile readily transplants and a bed should be kept to fill in any bare patches in the lawn. If the creeping thymes are also to be used thin the chamomile to 20 cm (8 in) apart, but the thymes are best used on their own, planting several varieties 30 cm (12 in) apart, and when in bloom will produce a carpet of brilliant colour.

The chamomile may also be sown in drills, in the same way that many other herbs can be raised. Make the drills 15 cm (6 in) apart and sow thinly, just covering the seed. If sown early in April the young plants will be ready to make the lawn in July, usually a rainy month, when they will soon re-establish themselves. In dry weather keep the plants moist at the roots; a chamomile lawn will greatly benefit from a daily spraying during warm, dry weather when it will take on a deep emerald green shade.

The lawn must be kept weeded the first year and by the end of the summer the plants will have almost closed up, to hide any bare patches of soil. Do no clipping the first year and do not walk over the lawn except to weed it. By the following summer it will have become a mass of plant growth and can be walked upon and rolled. Early in autumn trim the plants with shears. This will encourage them to grow sideways rather than upwards. Once established the lawn will remain bright green during the hottest weather when grass lawns have turned brown, and when walked or sat upon it will release its delicious, refreshing scent of ripe apples. From their second year the plants will close right up and so prevent any weeds growing between them. For a lawn the best form of chamomile is *Anthemis nobilis* 'Treneague', which has brilliant green foliage and does not flower. This variety is of no use, however, if required for making tonic 'teas' from chamomile flowers.

Herbs for a dry wall

A dry stone wall is always an attraction in a garden. It may be made on one side of a terrace or patio, to separate it from the rest of the garden. Or a low wall, with a core of earth, may be made around a small herb garden, for there are many herbs that will grow well at the top of a wall. A brick wall can be constructed to hide an unsightly corner, or to retain a bank which can be planted with low-growing herbs which will remain green all winter.

If a dry wall with a core is made alongside a path to a height of 1 m (about 3 ft) it will, if planted with low growing herbs, be a constant pleasure to older people and those who are blind for, without stooping, the various leaf scents of the herbs can be enjoyed by pressing the leaves as one walks along the path.

To make a wall with a core of soil, which will need to be about 40 cm (16 in) wide overall, remove soil from the base to a depth of 10 cm (4 in) and to the measurements of the wall. The soil will be used for the core. If stones are being used these can be of any size, but the wall will be more durable if a row of larger stones is used for the base, and these can be alternated with a row of smaller stones, to the top of the wall. If possible, select stones of a uniform thickness for each layer, and tie-in the rows as when building a wall round a field, placing a stone over each joint of the lower course. This will give added stability.

If the wall has a core a double row of stones will be needed, and they should be built up with the aid of a builder's spirit level so that the two walls are built to a similar height as the work progresses, and using a line on both sides as each course is built up. This will make for a professional job. Allow about 15 cm (6 in) for the core and about 13 cm (5 in) for the thickness of each wall.

Select the stones with care, using those of about the same thickness for each course. Fill in the space between the walls to a height of about 60 cm (2 ft) with rubble such as bits of stone, broken brick, rubble or mortar, making it compact as the work proceeds. This will give added strength to the wall. The soil core is added to the top 25–30 cm (10–12 in). The roots of the herbs will not penetrate much deeper than this.

The soil is added when the wall is complete. Use the soil removed for the base of the wall and mix with it lime rubble or some crushed chalk, or give a liberal dusting with hydrated lime. Mix in some used hops, usually obtainable from a brewery for the asking, or some old mushroom bed compost. Fill the central cavity to the top, allowing it a week or so to settle down before planting. The soil will settle to about 2.5 cm (1 in) below the top so that heavy rain will not cause the soil to be washed over the top. It should be remembered that a wall to be planted with herbs must be in a sunny position, and so the compost should contain some humus-forming material to prevent it drying out too quickly in hot weather.

As an alternative to stone, brick can be used to construct a wall which could be made with pleasing effect on either side of an archway, also made of brick, and with a wrought iron entrance gate leading to another part of the garden. Semi-circular steps joining the two walls and leading up to the entrance will enhance the scene. On either side of the steps plant rosemary which will grow over the steps; those who pass through the entrance gate will brush against the plants and their clothes will become scented with its resinous quality.

A brick wall is easier to make than one of stones for all the bricks are of the same size, and there is no sorting to be done and no manipulating when building up the courses. Otherwise the work should proceed in the same way, the lower 60 cm (2 ft) being filled with a rubble core and topping it with soil.

Those herbs suitable for a low wall will include wall germander (*Teucrium chamaedrys*) which is to be found on old walls, growing between the stones. It is a woody perennial, bearing large, handsome flowers of rosy-purple, but it is best confined to sheltered gardens where it will retain its leaves all winter. Parkinson said: 'It must be kept in some form by cutting and the cuttings are much used as strewing herbs for houses, being pretty and sweet, with a refreshing lemony scent'. The dried leaves, with those of rosemary, were placed in muslin bags and kept in the pocket or handbag to smell when the weather was warm or when one encountered unpleasant smells. Plant near it the lemon-scented thyme, *Thymus × citriodorus*, which grows 20 cm (8 in) tall and is used in the same way; it is also included in stuffings. Plant winter savory as well, which grows slightly taller, and which can also be included in stuffings and pot-pourris. It was at one time as popular as fennel and parsley to make a sauce to serve with fish. By removing the taller shoots, the plants can be kept short and bushy.

Hyssop, too, may be grown on a wall and kept trim in the same way; it also stays green all winter. It will seed itself in the crevices of walls. It was also used for strewing and to include in pot-pourris; used sparingly, the leaves impart a pleasant, sharp taste to soups and stews. French marjoram, which has a pungent minty scent due to the essential oil it secretes from its stems, is another suitable for a wall. It was used to make sweet bags and washing waters and it figures in Isaac Walton's instructions for dressing a pike. It makes a delicious sauce to accompany fish and its leaves may be included in soups and stews. Hyssop and marjoram are loved by bees and butterflies.

Include also the dwarf lavenders with their silver-grey foliage. Gertrude Jekyll's 'Munstead Blue' and 'Twickle Purple' are compact and remain long in bloom. The pot marigold, *Calendula officinalis*, is also suitable for a wall. Its flower petals add a unique pungency when a few are included in soups and stews, while marigold 'tea', made by pouring half a litre (1 pint) of boiling water onto a handful of petals, will promote sound sleep. The chopped petals can also be included in salads, and the brilliant orange and yellow large, handsome flowers are most striking in the garden and provide their old world charm indoors when cut and placed in a vase of smoky glass. Plant also the wild thymes, letting them trail over the wall; the catmint, *Nepeta × faasenii* and the trailing ground ivy *N. glechoma*, which is a diuretic and blood purifier. The alpine pinks can also be included and their clove-scented flowers used in pot-pourris. Like all these herbs pinks grow best in a sunny position and are tolerant of long periods without much water.

5
Propagating herbs

Ways of growing herbs

Herbs are among the easiest of plants to propagate, requiring no artificial heat and no special horticultural skill. Herbs are propagated in three ways: *(a)* from seed; *(b)* from cuttings; *(c)* by root division.

Almost all herbs are readily raised from seed, which is an inexpensive way of obtaining a stock, but if certain forms of a herb are required these have to be increased by vegetative methods, either by root division or from taking and rooting cuttings. There are a number of annual and biennial herbs that are raised only from seed; sown in drills and the seedlings transplanted, or sown directly into the ground where the plants are to mature. It is not generally realized, however, that most of the large shrubby herbs like rosemary and lavender can also be raised in this way. In a dry and not too cold garden they will grow vigorously in the gravelly soil and seed themselves on the paths. Annual herbs are raised each year and sown about April 1st, as soon as the soil is friable after the winter frosts and snow. Those herbs such as borage which are of biennial habit, which means they mature the year following that in which the seed is sown, are sown in July or August. This enables them to make good size plants before the winter, which they must survive to reach maturity the following year.

Herbs from seed

Seed is sown in drills in the open ground if the plants are to be transplanted, or when they are being grown for a commercial seed crop; most annual herbs are grown for their seeds. Alternatively seed is sown in a border where the plants are to grow. Here they are sown in circles of about 40 cm (16 in) diameter, which should be physically marked in the border (between already established perennial plants) with chalk or lime. Before sowing place a wooden label in each circle with the name of the herb, and remember to sow the taller-growing herbs at the back, grading them in height from back to front of the border. At the end of autumn after harvesting the seed, or when the plants no longer produce fresh green foliage for use in salads and sauces, the plants are pulled up and destroyed, and the ground dug over and made ready for more sowings next spring. Unless the ground is still frozen, do not delay sowing after the first days of April, because most annual herbs grown for their seed, for example dill and chervil, require a long growing season and plenty of dry, sunny weather to ripen properly. For this reason those herbs grown for their seed will ripen better where summers are normally warm and sunny.

If sowing in drills make them north to south, so that all parts of the young plants can obtain as much sunlight as possible, and about 15 cm (6 in) apart, unless the plants are to be grown on to maturity where they are sown. If so, make the drills 25 cm (10 in) apart and thin out the plants to 15 cm (6 in) apart in the rows. Use a garden line to keep the drills straight, and make them with the back of a rake or use a strong stick or garden label. Make the drills 1.2 cm ($\frac{1}{2}$ in) deep. The seed bed should be cleared of all weeds and large stones, and before sowing rake into the surface some peat or decayed manure, and give a 35 g per sq m (1 oz per sq yd) dressing of superphosphate of lime to promote vigorous root action. Bring the surface to a fine tilth before sowing, and afterwards keep the seed moist in dry weather to hasten germination. The same procedure should be followed where seed is sown in a border, but here the seed will be sown in circles, scattering it at random and raking it in. It should be noted that those annual herbs grown for their seed should be grown on where they are sown, for to transplant them will cause a check in their growth and in a poor summer the seed may not ripen in time. In any case, they resent root disturbance and do not transplant well.

There are several herbs, for example sweet basil and summer savory, which are native to the Far East and are only half-hardy, not surviving long periods of frost. These are best raised in boxes or seed pans in a frame or sunny window, sowing the seed in one of the standard seed sowing mixes in March, and planting out, when frosts will no longer be expected. Most of the perennial herbs may also be raised in this way; as their seed usually takes longer to germinate than annuals it is best sown directly into a frame, or in boxes placed in a frame, or covered with a sheet of glass and placed on a terrace or verandah in full sun. Seed sown in this way can be more carefully supervised than in the open ground, and if it takes a long time to germinate it is less likely to be taken by birds and mice.

Where sowing in boxes or pans do not use ordinary garden soil; this will often be full of weed seeds and disease spores, each of which will be in competition with the seedlings. Use a proprietary, peat or loam based, seed-sowing medium. Fill the boxes or pans almost to the top. Make it level and gently firm it; then sow the seed evenly over the entire surface. Lightly cover it with the soil and water in. Then place in a frame or cover with a sheet of glass. At no time must the boxes or pans be allowed to dry out, but do not keep them saturated. They should be kept nicely moist.

The seeds of some herbs will germinate within two weeks; others may take two months, but as soon as the seedlings are large enough to handle, that is when they are 3 cm (about 1 in) tall, they are moved to small pots. They are then grown on in a frame or in the open until they are large enough to be planted out in permanent beds or sold.

Small plastic or earthenware pots are ideal and these are filled with fresh potting soil; peat pots are also excellent. The pots are filled with the soil in the ordinary way but the roots will also grow into the pots and so obtain extra nourishment. As the herbs are sold or planted out in the pots there will be no root disturbance. If sown in spring, many plants will be ready to set out in July, which will enable them to become established before winter.

Annual and biennial herbs raised from seed: (HH = Half-hardy where regular frosts are experienced)

Herb	Uses	Height
Alexanders	Culinary	1 m (3–4 ft)
Alkanet	To flavour drinks	50 cm (20 in)
Angelica	Culinary; medicinal	1.5 m (5 ft)
Anise	Confectionery	45 cm (18 in)
Basil (HH)	Culinary; medicinal	40 cm (16 in)
Borage	To flavour drinks	60 cm (2 ft)
Burdock	Medicinal	1 m (3–4 ft)
Caraway	Culinary; medicinal	60 cm (2 ft)
Centaury	Medicinal	20 cm (8 in)
Chervil	Culinary; medicinal	40 cm (16 in)
Coriander	Culinary; medicinal	25–30 cm (10–12 in)
Cumin	Culinary; medicinal	50 cm (20 in)
Dill	Culinary; medicinal	1 m (3 ft)
Marigold	Culinary; medicinal	30 cm (12 in)
Mullein	Medicinal	1.5–2 m (5–6 ft)
Nasturtium	Culinary	Trailing
Parsley	Culinary; medicinal	20–25 cm (8–10 in)
Savory (summer) (HH)	Culinary	20 cm (8 in)

It is not generally realized that most of the perennial herbs can be raised from seed as readily as the annuals. Even the herbs of shrubby habit such as lavender, sage and rue germinate without difficulty and in hot, gravelly soil, will often sow themselves.

Chamomile has long been used as a grass substitute in lawns – hence this chamomile 'seat' which forms the centre piece of this mixed herb garden at Kew.

A small mixed herb garden
showing use of paving stones
to separate the various herbs,
and which also gives a
visually pleasing effect.

A colourful border showing,
in the foreground, the herbs
thyme *(Thymus vulgaris)* and
lavender *(Lavandula spica).*

Perennial herbs often raised from seed

Herb	Uses	Height
Balm	Culinary	60 cm (2 ft)
Chamomile	Medicinal	10 cm (4 in)
Chicory	Culinary	30 cm (12 in)
Chives	Culinary	15 cm (6 in)
Cowslip	Culinary	15 cm (6 in)
Dandelion	Culinary	10 cm (4 in)
Elecampane	Medicinal	1.2–1.5m (4–5ft)
Feverfew	Culinary	38 cm (15 in)
Fennel	Culinary	1.2–1.5 m (4–5 ft)
Hyssop	Culinary	60 cm (2 ft)
Marjoram	Culinary	30 cm (12 in)
Rue	Moth preventive	60 cm (24 in)
Sage	Culinary; medicinal	50 cm (20 in)
Sorrel	Culinary	25 cm (10 in)
Tansy	Culinary	60–90 cm (2–3 ft)
Thyme	Culinary; medicinal	15–25 cm (6–10 in)
Wormwood	Medicinal	30 cm (12 in)

These can be sown in boxes or pans, in a frame or covered with cloches. In those areas enjoying a mild climate they can be sown in drills in the open ground, as for annuals and biennials.

Propagation from cuttings

It is mostly the hard-wooded herbs, those of shrubby habit, that are propagated by cuttings because they take several years to make substantial plants if grown from seed, and as they usually grow from a central or thick basal stem, root division is not practical either. Except where winter temperatures regularly fall below −18° C (0° F) these herbs may be grown in the shrub border. They associate admirably with artemisias, with their silvery-grey foliage and with others such as *Senecio greyii; Elaeagnus argentea; Phlomis fruticosa*, the Jerusalem sage; *Weigela variegata*, and many others of equal beauty. Once planted in a soil cleared of weeds (and ordinary soil suits them well) these plants, with their handsome evergreen foliage, will be colourful all the year. All the attention they require is to trim back any unduly long shoots; the herbs are kept in control by removing the shoots to use in the kitchen and for other purposes about the home. These herbs are of shrub-like habit:

Herb	Uses	Height
Bay laurel	Culinary; medicinal	2m (5–6 ft)
Cotton lavender	Moth preventive	60 cm (2 ft)
Curry plant	Culinary	40 cm (16 in)
Germander	Medicinal & pot-pourris	30 cm (12 in)

Hyssop	Culinary & pot-pourris	60 cm (2 ft)
Lavender	Medicinal & pot-pourris	30 cm–1 m (12–36 in)
Rosemary	Culinary; medicinal	2 m (5–6 ft)
Rue	Moth preventive	1 m (2–3 ft)
Sage	Culinary; medicinal	45–50 cm (18–20 in)
St. John's Wort	Medicinal	60 cm (2ft)
Savory, winter	Culinary	30 cm (12 in)
Southernwood	Moth preventive	1 m (3 ft)
Tansy	Culinary; medicinal	1 m (2–3 ft)
Tarragon	Culinary; medicinal	1 m (2–3 ft)
Thyme	Culinary; medicinal	30 cm (12 in)
Wormwood	Medicinal; moth preventive	40–45 cm (16–18 in)

The best time to take cuttings is in July and August when the plants have made some new growth in summer, for cuttings of new or half-ripened wood will root more easily than will the hard shoots of old wood. In any case, to help them with their rooting, it is advisable to treat them with a 'hormone' rooting powder obtainable from a garden shop. Select a cutting about 7.5 cm (3 in) long; this is best removed from the plant by gently pulling it from a main branch or stem so that it will come away with a wafer of stem attached. This is known as a 'heel', and the cutting will root more quickly as there will be a larger area of wood to form roots than if the cutting was severed cleanly from the plant.

After removing as many cuttings as needed for rooting, take a piece of damp cotton wool (cotton); dip this into the hormone powder and transfer it to the base of the cutting after removing any excess leaf near the base. The cuttings will root well in a proprietary compost. Cuttings like to be in contact with the inside of an earthenware pot, and where these are available insert the cuttings round the inside and about 2.5 cm (1 in) apart, with about 2.5 cm (1 in) of the base inserted into the compost. If using a loam-based soil make quite firm by pressing with the thumbs on either side of the cuttings. They may also be planted in boxes filled with 5–7.5 cm (2–3 in) of potting soil, and set out 2.5 cm (1 in) apart. If a frame is available, the cuttings can be set directly into a rooting medium at the same distance apart; they can also be placed under cloches. The cuttings should be kept comfortably moist, and on sunny days they should be syringed with water to prevent them from flagging.

By early autumn they will have begun to form roots but they are best left undisturbed until spring, giving them only a minimum amount of moisture during winter, just sufficient to keep them alive and to prevent them being attacked by mildew. Dust them with flowers of sulphur in October.

Early in April lift the cuttings carefully, so as not to sever the roots, and re-plant them into small individual pots of plastic or earthenware, or into the peat pots containing a good potting mix.

Plant firmly and keep the plants growing on until July or August when they can be planted out where they are to grow, or sold in the pots. Without further root disturbance they will quickly become established, and will have made good sized plants before winter. If gardening in colder parts, it may be advisable to keep the plants in the pots until the following April.

In addition to the hard-wooded herbs, mint and balm, catmint and winter savory, mugwort and elecampane can be grown from cuttings of the young shoots taken in the summer.

Propagating by root division

This is the most satisfactory method of increasing the stock and should be used wherever possible. It cannot be used for most hard-wooded plants which grow from a single main stem, with the possible exception of garden thyme, but even this herb grows better from cuttings and seed. Those herbs that are suitable for root division are the herbaceous perennials, the herbs that associate well in the flower border and which are soft- rather than hard-wooded.

These herbs are propagated by root division:

Herb	Uses	Height
Agrimony	Culinary; medicinal	60 cm (2 ft)
Balm	Culinary; medicinal	60 cm (2 ft)
Bergamot	Medicinal & in pot-pourris	60 cm (2 ft)
Bistort	Culinary; medicinal	45 cm (18 in)
Calamint	Medicinal	25 cm (10 in)
Catmint	Medicinal	40 cm (16 in)
Clary	Culinary; medicinal	30 cm (12 in)
Comfrey	Medicinal	60 cm (2 ft)
Costmary	Culinary; medicinal	1 m (3 ft)
Cowslip	Culinary; medicinal	15 cm (6 in)
Germander	Medicinal	25 cm (10 in)
Herb bennet	Culinary; medicinal	40 cm (16 in)
Lady's smock	Culinary	40 cm (16 in)
Lovage	Culinary; medicinal	1 m (2–3 ft)
Marjoram	Culinary	30 cm (12 in)
Meadowsweet	Culinary; medicinal	1.25 m (3–4 ft)
Mint	Culinary; medicinal	45 cm (19 in)
Pennyroyal	Culinary; medicinal	5 cm (2 in)
Rose root	For sweet waters	40 cm (16 in)
Salad burnet	Culinary	40 cm (16 in)
Sweet cicely	Culinary	1.5 m (5 ft)
Tansy	Culinary; medicinal	1 m (2–3 ft)
Tarragon	Culinary	1 m (2–3 ft)
Valerian	Culinary; medicinal	1 m (2–3 ft)
Yarrow	Medicinal	40 cm (16 in)

All these herbs can be lifted and divided in November after harvesting, or after using the flowers or leaves during summer; they may also be lifted and divided in spring. This is a better time for those who are gardening in the colder parts for the plants will then have the warmer weather in front of them. The plants will be ready to divide when three–four years old, by which time they will have formed large clumps, and if they are not divided they will tend to die back in the middle. Lift them with a garden fork so as not to sever the roots; then, with the hands, tease apart the offsets.

Propagation by division. This is best carried out in spring or autumn, and herbs that grow in clumps such as chives should be divided in this way: (a) the soil around the plant should be watered, then loosened with a fork and the whole clump, roots and all, taken out of the ground; (b) shake the roots free of soil and separate them gently, being careful to break as few roots as possible; (c) pull the clumps apart and discard the centre; (d) replant the clumps separately, placing a layer of compost at the bottom of each hole.

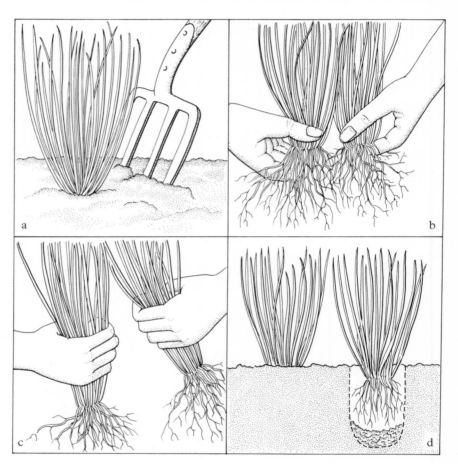

These are pieces of the plant which have been cut back to about 7.5 cm (3 in) above soil level after harvesting, and each piece will have a few roots attached. It is usual to divide the roots into four or five pieces or clumps and to replant them into clean, freshly prepared ground as soon as possible. Where herbs are grown for sale, each clump can be divided into numerous offsets and replanted 15 cm (6 in) apart in rows; the ground should be kept hoed and free of weeds between the rows. If the plants are divided in spring they will have grown large enough to sell by early autumn.

Herbs may also be divided by using two garden forks, back to back, and prising the roots apart; or a number of offsets can be removed from established plants by using a trowel, without lifting the whole root. These offsets are removed from the outer extremities of the clump without disturbing the rest of the plant.

When lifting old plants, if the central parts have decayed or died back, discard them, re-planting only the most vigorous outer parts. If the herbs are regularly divided, this will maintain the quality and strength of the plants, as well as increase the stock.

Mint is propagated by lifting the thin, pencil-like roots after cutting back the stems in November. Press the fork well into the soil, and after lifting and disentangling the roots, shake away the soil (or wash it off) and divide the roots into numerous pieces before re-planting 7.3 cm (3 in) deep into ground enriched with some decayed manure. Unlike most other herbs, mint requires a moist, well-nourished soil, and is happy in partial shade. All the mints should be grown in a specially prepared bed, perhaps near the kitchen, for the plants will be in constant use. They will benefit from a top dressing each year of fresh soil and decayed manure, applied in winter.

6
Harvesting and drying herbs

Herbs for drying

Greater care is needed in the harvesting and drying of herbs than in their growing. Many herbs are used fresh during summer, in salads and sandwiches, to cook with, or to make sauces to serve with fish and game. However, there are a number of herbs that can be dried to use in winter, to include in stuffings and sausages, and to add flavour to soups and stews. Indeed, these dried herbs are most potent only after drying, and chief among them are thyme, sage, marjoram and winter savory, the most popular of all culinary herbs for winter cooking. Properly dried, they will retain their qualities for at least four years and will be in good condition to use for a second and third year if a wet autumn should make drying too difficult. Large quantities of these herbs are in demand for sale in bunches when partly dried, and also when fully dried, by those who packet herbs for shop sale.

Most herbs which are suitable for drying will be harvested during late August and September, for in most years only by then will they have reached their maximum fragrance and flavour. Late August is the most suitable time to harvest lavender flowers, and in September, sage and thyme are cut and dried. The correct harvesting of herbs was most important in medieval times when they were the only physic available to the people, and when they were included in the cooking of almost every dish.

The large commercial growing of herbs is mostly confined to the sunnier regions of the world where drying presents no problems. In less suitable climates drying can be a difficult task unless a drying room is available. The herb grower needs to keep a sharp watch on the weather, just as the farmer does at harvest time when ripe corn must be harvested without delay. The same applies to herbs. If lavender flowers are left too long before cutting, they will shed themselves and leave nothing but bare stalks; this also happens with herbs such as dill and caraway which are grown for their seeds. Although they require a long season to ripen, they will either shed their seeds when too ripe, or the seed will turn mouldy in a wet autumn if left too long on the plants. In most seasons there is usually a suitable time, even if only a few days, when most herbs can be successfully harvested.

Herbs for drying will have reached their maximum fragrance by early autumn; afterwards the volatile oils return from the leaves to the base of the plant. The leaves then begin to fall and are lost. Before this happens the plants must be harvested, and this must be done at exactly the right time, weather permitting. Herbs must never be cut when the days are wet or when a heavy mist covers the plants with a film of moisture. Often the mist will have lifted by noon and a warm sun will dry off the plants by late afternoon, when they can be harvested. On rainy days do no harvesting. Wait for a dry, sunny day and until the plants are quite dry, although it may mean waiting two or three days until they have fully dried off. If damp, they will dry better in the sun and wind than they will indoors, however efficient the drying room may be. If harvested in a damp condition, it will be difficult to dry the herbs before they begin to turn mouldy; once they do so they will never regain their full flavour or scent, and will take on an unpleasant musty smell.

There are some plants, marigolds for instance, that are grown for their flowers, and although the plants will remain in bloom until almost the year end, it is advisable to begin saving some blooms for drying, before the end of summer, when they are most plentiful and most potent. Marigold flowers are used to flavour soups and stews, and are stored in wooden or cardboard containers.

It may also be desired to dry clove-scented pinks and the most highly scented roses, to use in pot-pourris. Of roses, those with the strongest perfume are: the hybrid shrub roses 'Constance Spry', with its large pink globular flowers, and 'Belle Amour'; the hybrid perpetual 'Mrs. John Laing', with its incurved blooms of purple-pink; and several modern hybrid tea roses such as 'Wendy Cussons' (old rose-red), 'Fragrant Cloud' (coral red), and the older 'Crimson Glory' and 'Ena Harkness' (crimson). There are no white, yellow or orange roses to compare with these for perfume. Nor must the old red rose (or apothecary's rose), *Rosa gallica*, be forgotten. It was used to adorn the shields of Persian warriors many hundreds of years before the birth of Christ. When dry, this rose retains its rich scent for several years and should be included in every well-made pot-pourri. It can be grown with the herbs for it also flourishes in a poor, dry soil as in its native Iran and the near east.

To dry rose petals gather the blooms when at their best. Do not delay or they will lose their scent. Late in June will usually see the roses at their most highly scented best, and they are cut in early morning, as soon as the sun has dried off the dew. Take them to a light, airy room but keep them away from the direct rays of the sun which cause them to dry too quickly. Pull away the petals and place them on wooden trays, and turn them daily to prevent them becoming mouldy when they will lose their perfume and spoil a pot-pourri. They will dry well in an attic which, in summer, is usually the warmest room in the home, being nearest the roof.

Roses will take two or three weeks to dry fully; when the petals are fully dried they should be placed in wooden drums, and securely fastened down to prevent the scent escaping, until they are required for making up a pot-pourri.

Harvesting seeds

Those plants grown for their seeds, such as sweet cicely, dill and coriander, must also be harvested with care. They must be ripe or they will not retain their flavour when dried, neither will the flavour and scent be fully developed. When grown in cool, damp climates therefore, seeds of most of the spice herbs will not reach the same quality as those imported from India and the Near East, unless the season has been unduly dry and sunny, continuing well into autumn, so that the plants have had a long growing season.

The seeds must be harvested before they start to shed or many will be lost. It is therefore important to look at them every day as they reach maturity, and to cut away the heads at the first sign of the seed pods opening, or as soon as the weather permits their harvesting. Handle the seed heads carefully, and after cutting them off, place them in a large cardboard box, using a separate box for each herb with the name written on the side. Remove them to a dry airy room, and either place the seed heads in large muslin bags and hang them up in the room (an attic is ideal), or spread them out on shelves lined with white ceiling paper which enables the seeds to be readily seen as they fall from the heads. Place them in the sun if the heads appear to be the slightest bit damp, and inspect them each day, turning them so that all parts will receive air and sunlight. In two–three weeks they should have become quite dry, although if damp when harvested they may take a while longer. Then remove the seeds which still remain in the heads, gather them all up and place them in wooden drums, small cardboard boxes, or glass jars. Do not use tin cans which tend to sweat.

When herbs are growing under the most suitable conditions, and given a hot, dry summer such as 1976, it may be possible to make two harvestings of sage and thyme, the first cutting being made at the end of June which is usually a warm, dry month. This will allow the plants time to make a second growth and be ready for harvesting again early in October. However it all depends upon the weather and soil conditions.

Cutting herbs

When cutting hard-wooded herbs such as sage and thyme use a sharp knife or sickle if cutting in quantity. Hold the stems with one hand and cut away from oneself, with the knife held in the other hand. With the upright thymes it is possible to bunch together the entire top of the plant with one hand and to cut neatly off about 7.5 cm (3 in) above the base. This will allow the plant to form new growth near the base and keep it free of old and often dead wood. The stems are placed on a sack in rows to make for easier bunching and drying.

The soft-wooded herbs such as balm and mint can be cut with a pair of large scissors, and the cuttings placed in a box or basket, to be taken indoors as soon as possible. Do not leave the cut herbs too long exposed to the direct rays of the sun as this will cause too rapid drying. The exception is if the herbs are being cut when damp, or the season has been wet and sunless, in which case exposure to the sun will be beneficial. Old plants of sage and southernwood, which may have grown 'leggy' and be carrying a lot of thick stems, are best cut with secateurs or shears to guard against pulling the plant away from its roots.

Some herbs can be cut and dried all through summer, angelica for example. It is the young stems that are used for candying to decorate cakes, and to stew with apples, rhubarb and pears, to impart a rich muscat-like taste. Mint and parsley can also be used fresh and be dried for winter use all summer, although parsley will usually retain its green during winter. Name them and place in a dark cupboard or closet to use as required. Well-dried herbs have many uses and a long life.

Nasturtium seeds, taken as they form on the plants from early July until the end of autumn, are pickled in malt vinegar.

Drying herbs

Herbs are dried either in the home or in a shed which has a wooden roof covered with bitumen-treated felt, and not a roof of corrugated iron or asbestos, for this will sweat and prevent the herbs from drying properly. For the same reason a cellar will be too damp for herbs although it will be ideal to store root herbs in during the winter. An attic is the most suitable place for drying herbs, or use a cupboard beneath the stairs, or an airing cupboard for clothes which is fitted with laths to allow the warm air to penetrate and complete the drying. If a cupboard is used, leave the door slightly ajar to allow any dampness to escape as the herbs are dried, and this will allow more air to reach them. Spread out the herbs on the shelves or trays and turn them daily for about three weeks and until quite dry. Then gather them up into bunches, the stems pointing in the same direction, and string them up to use as required. The drying must be completed as quickly as possible for the herbs to retain their maximum flavour and scent; if the herbs have been harvested when slightly damp, which may be necessary in adverse weather, mildew will set in and spoil the crop if they are not dried quickly.

A good way of storing herbs once they have been dried is to gather them up into bunches, tie the stems together and hang them up in a dry, well-ventilated room, such as an attic. If there is a possibility of seed heads dropping off, they should be enclosed in a perforated paper bag.

Parsley, with its thick crinkled leaves, is the most difficult of all herbs to dry and needs a warm oven. Leaving the door slightly ajar, heat the oven to a temperature of 32°–38° C (90°–100° F); this should be held for about ten hours. Because parsley will remain green all winter in the open, covered by a cloche in severe weather, and can be finely chopped to accompany chives to sprinkle over fish and scrambled eggs, there is rarely any need to dry it.

Mint is dried in the same way but does not need such a high temperature. Mint sauce to use in winter is best made in summer from the fresh green leaves.

Where a number of herbs are grown, specially contructed racks of simple design erected in the drying room will be of value. A number of trays 1.2m (4 ft) square can be made and these are held in place, one above another, by four posts of 5 × 5 cm (2 × 2 in) fixed at each corner of the trays. The frames for the trays are made from 2 cm ($\frac{3}{4}$ in) timber, as they will not have to take much weight, and builder's laths are nailed across the frames at intervals of 5 cm (2 in), over which pieces of hessian (burlap) 1.25 m (about 4 ft) square are tacked. This will retain the herbs yet allow for a free circulation of air which is necessary for quick drying. Allow 30–35 cm (12–14 in) between the trays for the turning of the herbs, but the rack may be made to any height depending upon the height of the room. Fix the first tray about 10 cm (4 in) above the floor. If the corner posts are obtained (or cut to) 2m (6 ft 6 in) in length, this will allow for the fixing of 5 trays, allowing 35 cm (14 in) between each, and with the lower tray 10 cm (4 in) above ground. Allowance is made for thickness of timber. The rack will allow for the drying of five different herbs at the same time and yet will take up little space. Two people will be able to move it quite easily, but to allow the herbs to be reached from both sides, and also for a free circulation of air, it is preferable to have the rack away from the wall.

A drying rack may be fixed to a wall and made 75 cm (2 ft 6 in) wide. It can be made with two upright posts and with the trays fixed to lengths of 2 cm ($\frac{3}{4}$ in) timber fastened to the wall at the required heights. The trays are made with a frame to which laths and hessian (burlap) are fastened as described above.

Where there are large numbers of herbs to be dried, on a commercial scale perhaps, a specially constructed drying room will be an advantage. It may be a wooden shed with an electricity supply from the home, which would enable a light to be available for evening and winter work, and an electric fan heater to be installed to help the herbs to dry quickly if the weather was cold or damp. Ventilation must be provided, for where there are large quantities of herbs in a room there will be moisture evaporation which must be allowed to escape or the herbs will be spoilt by mildew. A sliding side window on two sides of the shed will provide ample ventilation, as will roof windows which open and enable sunlight to reach inside, while vents in the shed just above ground will enable an air intake to pass through and come out at the top or sides. Racks or shelves are constructed as described.

Herbs will be dry if they 'crackle' when pressed by the fingers. Correctly dried they will have a pleasing aromatic smell, devoid of any mustiness. In this condition they will keep for several years. If dried herbs are to be sold in bunches, do so just before the leaves begin to fall from the stems otherwise much of the value will be lost between the shop and the buyer's home. But where the herbs are to be rubbed down for use at home, or to market in small cartons, they should be fully dry and the leaves should have begun to part from the stems. Place the herbs on a table over sheets of white ceiling paper and take up a number of stems together; rub them with the palms of the hands until every leaf has left the stems. If the leaves do not readily come away, this means that they are not fully dry and they should be left several more days before trying them again. Discard any stems except those of lavender; these can be treated with a saltpetre solution and burnt (like incense sticks) in a sick room, for they burn slowly and release the delicious lavender perfume.

After removing the leaves, place them through a fine mesh riddle to remove any chaff or dust, and then crush the leaves with a rolling pin before placing them in containers. If herbs are to be sold in packets they must be weighed and the quantity shown on the packet, together with the name of the herb and the grower.

Large quantities of herbs, whether for home use or for shop sale, can be stored in wooden drums or glass screw-top containers, but never in tins. Wood is preferable, for it will not absorb moisture from the air. The top should be well fastened down so that the fragrance and flavour of the herbs do not escape, and kept until required in a dry room, away from sunlight.

The good cook will blend his or her own herbs, like the best tobaccos, and in this way will obtain the best from them. Winter savory and thyme associate well together, and also marjoram and thyme, while the best mint sauce is made from mixing together the leaves of apple mint or 'Bowles Variety', both round-leaf mints, with spearmint. When you get to know them there are many relatively unknown herbs, such as pineapple sage and orange-scented thyme, that will bring an added interest to cooking. But, like many of the best tasting dessert apples, these choice herbs cannot be found in shops and must be grown in the garden.

Harvesting root herbs

Root herbs are as important as those grown for their seeds and foliage, for their leaves are used for flavouring soups and stews, and their roots are used to boil or braise or to grate raw into winter salads. Grown mostly in the vegetable garden, they may be lifted with other roots such as swedes and turnips, or stored in a cellar or shed through the winter, which is advisable if you are gardening in the colder parts of Europe. The foliage is used fresh throughout the summer, but by late autumn it will, in most cases, have begun to die back. This means that the roots will grow no larger, although they will retain their quality the better if left in the ground and used as required.

If it is required to store them over winter, lift them in late October when they have finished growing, before the soil becomes wet and sticky with winter rain. Use a garden fork and lift them with care so as not to damage them. This would cause deterioration during storage, and with some roots may cause 'bleeding' and loss of piquancy. If possible lift them on a dry day and spread them out on sacks for the soil to dry from them. Then take them indoors and place them in deep boxes (orange boxes or tea chests are ideal), with layers of peat between them. This will protect them from frost and prevent the roots shrivelling, although this will not happen if the roots are stored in a cellar. Remember to remove the foliage before placing them in the boxes. If boxes are unobtainable place the roots on the floor and build up the heap with a layer of peat between each row. If the house has no cellar a garage will be suitable; store the roots at the opposite end to the door. They will benefit if a length of 15 cm (6 in) wide boarding can be placed across the end of the garage about 60 cm (2 ft) from the end wall, held in position by two short pieces of timber fixed to the wall on either side; and into which the board can be slotted and removed as required.

Those roots required for grating raw, boiling or braising should be washed and scraped first. This is preferable to peeling them when much of the flavour is lost.

A number of the root herbs such as dandelion and chicory can be forced; dandelion where it grows, chicory in a cellar or garage. They can provide a nutritious addition to a winter salad or can be served with meat or game.

7
Pot-pourris and sweet bags

Herbs for all occasions

Besides their culinary and medicinal uses, herbs can be used in other ways. They can be used in beauty preparations, to make cold creams with a herbal background and to make sweet waters and bath essences to relieve aching limbs; they can rest the nerves, and be made into sweet bags or used to stuff pillows, to encourage sound sleep. They can also be used in pot-pourris to place about the home. For whatever purpose they are needed, herbs and the petals of those flowers that associate with them provide a lasting and delicious fragrance.

For pot-pourris, the scented roses and their harvesting have previously been mentioned. Just one plant of each of the most heavily scented varieties will provide quite large quantities of petals to include in sachets and sweet bags, with lavender and marjoram (sweet), and in dry and moist pot-pourris. The flowers must be gathered at their best when they are most fragrant. In roses, the essential oil is present in glands in the petals where it is stored in an inert form, as a mixture of oil and sugar, known as a glucocide. This is not released in the bud form, only when the flower opens. It is not released until a state of fermentation has begun and it continues only while the flower is alive. A rose is most heavily scented when it reaches perfection and it takes 2000 blooms to yield just 1 g of attar, or 113 kg (250 lb) of petals to produce 30 g (1 oz) of essential oil by distillation, the rose being one of the few flowers to withstand considerable heat without suffering change. With their thick leathery petals, roses retain their scent for several years after drying and are one of the most important ingredients of any pot-pourri.

To make a pot-pourri

To make a dry pot-pourri, to three parts of a small 1 pint size pudding basin of carefully dried rose petals, add a small cupful of dry thyme and rosemary together, a few crushed bay leaves, the powdered skin of a lightly peeled orange dried in a low oven, 14 g ($\frac{1}{2}$ oz) of crushed cloves and a small teaspoonful of allspice. Mix well together and place in a pot-pourri bowl or jar which can be kept tightly closed when a room is not in use. If required to scent a bedroom, perhaps a sickroom, close up the jar by day and open in the evening. In a warm room it will be especially potent. If an open bowl is used, the mixture will better retain its perfume if a piece of polythene is stretched over the top and fastened around with a piece of ribbon, when the room is not in use.

Those who prefer a less 'sweet' pot-pourri could replace the orange peel with that of a lemon and use lemon thyme with the rosemary. Add some dry leaves of the lemon-scented geranium and of southernwood, together with a pinch of powdered nutmeg and mix well together; the pot-pourri will release the crisp, refreshing scent of lemon verbena, the leaves of which could be included if growing in the garden.

A pot-pourri jar, such as would have been used in the 16th century.

Alternatively, make up a concoction of scented rose petals, some marjoram, thyme, lavender and rosemary and mix with them a small quantity of a proprietary brand of pot-pourri maker, containing as many as thirty ingredients and made to a secret formula. Place the mixture in a plastic bag, shake well and keep the bag closed for two weeks, shaking it several more times. Then place the mixture in a pot-pourri jar or bowl in a warm room, stirring it occasionally; it will last almost indefinitely if the ingredients have been correctly harvested and dried.

67

Sweet bags to perfume linen

Rose petal bags, made of muslin, were in great demand in Tudor times to place among clothes and bed linen, also with church vestments. To the rose petals, dried when at their best, were added the dried leaves of sweet marjoram, lavender and clove-scented pinks which were shaken up with a teaspoonful of powdered cloves before placing in the bags and fastening up. The bags may be placed beneath a pillowcase or behind a chair cushion and the delicious perfume is released whenever the chair is used. The bags too can be suspended from the headboard of a bed and will release a sleep-inducing perfume through the night.

Mary Doggett, wife of the Doggett who in his will, left a legacy for 'a coat and badge' to be contested yearly by Thames watermen, gives a number of interesting recipes in her *Book of Receipts* for perfuming linen and clothes. One is especially lasting and is made from a little ambergris or musk mingled with orange flower water or rose water. Into the liquid place a few whole cloves and leave them for several days. Then press the cloves while still wet into some pink or red rose buds and dry in a low oven, sprinkle with orris powder and grind the buds with a rolling pin. Place the mixture in muslin bags and they will retain their perfume for several years.

From the same period come several recipes for beauty preparations which will benefit the skin and may be used today. Mary Doggett recommends the use of rose water as a skin tightener and to remove wrinkles. An astringent lotion is made from 15 g ($\frac{1}{2}$ oz) of tincture of benzoin, 30 g (1 oz) of witch hazel and 140 g (5 oz) of rose water. Rosemary and chamomile water are also reliable astringents.

To make rose water, gather 0.5 kg (1 lb) of fresh pink or red rose petals and after half filling a large kettle with water, add the petals and put on a low heat, a gas ring being ideal for this. Attach a length of rubber tube to the spout leading to a glass bottle or jar; before reaching the bottle, the tube should pass through a basin of cold (preferably iced) water to cool the steam. Pure rose water of rich perfume will drip into the bottle until all the water in the kettle has evaporated. Cork the bottle and use as required to apply to the face and neck. The same simple method of distillation can also be done with 'mock orange' blossom, which is also unharmed by heat, and with the leaves of a number of herbs.

Another way of making rose water is even easier though the end product will not be so concentrated. It was used as an aid to beauty in many a Tudor home. Rose water was also found on every banqueting table, kept in silver sprinklers, like those used for castor (finely granulated) sugar of later date; it was used to sprinkle over food and also over one's clothes when sitting at table. Bowls of rose water were also provided for washing the hands.

Pink rose water is made by placing 0.5 kg (1 lb) of petals and

Angelica *(Angelica archangelica)*. This very tall (1.5–1.8 m; 5–6 ft) plant grows best in a moist soil, and will flourish in semi-shade. Every part of it has its uses (including the root) and is highly scented.

Basil *(Ocimum basilicum)*.
The 'Dark Opal' variety,
with its very striking, almost
bronze leaves which when
pressed, release a warm,
spicy scent.

Bay laurel *(Laurus nobilis)*.
The glossy, dark green leaves
of this evergreen hard-
wooded tree or shrub
produce a very distinctive
flavour when added to
marinades, preserves, roast
meats or fish.

0.5 litre (1 pint) of water into a pan which is covered with a lid or plate to prevent the scented steam from escaping. Simmer over a low flame for about twenty minutes, then allow to cool, keeping the lid on. Then strain into glass bottles or jars. Always use crimson red or deep rose-pink flowers for the water will then be of a pleasing pink colour and not a dirty shade which appears when roses of other colours are used; a few of these will be as heavily scented as pink and red roses.

In Tudor times, the gardens of the less well-off grew rose root *Rhodiola rosea* in place of roses and though not having the same rich perfume as that made from rose blooms, rose root yielded a water to be used for the complexion and in cooking, which had something of the rose perfume. The roots are lifted in autumn when the plants are divided, some being replanted to grow on, while pieces of the root are washed clean of soil and cut into small pieces. They are then placed in pans with water (about 1 kg (2 lb) of root to 0.5 litre (1 pint) of water) and simmered with the lid on for an hour or so. This is allowed to cool with the lid still on, and then strained into bottles.

During the Middle Ages, there were alcoholic waters made to secret formulas at monasteries everywhere. These waters were the forerunners of alcoholic perfumes and essences and were made entirely from herbs and spices. Perhaps the most famous was Carmelite Water, made at the Abbey of St. Juste and it was used as an elixir for many purposes, taken inwardly and used outwardly. It is made from 1 kg (2 lb) of balm leaves, 110 g (4 oz) of lemon peel, 60 g (2 oz) each of nutmeg, cloves and coriander seed, some cinnamon bark and dried angelica root. To this is added 2.3 litres (about $\frac{1}{2}$ gallon) of orange flower water and 4.5 litres (1 gallon) of alcohol. It should then stand for four to six weeks before being placed in a still and slowly distilled.

To make scented waters

An aromatic bath essence can be made by simmering together in a pan, the stems and leaves of rosemary (the tips of the shoots being most potent), lemon balm, bergamot, hyssop and southernwood, a little lemon thyme and some chamomile, preferably the flowers. There should be 0.5 kg (1 lb) of herbs to 0.5 litre (1 pint) of water. Simmer for five to six minutes and strain, then add to the liquid, a 1/5th part of whisky or brandy which will keep the liquid potent for some weeks. Use a little in a warm bath at bedtime when it will give the body and spirits a refreshing uplift.

To make a bath which soothes and cleanses the body, to 0.5 kg (1 lb) of barley meal and 1.8 kg (4 lb) of bran, add a large handful of borage leaves and one of balm and some marigold flowers. Boil together for half an hour, preferably in rain water and add to a warm bath. Soak in it for half an hour, adding more hot water as the bath cools and you will come out completely refreshed.

For a lip salve, take two tablespoons of olive oil and enough beeswax to fill an eggcup and pour into a small saucepan. Add several tips of rosemary shoots and simmer slowly for half an hour, pouring in a little rose water. Then pour into an old face cream jar and allow to set. If a little is applied to the lips at bedtime in cold weather, it will be found to be most efficient.

Comfrey and marigold water can be added to home-made cold creams and are soothing and healing when applied to the skin, especially when burnt by over exposure to the sun or chapped by cold winds. An extraction of elder-flower water and lemon juice to whiten the complexion was perhaps used by Elizabeth I of England as most paintings depict her with a face as white as driven snow. Parsley and tansy water, made by simmering the leaves for fifteen minutes, and allowing to cool, were used to remove freckles and other facial blemishes caused by the sun. To brighten and strengthen the eyes, euphrasia or eyebright obtained by simmering the whole plant in milk and when cold, applying to the eyes with lint, is as much in demand in herbal beauty shops today as it was in Stuart times.

To make a herbal cream for the face, in an enamel pan melt 30 g (1 oz) of white wax and 60 g (2 oz) of almond oil, over a low flame and add 5.6 cl. (2 fluid ounces) of rose water (or rosemary water if you prefer it), stirring in thoroughly. Then pour into small screw-top jars and place in a cool room to set. This will take about twenty four hours when the cream will be ready to use. With practice, a face cream can be made that is indistinguishable from those obtainable from beauticians and there is a healthy demand for creams made from natural products. To make a rose (or rosemary) scented toilet soap, obtain a small phial of rose oil and add a few drops to half a pint of water brought to the boil. Then add some thinly cut pieces of pure-white soap which will quickly dissolve; pour into a container used for poaching eggs. When cool, the mixture will set into circular 'cakes' which are removed from the poachers, leaving no trace of soap other than what washing in detergent and warm water can remove. The longer the soap 'cakes' are stored, the harder and more lasting they become; all soaps improve with keeping and they emit a rich perfume when used. Good soap is now expensive but by using various essential oils, one may make at home an interesting collection of top quality soaps for a very small outlay.

Oil of rosemary (or of any other flower or herb) is obtained by treating 0.5 kg (1 lb) of rosemary tips (the ends of the branches) which are most potent in early summer, with 4.5 litres (1 gallon) of proof spirit in a jar with a wide screw top. Allow to stand for a week or ten days, then distil it, using an old kettle kept for the purpose, as previously described. The oil may be used in a bath or to massage into stiff joints. Spirit of rosemary, which is an excellent hair restorer, is made by treating the essential oil with spirits of wine and is available, incidentally, at most chemists (druggists).

To scent a room

Mary Eales, Confectioner to Queen Anne, gives (1682) a pleasing way of perfuming a room which would be appreciated today where there is an open fire. Take three teaspoonfuls of dried and powdered rosemary (or the leaves of sweet bay) and a teaspoonful of castor sugar. Place in a perfume pan or in an old frying pan kept for the purpose and put over hot embers when it will fill the room and indeed, the house with its delicious scent. Even a few stems of rosemary, lavender or bay which may be obtained when older bushes are pruned will prove equally pleasant if thrown onto a low fire. This used to be the way of keeping sweet a sick room in winter when it was too cold and damp to open windows and when most bedrooms had an open fire.

Another way was to dry the stems of lavender after removing the flowers. The stems were then immersed in a saltpetre solution and dried. If the ends were stuck into a small piece of soap or wax and lit at the top, they burned slowly, like incense and gave off the rich lavender perfume. This today is still practised in cottage homes, not only in sick rooms but in winter, to counteract the often musty smell where there are stone floors and no central heating and windows that cannot be opened on cold and foggy days. Every part of every herb was put to good use and those such as rosemary which are evergreen, were used on every day of the year, for fumigating, to make a tonic bath, for the hair and complexion, as a carminative and to sweeten the breath, and to give its rich aromatic perfume to roast meats. Queen Anne is said to have especially loved the scent of rosemary and it was Napoleon's favourite perfume. It figures prominently in the manufacture of eau-de-Cologne which the French military commander used extravagantly throughout his life.

Seeds too, can be used to scent a room. Angelica seed was burnt in a firepan or chafing dish while from the seed of *Angelica archangelica*, an essential oil is obtained which has a musk-like perfume and is used by the monks of La Grande-Chartreuse in making their celebrated liqueur.

Another recipe used for scenting apartments consists of a glassful of rose water made by distillation, which is poured into a chafing dish over hot embers and then adding clove powder 'little by little ... when you shall make a perfume of excellent good order'.

In the 17th century it is recorded that university students at Oxford would burn juniper wood 'to sweeten their chambers' and the dried roots of elecampane were also much in demand for the same purpose for when placed on a low fire, they give off a powerful scent of violets, like that of orris, the powdered root of the Florence iris. Orris was much in demand for including in sachets, to place amongst clothes and linen, to impart its violet perfume. Dried lavender flowers and those of rosemary were often included with it but to keep away moths, the bitter rue and wormwood, also southernwood with its refreshing lemon scent, were more effective. Orris root formed the base of most talcum powders to dust onto the body and onto clothes and linen. Other ingredients consisted of the dried root of sweet calamus (sweet flag), a rush which grows near water, the dried and crushed flowers of lavender, the leaves of sweet marjoram and some ground cloves. The powder was blown on to bed linen and onto clothes while being worn, with bellows like those which at one time were found in every room, to revive a dull fire.

Today, we could well follow the example of Louis XIV of France, said to have been 'the sweetest smelling monarch that had ever been seen'; he always insisted that, after washing, his shirts were to be soaked in rose water with which some cloves, marjoram, lavender and rosemary had been simmered over a low fire. When dried, the shirts were impregnated with a rich perfume which they would retain for several days. Underclothes and bed linen were usually washed in lavender or rosemary water and this could be done at the present time and so provide them with a rich and wholesome perfume.

Herbs for smoking and snuffs

In addition to their many uses about the home, herbs can be dried to make a pleasing and healthy pipe smoke as an alternative to the more expensive tobaccos, just as they were before the introduction of tobacco at the end of the 16th century. The dried and crushed leaves of chamomile release a pleasant apple scent when smoked; the dried leaves of coltsfoot, obtained from the countryside and wood betony and a few leaves of thyme can be mixed in. The herbs must be thoroughly dried and rubbed down. The mixture must be well broken down but not into a fine powder. The herbs when mixed together should have their separate identity. They will then burn slowly over a long time. Coltsfoot and chamomile should make up at least half the mixture which should be kept in a tobacco jar. If smoked by those suffering from asthma or bronchial cough, it will give relief while a pipe smoked in the evening will encourage sound sleep.

The same herbs may also be used in snuffs, together with alehoof, orris powder, peppermint and woodruff which when dry, has the pleasing smell of newly mown hay. In Shakespeare's time, herbal snuffs were passed round after a banquet, to clear the head. Snuffs were kept in a pouncet-box which was also used to hold talcum powders though originally a pouncet-box was used for pumice which was used in the preparation of parchment for writing to prevent ink from spreading. Later, herbal snuffs were replaced by tobacco snuffs and it was Catherine de Medici who began the fashion at the French Court which later spread around the western world.

74

In *The Country Lady's Directory* (1732) is a recipe which tells how to make perfumed snuffs which can be made at home today in exactly the same way. Obtain a wooden box, line it with white paper and cover the bottom with a 2.5 cm (1 in) layer of ordinary tobacco snuff. Over this is placed a layer of highly perfumed flowers; alternatively use rosemary or peppermint. Then add more snuff and more flowers or leaves until the box is filled. Do not disturb for seven to eight days, then place through a sieve as used in the kitchen and store the highly scented snuff in glass or wooden jars to use when required to clear the head. The scent will be perpetuated if the same snuff is again treated with similar fresh flowers or herbs.

There are several herbs that will bring about sound sleep if used to fill a pillow. The narcotic effects of hops are well known to those who have to work among them for any length of time in a confined space. Placed in a pillow, dried hops release a delightful scent which acts immediately on the nerves, bringing about complete relaxation and sleep soon follows. This will be even quicker if the dried leaves of agrimony and woodruff can be included and like hops, their fragrance increases the dryer they become. If muslin bags are filled with the herbs and placed beneath a pillowcase or hung from the headboard of the bed, the effect will be similar.

PART II

Herbs A-Z
Their culture and uses

Herbs A–Z
Their culture and uses

Aconite (*Aconitum napellus*)

It has been included in herbals since Saxon times although it is a poison and used only under medical direction. It is known as wolf's bane or bait for its juice was rubbed on arrow tips which were used to destroy those troublesome animals when Northern Europe was covered in dense woodlands. Its name is derived from the Greek *akoniton*, a dart. The plant abounds in higher alpine woodlands from the Himalayas to Europe and was possibly taken beyond its natural range by the Romans.

Description. It is a hardy perennial growing 90 cm (3 ft) tall with a fleshy tap root and with dark green deeply divided leaves, being almost fern-like. Its purple flowers are shaped like a monk's cowl, hence its country name of monk's-hood. A handsome border plant, it blooms in June and July when the flowers are much visited by bees.

Culture. It requires a well-drained soil containing humus to retain summer moisture and the best time to plant (as for all blue flowering plants) is March when the new shoots arise. Lift and divide four to five year plants, replanting the pieces or pull-offs about 60 cm (2 ft) apart. It will grow in semi-shade. It is also grown from seed sown in a frame or in shallow drills under cloches in April, transplanting to the border in twelve months. It is very hardy.

Medicinal uses. All parts of the plant are poisonous so after planting, wash the hands. Preferably, wear garden gloves. For Extract of Aconitum which is used in cases of cardiac failure and in liniments used externally to relieve rheumatism and lumbago, the young stems are cut at the end of June when most potent and are sold to those who prepare the drug. It is the roots, however, which are in most demand. These are lifted in October and dried on shelves in an open shed. It will take about three weeks before they are fully dry so that they snap when pressed. Younger roots contain the principle aconitine in its most potent form and these are wanted by the druggists. All parts of the plant are poisonous to humans and to animals if eaten. Keep away from children.

Agrimony, Common (*Agrimonia eupatoria*)

It is common in fields and hedgerows in Europe, also growing in western Asia and north Africa. From its tall elegant flower spikes, it is known as 'church steeple'. It takes its name from the Greek, *argemone* which means 'shining' for it was thought to be able to remove cataract from the eyes.

Description. A perennial, growing 60 cm (2 ft) tall and of slender habit; its reddish stems are covered in small hairs, the leaves composed of three to six pairs of leaflets which have toothed edges. The small yellow flowers are borne in long spiky racemes, those of *A. odorata*, a closely related species, being scented of apricots, likewise the leaves and the blackish root. Agrimony blooms in July and August and if the plants are cut in early autumn, they will dye wool deep yellow if boiled in the water.

Culture. In the garden, it is readily raised from seed sown in boxes or pans in spring or in a cold frame. Transplant the seedlings when large enough to handle and plant in the border or herb garden the following April. Propagation by root division may be carried out in spring. Plant about 40 cm (16 in) apart and into a light, well-drained soil. It will tolerate a small amount of shade.

Medicinal uses. A decoction of the leaves and flowers of *A. eupatoria* used fresh as a gargle will ease a sore throat for its volatile oil contains a high proportion of tannin and tannin lozenges are an aid to ease an inflamed throat. Pliny, the Roman historian, considered it 'a herb of princely authoritie' for it had so many uses. Traditionally a concoction is taken for disorders of the gall-bladder; take a teaspoonful of flowers and leaves and infuse in a cup of boiling water. In the same way agrimony 'tea' is a valuable summer tonic drunk cold with a little lemon juice, or hot in winter when made from the dried leaves. It is pleasantly fragrant. The 'tea' when sweetened with honey is a valuable aid to indigestion and as a cure for skin eruption, while a handful of leaves in a warm bath will give relief to stiff and tired limbs and ease rheumatic pains.

Culinary uses. The young leaves make a pleasant addition to a summer salad whilst a delicious wine is made by simmering for twenty minutes half a litre (1 pint) of water, two large handfuls of the leaves and flowers with 110 g (4 oz) of ginger. Then pour it over two sliced lemons and two oranges and 2.7 kg (6 lb) of sugar in a large bowl. Leave for three to four days, then strain into large jars to ferment and use in about six months (early spring).

Other uses. Because the flowers and leaves of the fragrant agrimony (*A. odorata*) retain their scent after drying, it was in demand for making dry pot-pourris and for stuffing cushions and pillows. Used with hops in pillows, it brings about sleep. The stems of this agrimony are more leafy, while it grows slightly taller. All parts are fragrant.

Alexanders (*Smyrnium olusatrum*)

A native of the eastern mediterranean coasts, especially around Alexandria (hence its name), it was perhaps introduced into the rest of Europe by the Romans for it is widely naturalized. It is present in hedgerows and on waste ground, usually in calcareous soil and by the sea.

Description. It is a biennial growing 90 cm–1.2 m (3–4 ft) tall with smooth furrowed stems which are hollow and yellowish-green glossy leaves which are toothed. The flowers are borne in April and May in a round umbel and are followed by broad black seeds which when dry, omit a pleasant spicy smell and may be included in soups and stews, hence it was known as the black pot herb.

Culture. For the seed to ripen well in cooler climates than its native Mediterranean, sow in shallow drills made 40 cm (16 in) apart, in July. Early in spring, thin to 15 cm (6 in) in the rows and support the plants by lengths of twine taken along the rows when

about 60 cm (2 ft) tall. If the leaf stalks and central shoots are to be used, earth up the plants on each side of the rows from June onwards. The seeds are harvested in September.

Culinary uses. The large fern-like leaves which have the same myrrh-like taste and smell as those of sweet cicely, may be used to flavour soups and stews and used sparingly in salads. At one time, the leaves were found on costermongers' barrows during Lent to sell for making sauces to accompany fish. In winter, countrymen would lift the roots and boil them to serve with meats, as an alternative to parsnips. They are more tender when blanched.

Alkanet (*Anchusa sempervirens* (now *Pentaglottis sempervirens*) and *A. tinctoria* (now *Alkanna tinctoria*))

We know them better as the anchusas, biennial border plants which take their name from the Greek *anchousa*, paint or dye, since the roots when steeped in linseed oil, yield a red dye once used to impart a crimson tint to salves and ointments. Before the introduction of rouge, ladies would colour their cheeks with it.

Description. *A. sempervirens*, a native of western Europe, is a hairy plant growing about 50 cm (20 in) tall with broad ovate leaves and bearing purple-blue flowers in short axillary spikes. It blooms May – August. *Alkanna tinctoria* is native of the Near East but came into Europe in Roman times.

Culture. Both plants require a light soil and are readily raised from seed sown in July in the border where the plants will bloom the following year. It flowers all summer. In March, thin to 30 cm (12 in) apart.

Medicinal uses. While *Alkanna tinctoria* is used to colour drinks and medicines, *A. sempervirens* is a restorative, being rich in potassium salts, like borage and the leaves are added to cider and other summer drinks. An infusion of the flowers (a handful to 0.5 litre (1 pint) of water) in hot water and allowed to cool will help to stay looseness of the bowels if a wineglassful is taken twice daily.

Culinary uses. The blue flowers of *A. sempervirens* will add interest to a salad, to which they impart a cool, slightly bitter taste. The iced water in which they have been infused makes a restorative drink in summer while the flowers make a delicious conserve to accompany game.

Angelica (*Angelica archangelica*)

This is a native of northern Europe. It differs from the more widespread wild angelica *A. sylvestris*, in having smooth stems, free of any purple tinting. It was called angelica since, because of its many valuable properties, it was thought to be of heavenly origin in Iceland and Scandinavia.

Description. A perennial, it grows 1.5–1.8m (5–6 ft) tall, its leaves divided into segments, often 60–75 cm (2–2½ ft) across and it blooms in July and August when bees visit its umbels of greenish-white flowers for their nectar. The whole plant gives off a pleasant muscatel scent.

Culture. It is perennial but is usually treated as biennial, seed being sown in July at the back of a border or in shallow drills made 50 cm (20 in) apart. Thin to 30 cm (12 in) apart and support the plants as they grow tall. It grows best in a moist soil containing some humus. Every part of the plant has its uses and every part (including the root) is scented, *A. archangelica* more so than *A. sylvestris*. If one or two plants are allowed to form seeds and shed them each year, it will provide a continuous supply of new plants without the need to obtain and sow more seed. Angelica will flourish in semi-shade.

Medicinal uses. It is a carminative and aids the digestion, due to the principle angelicin it contains. An infusion made by pouring 0.5 litre (1 pint) of boiling water on to 30 g (1 oz) of the fresh root (or stems and leaves) after crushing, and sweetened with a little honey, will ease a tight chest, relieve a sore throat and bring about sound sleep if taken at bedtime. Where the roots (which

are dark brown and deeply wrinkled) are required, grow on the plants for three years, not allowing them to seed. The roots will then be most potent, and be as thick as one's arm. Lift in July, clean them of soil, dry off and store in containers which are as air-tight as possible, to preserve their aroma and medicinal qualities. If the roots are very large, slice lengthwise into two or more pieces. An aromatic oil is obtained from the roots and seeds, used by the monks of La Grande Chartreuse to impart the distinctive flavour (like juniper) to their famous liqueur. The seeds are used in making gin, together with or as a substitute for juniper.

Culinary uses. Young angelica stems will impart their unique muscat flavour to rhubarb and apples when cooked together. Use the freshly cut stems which also make a delicious sweetmeat when candied, to decorate iced cakes. To candy, cut into 7.5 cm (3 in) lengths and boil for a few minutes until soft enough to peel. Then boil again in a little water for a few more minutes, drain off the surplus moisture and cover with sugar. Leave for two to three days, boil again until the sugar clarifies and place the now brilliant green crystallized stems into a glass jar to use when required. Cut into small pieces to decorate cakes and pastries or enjoy it as a sweetmeat. From the fresh leaves, a stimulating drink or 'bitters' may be made when used with hops. To a handful of hops, and the same amount of angelica leaves by weight, add 0.5 litre (1 pint) of boiling water and a spoonful of honey. Strain when cool and drink without undue delay.

Other uses. Unwanted pieces of dried root, or the seeds burnt over a low fire will perfume a damp musty-smelling room.

Anise (*Pimpinella anisum*)

Native of N. Africa and the Near East, it is mentioned in St. Matthew's gospel for it was one of the tithes of Mosaic law. The seed, like caraway, was used in making bread and cakes but of more importance, its aromatic oil has the reputation of destroying lice and other pests. Requiring a long hot summer to ripen its seeds, it is now little grown in Europe, the small amount of seed used being imported from Spain (Alicante) and N. Africa.

Description. A half-hardy annual, it grows 45 cm (18 in) tall and has finely serrated leaves. It blooms in July and August, the tiny white flowers opening star-like hence its name, star-anise. They are followed by small round fruits (seeds) which contain anisic aldehyde which gives them their peculiar and not unpleasant smell.

Culture. It is a frost tender plant; seed is sown early April, and it is best where the summers are sunny to give time for the seeds to ripen. Even if they do not, the foliage can be used in salads through summer. Sow in shallow drills made 30 cm (12 in) apart and do not transplant. Leave the seed heads until the end of September before harvesting.

Medicinal uses. Aniseed 'tea' for indigestion is made by pouring a pint of boiling water on to a teaspoonful of seed. Strain when cool and take a wineglassful when necessary. For bronchitis, infuse 30 g (1 oz) of seed in half a litre (1 pint) of boiling water and skim off the oil which rises to the top. Mix it (1 part to 4 parts spirits of wine) and at bedtime take six drops in a wineglass of hot water. It will also encourage sleep.

Culinary uses. In Europe and the Near East, the crushed seeds are used in making bread and cakes served at the end of a meal and at one time the whole seeds were used in the confectionery trade to make aniseed 'balls', popular with children, in which the seeds are thickly coated with sugar. The leaves add interest to a salad but must be used sparingly as the taste is an acquired one.

Other uses. Oil of aniseed is used by eastern people against lice and by criminals to put dogs 'off their scent' for the powerful scent destroys all others.

Balm (*Melissa officinalis*)

It is usually known as lemon balm on account of its refreshing lemony smell; it was

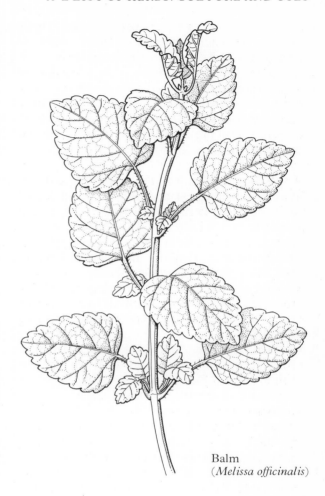

Balm
(*Melissa officinalis*)

much in demand for strewing and making into garlands and chaplets; the juice from the stems and leaves was rubbed on to oak furniture to which it would impart a high gloss and pleasing fragrance. It was also placed in ale to clarify it, as ground ivy would do.

Description. A hardy perennial, it grows 60–90 cm (2–3 ft) tall and bushy with stalked ovate leaves which are deeply wrinkled and serrate. They are brilliant green; there is also a variegated type, the leaves being splashed with gold but though attractive in the border, they are less highly perfumed. The small white flowers are borne in short axillary whorls during July and August, the calyx being covered in long white hairs.

Native of southern Europe, western Asia and N. Africa, it may have been taken to other areas of Europe by the Romans.

Culture. Of easy culture, it is propagated by root division in autumn or spring and from cuttings inserted into sandy soil in a frame in July and August. They are planted out the following spring into a soil containing some humus and in the middle of the border. It may require staking but is a plant of sturdy upright growth. It is not hardy in areas of severe frost and it is wise either to protect some plants or to bring them under cover. It is a plant that beekeepers should grow for its flowers provide a generous amount of nectar, hence its botanical name from the Greek *melissa*, honey. George Whitehead in *Garden Herbs* suggests that it emits 'the sweetest odour of all herbs' being similar to bergamot and enjoys the same soil conditions.

Medicinal uses. The juice has antiseptic and healing powers which was known to the Elizabethans for Gerard writing in 1596 said 'the juice glueth together green (new) wounds made by irons (swords)'. Balm 'tea' acts as a tonic and aids the digestion; it is also believed to promote long life and Mrs. Grieve in *A Modern Herbal* mentions John Hussey who lived to the age of 116 and always took balm 'tea' sweetened with honey for his breakfast. It is made by pouring 0.25 litre ($\frac{1}{2}$ pint) of hot water on to a small handful of fresh leaves. After a few minutes, strain, and add a few drops of lemon juice and a small teaspoonful of honey. This is also an excellent summer drink taken with ice in it. Balm 'tea' taken hot at bedtime promotes sweating and will help a severe cold or fever. It also acts as a carminative.

Balm was the principal ingredient of Carmelite Water, made by the nuns of the Abbey of St. Juste in the 14th century and which was used in the toilet of cultured people throughout mediaeval Europe. It is made from 1 kg (2 lb) of fresh balm leaves; 110 g (4 oz) of angelica root. These were slowly distilled with 2.3 litres ($\frac{1}{2}$ gallon) of orange-blossom water and 4.5 litres (1 gallon) of alcohol. It was rubbed on the body after washing and was also taken internally 'to renew youth'.

Culinary uses. A sprig placed in cider drinks will impart a cool lemony taste and the young leaves finely chopped make a pleasant addition to a salad or in cream cheese sandwiches. The dried leaves are used in stuffings and to make balm 'tea' in winter.

Other uses. The leaves, together with those of lemon thyme, bay and rosemary make a delicious 'green' pot-pourri and with cotton lavender in muslin bags, act as a moth deterrent.

Basil (*Ocimum basilicum* and *O. minimum*) Both the basils used in perfumery and cooking are native of the Far East and in cooler countries are best grown in pots in a sunny window or greenhouse. In India, the plants are held sacred to the Hindu gods, Krishna and Vishnu and are usually grown in pots, to be worshipped by the household while the name of the sweet basil, *O. basilicum* denotes its connection with royalty for it was an ingredient of a costly unguent used by royal households. Gerard said that 'the smell is good for the heart .... and taketh away sorrow that come with melancholie'. The plant has a warm spicy eastern smell and Tusser recommended it amongst herbs for strewing.

Description. *O. basilicum*, the sweet basil, is a branched half-hardy annual growing about 40 cm (16 in) tall and bushy, with dark green lance-shaped leaves covered in pellucid dots; it bears small white flowers in July and August. The form 'Dark Opal' is striking with its almost bronze leaves which are more heavily scented than the type, the scent being released when the leaves are pressed. *O. minimum* is of shorter habit and is known as the bush basil. It grows only half as tall as *O. basilicum* and was used by Tudor gardeners to surround beds of herbs and flowers but it too is only half-hardy.

Culture. Though the basils can be grown outside in temperate climates, they are best treated as indoor annuals where summers are cool. Seed is sown in shallow drills in April. Make the drills 30 cm (12 in) apart and thin to 15 cm (6 in) in the rows; or sow in small pots in a frame or sunny window or a gently heated greenhouse and grow on the plants outdoors in the pots on a terrace or verandah after hardening off, bringing them inside again at the end of September when the plants will remain green until Christmas. If there is overcrowding, transplant the seedlings to other pots and grow on. *O. minimum* can be grown in a sunny window box, but remember that the basils are only half-hardy and need protection from frost.

Medicinal uses. The essential oil when crystallized, is known as basil camphor and is used as an inhalant to clear the head. It has anti-bacterial qualities. The dried leaves, finely ground, were at one time used in snuffs, also taken to clear the head of colds and to ease a nervous headache.

Culinary uses. It once was used to give its distinctive flavour to 'Fetter Lane sausages' and it is the best of all herbs to accompany tomato dishes. A leaf in a glass of tomato juice will greatly improve the flavour and the chopped leaves in a tomato omelette or in a tomato salad will impart a warm, spicy taste. A delicious sauce to serve with fish is made from its fresh leaves while the dried leaves make a suitable alternative to sage in stuffings. To dry basil, cut away the whole plant at soil level late in September, tie into bunches and string up in an airy room or sunny window. When quite dry, remove the leaves from the stems and place in wooden containers to use when required. Where growing in pots in a sunny window, water sparingly during autumn and until the plants die back. Keep the plants cut back to make them grow more bushy.

Bay Laurel (*Laurus nobilis*)
A native of the Mediterranean and well known by the Romans who named it *laurus* (from which the plant's common name is also known) from the Latin *laudis*, praise; for it was esteemed above all other plants, crowning their poets and victorious warriors with chaplets and wreaths made from the leaves for it is always green. The plant was also believed to possess supernatural powers.

Description. It is an evergreen aromatic hard-wooded tree or shrub with lance-shaped leaves which are dark green and glossy; in May and June it bears small yellow flowers in clusters, followed by ovoid fleshy berries. The bark is smooth and in cool climates the plant needs winter protection if it is not to shed its leaves. Where temperatures regularly fall below $-18°$ C ($0°$ F) it can only be grown under glass.

Culture. It is raised from cuttings of the half-ripened wood which should be treated with 'hormone' rooting powder before inserting into a sandy compost around the side of a pot. Cuttings with a 'heel' will root more quickly. The bay or sweet bay as it is also called, lends itself to tub culture and makes an effective plant for a terrace or verandah or it will lend distinction if placed one on either side of an entrance. The plants can be clipped into pyramid shape with the stem well furnished with branches; or the stem may be grown like a standard rose, with the 'feathers' or lateral shoots removed as they form and until it reaches a height of about 1 m (3–4 ft). The top can be clipped to the size and shape of a football or to a cube with 30 cm (12 in) sides.

In summer, the foliage will respond to an occasional spraying in dry weather and by early October, the tubs should be placed under cover, in a greenhouse, garden room or a shed with windows where they remain until April. In the milder parts, protection from frost and cold winds can be given by covering the foliage with hessian (burlap) kept for the purpose. The plants will drop their leaves or they will turn brown at the edges if exposed to cold winds but will form new leaves in spring. The bay is distinguished from the poisonous cherry laurel by its waved and more pointed leaves which are also longer and narrower.

Medicinal uses. The Romans returning from battle or a long march would place a few leaves in their warm spring-water baths to ease their aching limbs and this may be done today. Add a sprig or two of rosemary with the bay leaves. The volatile oil of bay contains eugenol, geraniol and pinene which are relaxing and refreshing.

Culinary uses. A fresh leaf placed in a glass of milk for an hour before drinking or in a milk pudding before cooking will improve the flavour. A leaf is an important part of a bouquet garni for stuffings and roasting meats and one can be placed in the water in which salmon is poached to impart a distinctive flavour. A leaf will also add distinction to marinades and preserves.

Other uses. Bay leaves, after drying and pounding are an essential ingredient for pot-pourris and 'sweet jars'. To make a moist pot-pourri or sweet jar, place a thick layer of strongly scented fresh red or pink rose petals in a glass or earthenware jar, a teacupful of fresh lavender flowers and one each of orange blossom (Philadelphus will do) and clove-scented pinks or carnations. To these add a dozen fresh bay leaves finely chopped. Cover with 230 g ($\frac{1}{2}$ lb) of bay salt and 110 g (4 oz) common salt. Allow to stand for twenty four hours, then stir each day for a week. Then add 15 g ($\frac{1}{2}$ oz) of whole or crushed cloves, 110 g (4 oz) of orris, 15 g ($\frac{1}{2}$ oz) of cinnamon and a pinch of nutmeg. Thoroughly mix the ingredients together and fasten the top of the jar well down, opening it to release the powerful scent when required to perfume a room and closing it again an hour or so afterwards. Bay wood is deliciously scented and any clippings should be saved and dried, both leaves and twigs, to burn over a low fire. The perfume is especially appreciated in a sick room or where the room has a stone floor or is without a damp course.

Bergamot (*Monarda didyma*)

Native of North America it was introduced into Europe in 1774 and named after Dr. Monardes of Seville, who published the first authentic herbal on the flora of America in 1569. The name bergamot is from its likeness (when the leaves are pressed) to the scent of the bergamot orange of the Spanish peninsula. The plant gets its popular name from Oswego on Lake Ontario where the local Indian tribe used it for making a delicious and health giving drink, known as Oswego tea. Henry Phillips writing early in the 19th century said that its tea was preferred by many 'to that which came from China'.

Description. It is a hardy perennial growing 1 m (about 3 ft) tall with deeply grooved stems which are square and with bright green pointed lance-shaped leaves, hairy on both sides. The flowers are unique and most interesting, borne in whorls at the end of the stems and are red, pink or purple with pale green bracts. When in bloom (July–September), it is one of the loveliest plants of the herb garden.

Culture. A plant of great hardiness, it grows best in a soil containing a little humus to retain summer moisture but it flourishes almost anywhere, and in partial shade or full sun. Propagation is by root division in autumn or spring, replanting the pull-offs with their mint-like roots, 40 cm (16 in) apart. It grows upright and bushy and the stems are so sturdy that it does not need staking in a sheltered garden. At the end of autumn, the stems are cut back to about 7.5 cm (3 in) of soil level when new stems begin to grow up in spring. There are several handsome named varieties of which the best are 'Cambridge Scarlet' and 'Croftway Pink'. Bees love the flowers which secrete plenty of nectar. It is now occasionally found naturalized in open woodlands in England. All parts of the plant are pleasantly fragrant, the leaves and stems as well as the flowers and roots.

Medicinal uses. The 'tea' is a valuable tranquilliser and should be taken instead of Indian tea in the morning 'break' and at bed-time. It is made by pouring a quarter of a litre ($\frac{1}{2}$ pint) of boiling water on to a small handful of leaves. Leave for a couple of minutes, strain and add a few drops of lemon juice and sweeten with a little honey. Drink hot in winter or ice-cold in summer. The fresh leaves and stems added to a bath will sooth and refresh tired and aching limbs.

Other uses. The fresh leaves can be included in a 'green' pot-pourri to which they give an orange scent and the dried stems and roots (after washing) can be cut up and used in a dry pot-pourri or sweet jar.

Bistort (*Polygonum bistorta*)

Native to Europe eastwards to central Asia, it takes its name from *bis*, twice, and *torta*, twisted, because of its twisted rootstock, hence its common name of bistort or snakeweed. It is the roots that are of most value though at one time the young shoots were cooked and eaten in spring.

Description. An unbranched perennial, its large arrow-shaped blue-green leaves arise directly from the rootstock which is black on the outside, red within. The small pink flowers are borne in July and August and followed by seeds which are an important part of a bird's diet. It is most often seen in damp meadows and pastures on acid soils.

Culture. Not usually a garden plant though it has character. It is propagated by root division and grows well in any moisture-retentive soil. It is also grown from seed sown in spring in shallow drills and transplanted to 40 cm (16 in) apart. The variety 'Superbum' is a handsome border plant bearing spikes of pinkish-red on 60 cm (2 ft) stems.

Medicinal uses. The roots, when dried and powdered and taken in a little red wine, are a traditional remedy for bleeding piles while the same concoction was at one time taken to help with jaundice. The distilled water of the roots or leaves relieves sore gums and toothache.

Culinary uses. The dried leaves were once used in stuffings and the young shoots cooked and served with meats and the water, with its valuable mineral salts, included in soups.

Blessed thistle (*Cnicus benedictus*)

It was, with angelica, believed to cure all ailments and was known as the blessed thistle.

Description. An annual, it is a native of S. Europe and the Near East and may have come to western Europe with the Romans or by those returning from the Crusades. It was cultivated in cottage gardens for its medicinal qualities and is often found in the wild, on stony waste ground, as a garden escape. It is a much branched plant growing 60 cm (2 ft) tall with long, stem-clasping leaves with spines at the margin and covered in down. The thistlelike flowers are yellowish-green and appear in mid-summer.

Culture. It is worthy of planting in a border for it is a handsome plant and is propagated from seed sown in early autumn or in early spring. Scatter the seed in small groups and thin to about 40 cm (16 in) apart. Ordinary soil is suitable.

Medicinal uses. It is a tonic and blood purifier and given to reduce a high temperature. It also stimulates the appetite. An infusion of a large handful of leaves and the flowering tops in half a litre (1 pint) of hot water can be taken, a wineglassful at a time, to reduce a temperature, used cold as a tonic or hot at bedtime. Though an annual, it will remain green through winter.

Bogbean (*Menyanthes trifoliata*)

Also known as marsh trefoil and buckbean it grows on wet land and is so named because its leaves resemble those of the broad bean.

Description. A glabrous perennial with a creeping rootstock, its leaves being held on long petioles. The pale pink flowers have red stamens and are borne from May to July in a thick spike. Growing to about 45 cm (18 in) high, the plant is found in marshlands throughout the northern hemisphere from Greenland to Morocco.

Culture. Readily propagated by division or from seed in spring, it is a plant for low lying land rather than the herb garden but ordinary soil is suitable if given a liberal dressing of peat or leaf mould, for the roots must be kept moist. Plant 45 cm (18 in) apart.

Medicinal Uses. The leaves contain a bitter principle and act as a spring tonic as well as providing vitamin C; thus it was used in salads and sandwiches to accompany cheese or pickles. To make a tonic drink, immerse a handful of leaves in half a litre (1 pint) of boiling water, strain and when cool, take a wineglassful daily. An infusion of the dried leaves (a tablespoonful to 0.5 litre (1 pint) of water) can be taken during winter and it will keep the skin clear of blemishes as well as being a tonic drink. The dried leaves can also be included in herbal smoking mixtures.

Borage (*Borago officinalis*)

Another herb of Mediterranean origin but naturalized in many parts of Europe and N. America. The ancient Greeks called it *Euphresynon* because as Gerard said 'when the flowers and leaves are put into wine, it makes men and women glad and merry' but the name borage is derived either from the Latin *burra*, rough hair, which refers to the hairy leaves or from the Celtic *borrach*, courage, for it was believed that an infusion gave people courage. 'I borage, always brings courage', was an old country saying.

Description. An annual growing 65 cm (2 ft) tall, all parts of the plant are covered in bulbous hairs which give the oval leaves a grey appearance. The flowers are brilliant sky-blue with black contrasting anthers borne in forked cymes, which fold over to form a central cone. A large quantity of nectar is secreted at the base of the stamens and from June until late August, the flowers are much visited by bees.

Culture. Seed is sown in July in drills made 25 cm (10 in) apart and in spring the plants are thinned to 20 cm (8 in) in the rows; or sow in a frame in August and move to the open ground about April 1st when another sowing can be made in the open to continue the display and supply of flowers and leaf through summer and autumn. The plants require a sunny position and a well-

Borage
(*Borago officinalis*)

drained soil. Those over wintering will seed themselves.

Medicinal uses. John Pechey in his *Herbal* (1695) described it as one of the 'four cordial-flowers' and said 'the distilled water and conserve of the flowers, comfort the heart, relieve the faint, cheer the mel-

Bergamot *(Monarda Didyma)*, 'Cambridge Scarlet' variety. This very hardy plant, with its unique red and purple flowers, is one of the most striking plants in the herb garden. Its leaves can be used to make tea, and the stems and roots can be dried and added to pot-pourris or sweet jars.

Chives *(Allium schoenoprasum)*. This hardy perennial herb is very easy to grow and increases rapidly. In the kitchen its mild onion flavour is used in a wide range of dishes such as soups, salads and cheese savouries.

Burnet *(Poterium sanguisorba)*. A very useful plant, particularly as it grows through the winter. Traditionally it was used to heal wounds and to cure gout and rheumatism. It makes a pleasing addition to salads and summer drinks.

ancholy, and purify the blood'. The distilled water will ease a sore throat if used as a gargle when warm. The older writers have been proved correct when they said that borage cheers up the melancholy, gives one a sense of well-being and will revive one during hot weather. Hence the leaves were included with cheese, in a ploughman's lunch, washed down with cider. For the same reason, the leaves may be put in most summer drinks such as cider, tonic water and Pimms No. 1.

Culinary uses. A delicious 'cool tankard' is made by simmering two lemons with an ounce of sugar and a small handful of borage leaves. When cool, add a bottle of white wine, strain and use as a summer drink from the refrigerator. Borage leaves (which should be cut across to release the juice from the veins) in cider and lemonade drinks, give a cool, cucumber-like flavour while the flowers and leaves add the same qualities to a salad and are invigorating when used in this way. The leaves fried in batter make appetizing fritters, especially if covered with grated cheese. The flowers can be candied like violets and used to decorate cakes. This is done by dipping the flowers in a solution of gum arabic and rose water, then sprinkling with fine sugar before placing on trays in a warm oven to dry. Keep them in boxes between tissue-paper layers until required.

Brooklime (*Veronica beccabunga*)

In Anglo-Saxon leech-books this plant was called *broke lemp* (growing in the slime or mud of brooks). It has a bitter taste. Drake's sailors would gather it from ditches before sailing as it kept away scurvy, due to its vitamin C content, for which purpose it was sold in the streets of London.

Description. An almost prostrate perennial rooting from the leaf nodes as it trails over the ground. It has glossy dark green oval leaves and bears tiny bright blue flowers in racemes from May to September. It is widespread in damp places, in ditches and by the side of ponds and streams from western Europe eastwards to Japan.

Culture. It is rarely grown in gardens. If required, seed is sown in boxes in spring and the plants set out 15–20 cm (6–8 in) apart in a moisture-holding soil; or sow in shallow drills in the open and thin out to the same distance apart.

Medicinal and culinary uses. The two go together, the plant being used in salads all the year round as a source of vitamin C and as an alternative to watercress. An infusion of the leaves and a wine glassful taken once daily for seven to ten days will clear the blood and the skin of blemishes.

Burdock (*Arctium minus*)

It takes its botanical name from the Greek *arktos*, a bear, from its long hairy burrs which have hooked spines and stick to the clothes when thrown, hence they were used by girls to throw at their lovers and if they stuck, it proved true-love! It takes its country name from its burrs and from the dock-like leaves.

Description. It is a biennial growing 1 m tall (3–4 ft) with large wavy heart-shaped leaves, depicted in the landscape paintings of Turner and Wilson. The long-stalked thistle-like flower heads are borne in July and August.

Culture. It is common on waste ground throughout Europe and has been introduced into N. America. It is an obnoxious weed in the garden, depriving the soil of its goodness. It will seed itself anywhere in late summer, the plants reaching maturity in twelve months.

Medicinal uses. Since early times the roots have had the reputation of being the best of all blood purifiers for which purpose it is still widely grown in the north of England and in the United States and Canada where an average crop will yield 2000 lbs of root per acre. The dried root is used with that of the cultivated dandelion, 'Dandelion and Burdock' being a popular blood purifying spring and summer beverage. Like docks, the juice of the leaves rubbed on wasp stings will give instant relief.

Where grown commercially, the plants

Burdock (*Arctium minus*)

are sown in drills 60 cm (2 ft) apart in August and the roots lifted in autumn the following year, after first removing most of the top growth. The roots are washed and dried before crushing them into powder. Dandelions are treated in the same way.

Burnet, Lesser or Salad (*Sanguisorba minor* or *Poterium sanguisorba*)

It is a common plant of downlands, especially of a chalky nature and Shakespeare told us that it was associated with good husbandry. Sheep love to feed on it. According to Pliny, it takes its botanical name from the Greek *poterion*, a drinking cup, for it was used to impart its cool, cucumber-like taste to wines and cider drinks, like borage. It is common in Europe, east to Persia and south to Morocco and is also naturalized in N. America. It was one of the plants which Francis Bacon, in his *Essay of Gardens* said 'perfume the air most delightfully ... when trodden upon and crushed, are burnet, wild thyme and water mint', and he suggested planting 'whole alleys of them'.

Description. A glabrous erect perennial growing about 30 cm (12 in) tall with serrated leaves, borne in pairs all the way along the stems, so well described by William Turner, Dean of Wells, in his *Herbal* (1551) as 'like unto the wings of birds ... setteth out when they intended to fly'. He said also that 'the Dutch call it (the plant) "God's little bird"'. The leaflets are borne six to twelve to a stem, directly opposite each other. The tiny purple and green flowers are borne in a capitate cyme but should be removed as they form for they exhaust the plant and serve no purpose. They appear June to August. It is a useful plant for the herb garden and also in pasture as it continues to grow all winter and can be used in salads all the year through.

Culture. It requires ordinary well drained soil and an open sunny situation. Seed is sown in April in a box or frame and the young plants set out 25 cm (10 in) apart when large enough to handle. Do not remove the leaves until the second year.

Propagation of established plants is also by root division in spring or autumn.

Medicinal uses. It has the same styptic qualities as the greater burnet, healing wounds made by carpenters' tools and swords by taking an infusion of the leaves. Turner advised steeping the leaves and stems in wine or ale and taking a little each day to cure gout and rheumatism.

Culinary uses. The leaves make a pleasing addition to a salad, especially in winter and spring when lettuce is in limited supply. They are also used to impart a 'quick' taste to summer drinks which will refresh one in the same way as borage and balm. They are delicious when included in cream cheese sandwiches.

Burnet, Great (*Sanguisorba officinalis*)
Both this and salad burnet may be enjoyed in summer salads and both are plants of similar appearance though salad burnet grows to only half its height. The salad burnet is of greater importance.

Description. A perennial plant growing 1 m tall (about 3 ft) with dull green oblong leaves and bearing purple-brown flowers in July and August. It is found in pastureland and by the side of woodlands through Europe and N. Asia and was once grown as a fodder crop. It is also naturalized in N. America.

Culture. It requires a light friable soil and an open sunny position. Plant in spring and propagate by root division, lifting and dividing every three to four years.

Medicinal uses. It is an astringent and was at one time used in cases of diarrhoea and dysentery, also for internal haemorrhages. An infusion of the leaves (a handful to half a litre (1 pint) of boiling water) or of the dried roots should be taken, a wine glassful at a time, two to three times daily.

Culinary uses. The leaves may be used in salads but they are not as pleasant as those of salad burnet while the roots and leaves may be used to make a tonic herb beer which will also clear the blood of impurities.

Calamint (*Calamintha ascendens*, formerly *C. officinalis*)
Also known as basil thyme and mountain mint, it takes its botanical name from the Greek *kalos*, beautiful or excellent, and *minthe*, mint.

Description. It is an aromatic hairy perennial of shrubby habit, growing 25 cm (10 in) tall and is present on banks and mountainous slopes of a calcareous nature. It is found throughout Europe and also in N. Africa. The ovate leaves have serrated edges and the lilac-pink flowers are borne in forked cymes during July and August. The lower lip of the corolla is lobed and covered with purple spots. It is evergreen.

Culture. It requires an open situation and a well-drained soil and with its shrubby habit may be used to edge a herb garden. Propagation is by cuttings of the half-ripened wood taken in August (preferably with a 'heel' attached) and rooted in a sandy compost in a frame; or by root division in spring. Plant 25 cm (10 in) apart.

Medicinal uses. An infusion of the stems in a pint of boiling water, with a few drops of lemon juice, makes a 'hot' aromatic 'tea' which warms the stomach on a cold day and is a splendid remedy for flatulence and indigestion. The dried leaves which are collected in July and August can be used in the same way. Culpeper said an infusion relieved colic of the stomach and bowels. Its pleasantly warming feeling is due to its camphoraceous volatile oil.

Caraway (*Carum carvi*)
It takes its name from Caria in Asia Minor where it grows naturally, amongst rocky outcrops and in considerable heat but it is prominent over northern Europe and much of Asia. The Romans used it in making bread and cakes as in Italy, Ireland and Germany to this day.

Description. A hardy biennial growing 60 cm (2 ft) tall, with hollow stems and bipinnate leaves. All parts of the plant have the peculiar scent including the root which grows as long as a parsnip. The white flowers are borne in umbels during June and July but they fruit only where summers are long and hot. The seeds (carpels) are oblong, with ridges and the essential oil has a camphor-like smell. This is more pronounced from plants grown in the East for commercial seed production. The seed was used to make a spiced wine known as *aqua compositis* which Henry VIII greatly enjoyed. Today, the essential oil is used to flavour the liqueur Kummel. In Shakespeare's time the seed was roasted with apples, to which it imparted its unique 'warm' flavour and is still served with apples in Hall at Trinity College, Cambridge, England.

Culture. For the seed to have any chance of ripening, treat it as a biennial, sowing in July where the plants are to mature, in circles in the herb border, or in drills in the vegetable garden, made 40 cm (16 in) apart. In April, thin the seedlings to 20 cm (8 in) apart in the rows. An open situation is required and a well-drained soil. Leave the plants as long as possible for the seeds to ripen, then cut away just above soil level and use the roots as a winter vegetable.

Medicinal uses. To relieve flatulence, infuse 30 g (1 oz) of seed to 0.5 litre (1 pint) of boiling water and when cool, take a teaspoonful when required. It is warming and comforting. A little of the powdered seed taken with a teaspoonful of sugar in a wineglass of hot water will relieve colic.

Culinary uses. The leaves when placed in soups and stews impart their special flavour while the seed is put into bread and cakes, but its taste is not to everyone's liking. It was served with fruit as it was known to expel wind and in Holland and Germany, the seed is put into cheeses. The young roots can be braised or served with white sauce to accompany meats and as Parkinson said, are as agreeable as parsnips.

Catmint (*Nepeta cataria*)

It is so-called because of its fascination to cats, attracted by its pungent smell and when the plants are dry and the weather warm, they roll about them for hours. The plant has useful medicinal qualities. It is not the same plant as the garden catmint.

Description. A hardy perennial growing 60 cm (2 ft) tall, all parts being covered in soft hairs which give it a frosted appearance. The flowers are pale pink with crimson anthers and are borne in whorls from early July until September. It is the flowers and upper leaves which have the most valuable properties. The plant is present normally on chalky soils from Portugal east to Kashmir. It is also naturalized in N. America and S. Africa.

Culture. It grows well in ordinary soil and is tolerant of semi-shade. Propagation is by root division in autumn or spring and by cuttings taken in July and rooted in a sandy compost in a frame. It is also raised from seed sown in spring in shallow drills or a frame, transplanted to 25 cm (10 in) apart.

Medicinal uses. It is the flowering shoots that are used; a handful infused in half a litre (1 pint) of hot water and sweetened with a little honey will, if a wineglassful is taken at bedtime, cause the body to perspire and bring out a fever or heavy cold. It is also a carminative and will relieve a nervous headache brought on by tension. For this, take a little when the infusion has cooled.

Culinary uses. The leaves and young shoots can be used for seasoning and in stuffings and have a similar taste and smell to pennyroyal which is used in the same way. Dry the leaves for winter use.

Centaury (*Centaurium erythraea*)

It was named after the Greek centaur Chiron, who was skilled in the use of herbs and at one time it was called chironia or red centaury on account of its rose-red flowers. It was one of the fifteen 'herbs of magic' of ancient England, 'all-powerful against wicked spirits'.

Description. It is a glabrous annual growing about 15 cm (6 in) tall and forming a rosette of pale green pointed leaves from which rise its rose pink flowers, borne July and August in terminal clusters. It is a common plant of dry places throughout

Europe, into N. Africa and W. Asia. It is also naturalized in N. America.

Culture. It is rarely grown in gardens but it is a pleasing little plant of medicinal value. Sow in spring in small groups to the front of a border and thin to 15 cm (6 in) apart. Ordinary soil is suitable.

Medicinal uses. A handful of flowers infused in a pint of boiling water will relieve indigestion if a little is taken after a rich meal. Countrywomen would wash the face with centaury water to keep the skin clear of blemishes. Another traditional use is in strengthening the bladder of old people and preventing children from wetting the bed. The leaves should be used with those of St. John's wort, a small handful of each to half a litre (1 pint) of water and after simmering for several minutes, strain, sweeten with a little honey and drink warm at bedtime.

Chamomile (*Anthemis nobilis* now *Chamaemelum nobile*)

It grows over much of Europe and N. Africa and was revered by the ancient civilizations for its many health-giving qualities. Tudor gardeners used it to make their lawns and Drake would be playing bowls on a well-cut and rolled chamomile 'lawn' when news reached him that the Armada had been sighted. It derives its name from the Greek meaning 'earth apple' on account of its fruity smell. In Spain it is *manzinella*, little apple.

Description. Common chamomile is an almost prostrate perennial with a much-branched stem so that it soon forms a thick mat covering an area of about a square foot. The leaves are finely cut into segments and when trodden upon emit a rich fruity scent. The flowers are borne solitary in July and August, the ray florets being white, the disc florets yellow. It must not be mistaken for the much commoner, but foetid, stinking mayweed, *Anthemis cotula*.

Culture. It is readily raised from seed sown in spring, an ounce of seed producing about 1000 plants. Sow broadcast, into a sandy soil

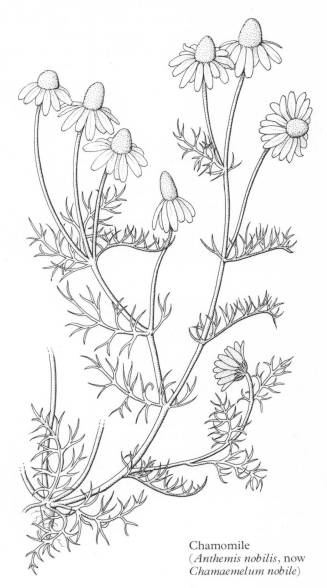

Chamomile
(*Anthemis nobilis*, now
Chamaemelum nobile)

containing some humus but in ground that is well-drained, raking the seed into the surface. Thin to about 25 cm (10 in) apart. For a chamomile 'lawn', plant at half the distance.

Medicinal uses. Chamomile 'tea' has many uses. It will sooth tired nerves and relieve indigestion if a wineglassful is taken once daily, and the same may be used for a tonic hair rinse. To make the 'tea' remove the daisy-like flowers when fully open and use a handful to half a litre (1 pint) of boiling water. Leave for ten minutes, then strain and use as required. It is also a valuable sedative. The flowers may be dried to use when the plants are not in bloom. The medicinal qualities are contained in the central florets and English grown chamomile is the most powerful. To ease neuralgia, fill a small muslin bag with flowers, immerse it for a coupe of minutes in boiling water, drain and apply to the face as warm as possible. The same treatment can be applied to sores when healing will be rapid.

The flowers and leaves of this plant, when dried are the chief ingredient of herbal smoking mixtures and will calm the nerves and bring about sound sleep. The dried leaves are also taken as snuff. Chamomile 'tea' sweetened with a little honey is the best of all remedies for those who suffer from nightmares and it acts as a tonic. Those who take a wineglassful each day, report how well it invigorates and tones the body and brings about sound sleep. The plant may also be used to make a tonic beer and with a little ginger, is warming to the stomach on cold days if taken hot and is excellent for colic and diarrhoea. Water obtained from the dried flowers and rubbed on to the hair will, with perseverance, dye it blond.

Chervil (*Anthriscus cerefolium*)

It takes its botanical name from *cheirei* and *phyllum* meaning 'that which rejoices the heart' because of its warming properties. All parts of the plant can be used and they have a distinct aniseed smell.

Description. A pubescent annual growing 40 cm (16 in), its hollow stems covered with silky hairs. Its tripinnate leaves are pubescent on the underside while its flowers, which appear in May and June are borne in lateral umbels. They are followed by smooth fruits with a long beak. It is present as a native in Europe and Western Asia and is found naturalized in every continent.

Culture. It quickly runs to seed if transplanted and before making much leaf so sow thinly in April in shallow drills made 30 cm (12 in) apart and do not transplant. Alternatively, treat as biennial where the soil is well-drained and sow in August. The plants will then have a longer season for the leaves to be used and for the seed to mature. Gerard wrote that its handsome fern-like foliage 'is deeply cut, of a very good and pleasant smell ... which has caused us to call it sweet chervil'.

Medicinal uses. Countrywomen bathe the face in chervil water and rub the juice on to blemishes which are quickly removed. The juice is aperient but must be used sparingly, only two to three drops in water.

Culinary uses. At one time the long taproots were boiled and candied and taken as sweetmeats 'to warm and comfort a cold phlegmatic stomach' wrote Parkinson. However, the roots must be boiled first otherwise they are poisonous. The leaves make a welcome addition to a summer salad with their slight aniseed taste while a delicious sauce to accompany fish is made from them. If spring sown plants are covered with cloches in October, they will remain green all winter and those sown in August will be ready to take over in spring, thus providing a year round supply of fresh leaf, so useful for garnishing as an alternative to parsley.

Chicory (*Cichorium intybus*)

Also known as succory, this is a most appetising vegetable; the dried roots are used as a substitute for coffee. Countrymen also knew it as turnsole for its flowers turn to face the sun each day as it moves round in its orbit. Linnaeus used it as a flower clock for at Upsala the flowers open at about 6.0 a.m. and close at 10.0 a.m. It takes its name from the Latin *succurrere*, to run under, as the root penetrates deeply in well-dug land.

Description. It is perennial, with a long tap root and alternately branched stems arising to a height of about 60–120 cm (2–4 ft) with clasping leaves and bright blue sessile flower heads. It is a plant of grasslands and is found all over the temperate world where it has been introduced by man.

Culture. It is grown in gardens chiefly for its roots which are forced in winter to serve as a vegetable and included in salads. Seed is sown about June 1st, not earlier or the plants may run to seed. Sow in drills made 40 cm (16 in) apart and thin to 20 cm (8 in) in the rows. A deeply worked soil is necessary and to retain moisture, dig in some humus and decayed manure or used hops. If the weather is dry, keep the plants well supplied with moisture. In late autumn when the plants have died back and the roots are almost as thick as a man's wrist, they should be carefully dug up, trimmed of all small roots and forced. This is done in the dark, in a cellar, shed or garage, or beneath the greenhouse bench and if possible, a small amount of heat should be used to complete the forcing within four weeks. Fill a deep orange box to a depth of 15 cm (6 in) with composted straw or manure which will retain some heat and over it, place 15 cm (6 in) of fine soil. Into this, the roots are set close together, with the crown just below soil level. Water in and cover the box with sacking or hardboard to exclude light. 'Giant Witloof' is the best variety for the heads of the tightly packed and blanched leaves are large, solid and pure white when forced, which makes for sweet and tender eating. When about 20 cm (8 in) high, the shoots are broken off to use. But leave the roots undisturbed for there will be a second crop of smaller shoots in a month's time. Chicory can also be forced in large plant pots, with some manure at the bottom and filled up with soil. Into this, the roots are planted. To exclude light, place an inverted pot over that containing the roots and grow on under the kitchen sink.

Medicinal uses. An infusion of the tops of the plants, including the flowers, can be made between late July and mid-September and will cleanse the skin if applied to the face with lint. The same may be used to bathe the eyes; it will relieve them of tiredness and give them a sparkle. Again, it may also be taken (a wineglassful daily) in cases of liver upsets and when the tops are placed in soups and stews, they will sustain those made weak by long illness.

Culinary Uses. The forced heads are delicious when grated raw (with celery) into a winter salad and the fresh leaves can be used in salads from mid-July until late September. The forced heads make a delicious winter vegetable to serve with game and meats. Remove the shoots just before cooking, place in a saucepan and cover with salt water for several minutes. Drain off and add a few pats of butter and simmer for about an hour until tender. Serve with white or cheese sauce or with melted butter.

Chives (*Allium schoenoprasum*)

It is present throughout the northern hemisphere but it is not a common plant anywhere. It grows on mountainous slopes and rocky outcrops, possesses extreme hardiness and is the smallest and mildest of the onion family. No other herb has more culinary uses. Since earliest times it grew in every cottage garden for it is green almost all the year. Tusser included it in his *Herbs* for the kitchen, calling it seithes and it was also known as sieves and cives.

Description. A hardy perennial reproducing itself from small bulbs from which arises a dense tuft of hollow shiny green rush-like leaves growing 15 cm (6 in) tall. The botanical name of the plant does in fact mean 'rush-leek'. The leaves are removed just above soil level and are chopped into pieces about 1 cm (about ½ in) long, to sprinkle over those foods for which they are a suitable accompaniment. The plants bear pretty ball-shaped flowers of soft pink with blue anthers during August and September, being in appearance like thrift, with paper-like bracts.

Culture. Of the easiest culture, it is propagated by division every three or four years, the clusters of small bulblets being pulled or 'teased' apart and replanted into rich soil, about 20 cm (8 in) apart in autumn or spring. They make an attractive edging to a border or for knot gardens. Plants may also be raised from seed sown in shallow drills in April. Thin to 15 cm (6 in) apart, transplanting the thinnings. The plants should not be cut until their second year. They take up little ground and remain in constant use.

Medicinal uses. Like all the onion family, chives are mildly antibiotic, stimulate the appetite and lower blood pressure.

Culinary uses. A dish of fresh chives, perhaps mixed with chopped parsley, should be on every luncheon table for both are amongst the most health-giving of foods. Chives have a mild onion-like taste and may be sprinkled on to soups and stews and over scrambled eggs. Include them in omelettes and in sandwiches filled with cream cheese, tomato or hard-boiled eggs. They are a pleasant complement to all egg and cheese dishes and no salad is complete without them. Chives can also be included in rissoles and shepherd's pie and sprinkled over mashed potatoes. The more often the plants are cut, the quicker they grow. Water them in dry weather to maintain the supply and half a dozen plants will prove most rewarding.

Clary (*Salvia sclarea*)

Its popular name is a shortened version of clear eyes as an infusion of the leaves will relieve tired and inflamed eyes, hence its other names, eyebright and seebright. It was also included in ale to make it more potent and the Germans make a wine from the leaves which is known for its narcotic qualities.

Description. It is a short-lived perennial from southern Europe with erect, 30–100 cm (12–40 in) stems which are sticky to the touch and strong smelling, with softly hairy, wrinkled, oblong, heart-shaped leaves having toothed margins. The flowers are pale blue, each about 2 cm (1 in) long, set off by conspicuous membranes, and rosy-white or pale violet bracts. These are borne in whorls on branching spikes and appear from May to September.

Culture. It is best grown as a biennial, raised from seed sown in April in boxes or a frame, and the seedlings transplanted to about 50 cm (20 in) apart.

Medicinal uses. An infusion of a small handful of leaves in boiling water will, after being cooled and strained and applied to the eyes with lint, sooth and remove any soreness. The dried and finely ground root taken as snuff will clear the head.

Culinary uses. The flowers and leaves can be included in a salad and in omelettes and the leaves, dipped in batter and served with orange juice are a delicious accompaniment to fried ham or bacon.

Coltsfoot (*Tussilago farfara*)

It takes its name from *tussis ago*, to drive away a cough for which purpose it has always been used by apothecaries. It takes its name coltsfoot or foalsfoot from the horse-shoe shape of the leaves.

Description. A low growing perennial with circular leaves and bearing in February and March, drooping flower heads on short leafless stems. The yellow flowers with rayed petals appear before the leaves. It is present throughout the northern hemisphere on waste ground everywhere and is an obnoxious weed in the garden, difficult to eradicate.

Culture. Too common to be worthy of garden culture but if required, seed is sown broadcast in spring where the plants are to grow and an unused corner of the garden should be selected. Thin to 20 cm (8 in) apart.

Medicinal uses. Pliny said that the smoke from the leaves when inhaled, gave immediate relief to a tight chest and hard cough. For bronchitis, place 30 g (1 oz) of leaves in a saucepan with 1.7 litres (3 pints) of water and simmer for thirty minutes, strain, sweeten with honey and take a cup at bedtime, preferably hot. The plant contains tannin and the same infusion can be used for a gargle to ease a sore throat. For the relief of asthma, make up a herbal mixture to smoke, composed of the dried leaves of coltsfoot, chamomile (also flowers), betony, lavender and thyme and enjoy a pipeful

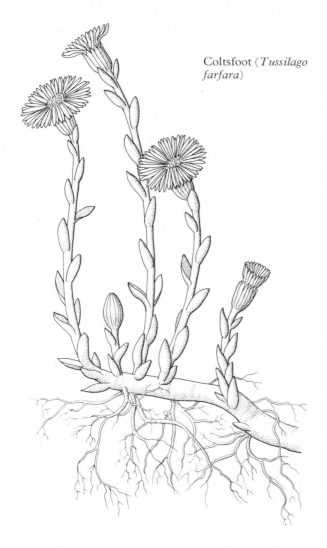

Coltsfoot (*Tussilago farfara*)

effect on sprains and bruises, quickly reducing swellings.

Description. A handsome hairy perennial growing 60 cm (2 ft) tall with branched stems and leaves which taper to a point. The flowers are purple, pink and white and borne in two-forked clusters during July and August. The plant grows in damp places through Europe east to Siberia and is attractive in the border. It must not be confused with the Russian comfrey, *S. × uplandicum* which is to be found on many dry roadsides and in waste places.

Culture. It requires a moist soil and is tolerant of semi-shade. It is readily raised from seed sown in spring in a frame or in shallow drills, transplanted in July to about 50 cm (20 in) apart, or propagated by root division in spring.

Medicinal uses. With arrowroot, marshmallow and slippery elm, it is a demulcent. A teaspoonful of a decoction made from the dry roots has a reputation for controlling bleeding of the bladder, bowel and piles. The roots contain an abundance of mucilage and are given for diarrhoea and dysentery and to heal stomach ulcers. Its healing action is due to asparagin which is present in the plant but is now manufactured synthetically. Due to its presence, the fresh leaves when bound over a cut or wound, bring about its healing.

Coriander (*Coriandrum sativum*)

It takes its name from the Greek koriandrum. Unripened seed has an unpleasant smell but when fully ripe, this is replaced by a rich aromatic scent and the longer the seeds are kept, the more pleasing does the scent become, taking on a sweet orange fragrance. It is native to N. Africa; Pliny said the best seed came from Egypt as it still does. It is one of the principal ingredients of curry powders.

Description. An annual, it grows 20–30 cm (8–12 in) tall with solid stems which are ridged and bipinnate dark green leaves, deeply divided. The flowers are borne in umbels during July and August and are

before bedtime. Leaves of Coltsfoot are collected in summer and after drying, store in a wood or cardboard box.

Culinary uses. The leaves, fried in batter can be included in omelettes and served with mustard sauce.

Comfrey (*Symphytum officinale*)

Closely related to borage, it was also called knitbone and boneset for the crushed root when bound to a broken limb brought about rapid healing while the leaves have the same white or pale mauve. They are followed by round pale yellow fruits which yield an essential oil of which the alcohol coriandrol is the principal ingredient.

Culture. The seed is sown in April, in drills made 20 cm (8 in) apart. Ordinary soil is suitable and an open, sunny situation is necessary for the plants to obtain full sunlight to ripen their seeds. They will do so only in a dry summer and autumn.

Medicinal uses. It was one of the ingredients of carmelite water and coriander water relieves flatulence and aids the digestion. It is made by pouring 1.1 litres (2 pints) of boiling water over 15 g ($\frac{1}{2}$ oz) of seed. Take warm or cold, a wineglassful whenever necessary. It is an excellent carminative and encourages sleep if taken before bedtime.

Culinary uses. The seeds and fresh leaves will impart their flavour to soups and broths but the seeds are best kept for six months before they are used when they will also impart their orange flavour to junket and blancmange. They are used in currys for which purpose the seed is grown commercially near Bombay, in India.

Corn salad (*Valerianella locusta*)

Also known as lamb's lettuce for it is ready in the lambing season and lambs enjoy the fresh leaves at this time. A plant of cornfields and waste ground throughout Europe, N. Africa and W. Asia, Gerard said 'we know lamb's lettuce as 'hoblollie' and it serves in winter as a salad herb'. In France it was known as the white hot herb or milk grass for its leaves and stems emit a milky juice. It first came to be appreciated in the 16th century.

Description. Found by the wayside and in cornfields, it is a low growing glabrous annual with bright green oblong leaves about 7.5 cm (3 in) long which appear early in summer when 'green' food is appreciated in salads.

Culture. Though common about the countryside, it should be more often grown in gardens, as a vegetable, the seed being sown early March in shallow drills 20 cm (8 in) apart. Ordinary soil is suitable. To maintain a supply, make another sowing early May and again early July.

Culinary uses. Use the young leaves with or as an alternative to lettuce in salads and sandwiches.

Costmary (*Tanacetum balsamita* syn. *Chrysanthemum balsamita*)

It is also known as alecost for before the use of hops in brewing, it was used to impart its aromatic flavour to ale. The plant is said to be dedicated to St. Mary Magdalene and named after her, though it is more likely that the name is from the Latin *Costus amarus*, a bitter shrub.

Description. A perennial growing 60–90 cm (2–3 ft) tall with dark green entire leaves and in July and August it bears heads of deep yellow flowers. The plant increases by a creeping rootstock. Native of central Asia, it was established early in Europe, Gerard saying that 'it groweth everywhere in gardens' and Parkinson said that it was one of the sweetest herbs and 'tied up with lavender to lie upon the tops of beds', on pillows and between the sheets, to which it imparted its balsamic perfume.

Culture. It is propagated by root division in spring, setting the offsets about 30 cm (12 in) apart and it prefers a well-drained sandy soil. It is also increased by seed sown in a frame or in boxes in spring, setting out the young plants late in July.

Medicinal uses. An infusion of the leaves (a large handful to half a litre (1 pint) of water) taken hot is good for colic and an upset stomach and from its leaves, boiled with half a cupful of olive oil, a tablespoon of turpentine and a little beeswax, a healing ointment is made. After heating for ten to fifteen minutes, strain and pour into ointment jars and allow to cool when it will set; it is used to heal spots and sores.

Culinary uses. The leaves put in ale will impart a balsamic taste, likewise in soups and stews; a few finely chopped may be used in salads.

Cotton lavender (*Santolina chamaecyparissus* syn. *S. incana*)

Also called lavender cotton, it is of the compositae order of plants, in no way related to the English lavender, in spite of its name. In Europe it was held in great esteem, to put amongst clothes and vestments for it gave protection from moths better than all other plants and also imparted to them its pungent, resinous scent. In France it is called *garde-robe*. Tusser included it amongst the best of all herbs for strewing.

Description. A hardy perennial shrub, resembling lavender in its hardiness though it is native of S. Europe. Growing up to 60 cm (2 ft) high and the same across, it has small fleshy linear leaves, silvery-grey in colour and the plant is able to survive long periods without water and also intense heat. But though it grows bushy, it will stand clipping better than most hard wooded plants and can be kept at any height up to 60 cm (2 ft). It is ideal for surrounding small beds of herbs or edging a border, being a valuable wind protector as well as retaining its foliage all the year except in very severe climates. In July and August, it bears masses of small yellow button-like flowers which are most attractive above the grey foliage but which have the unpleasant smell typical of the Order.

Culture. It is propagated from cuttings of the half-ripened wood, removed in late July, preferably with a 'heel' attached for quicker rooting. Insert into sandy soil, 5 cm (2 in) apart in a frame or under cloches and do not disturb until the following spring. This is the best time to set out the plants 30 cm (12 in) apart if making a low hedge; or allow twice the distance for the shrub border where the plants can be grown to their full height. *S. c. nana* is more compact than the type. Another beautiful form is 'Weston' which also grows to a height of 25 cm (10 in) and has tightly twisted leaves like tiny woolly lamb's tails and is so heavily silvered as to appear frosted. *Santolina neapolitana* grows to 1 m (about 3 ft) tall with finely cut foliage and it has attractive lime-yellow button-like flowers while a hybrid, 'Lemon Queen', grows only 30 cm (12 in) tall and has creamy yellow flowers. *S. virens* syn. *S. viridis* is slightly more demanding in its culture, requiring a warm sheltered garden. It has bright green foliage without the grey or silvering of the others. All are fully evergreen.

Medicinal uses. The dried leaves can be included in herbal smoking mixtures to ease asthma or a cough, with chamomile and coltsfoot. It will also act as a stimulant and tonic.

Other uses. As a moth deterrent it has no equal and the dried leaves should be mixed with rosemary or lavender (to add sweetness) and placed in small muslin bags to put amongst clothes and carpets not in use. The dried leaves are also used in pot-pourris and sweet bags.

Cowslip (*Primula veris*)

One of the loveliest of wild flowers, it is equally attractive in the garden. Shakespeare associated it (with burnet and clover) with good husbandry. It takes its name from the Anglo-Saxon *cusloppe*, the breath of a cow, but its scent more closely resembles a baby's breath. The plant is also known as paigle, from the Latin *prata*, a meadow, where cowslips grow. In the United States, the term cowslip is applied to two unrelated plants of the buttercup and borage families. The true cowslip is a relation of the primrose.

Description. A hardy perennial, native of Europe and much of Asia, with obovate leaves tapering downwards and deeply grooved, down which moisture can flow to the roots before it evaporates. The leaves are hairy on the underside whilst the drooping flowers are borne in umbels of six to eight on short downy peduncles at the top of a 15 cm (6 in) stem. The flowers are yellow with an orange spot at the base of each petal. The inflated calyx is bell-shaped and bright green and the flowers are borne April-June, shortly after the new leaves appear.

Culture. It is propagated by root division in July or in early spring, planted into soil well supplied with humus to retain summer moisture. It is also readily raised from seed sown in boxes or pans of potting compost in a sunny window, or in a greenhouse or frame. Sow about April 1st and begin transplanting the seedlings to boxes or directly into the open ground in May or June. Keep the young plants watered in dry weather and they will grow well in semi-shade though cowslips do like more sun than primroses. Work into the soil some peat or leaf mould or decayed manure before planting.

Medicinal uses. In early times it had many uses. Cowslip 'tea' to calm the nerves and bring about sound sleep is made from an infusion of the flowers (a handful to half a litre (1 pint) of water) which is taken warm or cold at bedtime, sweetened with a little honey. The same infusion applied with lint pads will cleanse and improve the complexion, to which Shakespeare alluded in *A Midsummer Night's Dream*. The flowers were also immersed overnight in white wine which was then applied to the complexion in the same way, acting as an astringent.

Cowslip wine, to calm the nerves and induce sleep, is made from the peelings of two oranges and two lemons put into an earthenware pan. Over them pour 4.5 litres (a gallon) of hot water into which 0.75 kg (1½ lb) of sugar has been dissolved. When cool add the juice of the peeled fruits, a small cupful of fresh yeast and a shoe-boxful of cowslip flowers. Do not take plants from the wild, as they are becoming rare in many areas as old meadows are ploughed. Remove each flower from its calyx. Allow to stand for three to four days, stirring often, then strain into another jar and leave for two weeks, until fermentation has ended. Then close up the jar or place in bottles and leave for three to four months. Cowslip wine is the most delicious of wild flower wines but if kept too long is very intoxicating and must be taken a little at a time.

Culinary uses. The flowers can be included in a spring salad, also the leaves which act as a tonic. They are pleasantly bitter, like watercress, which may be included with them. Include them in cream cheese sandwiches and the younger they are, the more pleasant will they be. The leaves can also be used with other fresh herbs for stuffings.

Cumin (*Cuminum cyminum*)

It is mentioned in Isaiah and in the Near East, of which it is native, the seeds were mixed with flour to bake into bread. It is still grown commercially in Egypt, Malta and Ethiopia, also in India and is used in Germany in large amounts in cake making and in Holland to impart its warm spicy taste to cheese. It requires a long hot summer to ripen its seeds properly.

Description. It is an annual, growing 30–60 cm (1–2 ft) tall on slender branching stems. The fern-like leaves resemble those of fennel and are dark green. The white or rose-pink flowers are borne in umbels during July and August and are followed by large elongated seeds which are distinguished from those of caraway (which are boat-shaped) by their straightness. They are also hairy, those of caraway being smooth.

Culture. A well drained soil and an open, sunny situation is necessary. Sow in shallow drills made 30 cm (12 in) apart in early April and thin to 15 cm (6 in) in the rows.

Medicinal uses. Like caraway, coriander and dill, cumin water relieves flatulence and colic pains. It is warming and in Malta where grown commercially, is known as *Cumino aigro*, hot cumin, hence its value in curries. It is also valuable for calming the nerves when three drops of cumin oil should be taken on a lump of sugar. The oil will also give relief to rheumatic pains and sprains if gently massaged in. Gerard mentions that the seed if crushed and placed in a muslin bag and applied hot to strains and bruises will quickly remove the inflammation and he also mentions that the washed and crushed root can be used in the same way. Cumin is used in veterinary prescriptions.

Culinary uses. It is included in most Indian curries and in chutneys and pickles.

For a really hot curry, use 110 g (4 oz) of seed and the same of coriander, 110 g (4 oz) turmeric and 15 g ($\frac{1}{2}$ oz) of allspice, ground in a mortar. Place in a screwtop jar, using as required. Cumin will add interest to red cabbage when pickled. Shred the cabbage, sprinkle with salt and leave overnight. Then place in an earthenware jar and pour over it after straining, a litre (2 pints) of malt vinegar in which was boiled 15 g ($\frac{1}{2}$ oz) red peppers, and 15 g ($\frac{1}{2}$ oz) of cumin and coriander seed mixed.

Curry plant (*Helichrysum italicum*, syn. *H. angustifolium*)
This native of southern Europe is less hardy than many mediterranean herbs and will survive only in a mild winter climate; it would be killed off at about −12° C (10° F).
Description. A shrubby perennial in suitable climes, it makes a low spreading bush about 50 cm (20 in) tall and the same across with handsome silver-grey foliage which is aromatic and in July and August bears small yellow everlasting flowers in umbels, held on 30 cm (12 in) stems. They can be dried and used for winter decoration.
Culture. Plant in April 60 cm (2 ft) apart, in dry sandy soil and in an open, sunny situation. Propagation is from cuttings of the half-ripened wood removed in July and rooted in a frame or in pots in a sunny window. The newly rooted plants should be given glass protection over winter. Outdoor plants may be cut down during hard frosts but usually will begin to grow again in spring. To have the plants retain their leaves in winter, grow the rooted cuttings in 8–10 cm (3–4 in) pots and in early October, bring them inside a greenhouse or garden room where they remain until April. During winter, water sparingly. The leaves can be used fresh or when dry. To dry them, remove from the woody stems, a few at a time during summer and place on sheets of paper in an airy room until quite dry. Then place into wooden boxes and use as required.
Culinary uses. The hot curry-like flavour of the leaves adds interest to soups and stews during winter. Use them sparingly for the flavour is pronounced. They may also be used either fresh or dry in stuffings, to accompany veal and venison.

Dandelion (*Taraxacum officinale*)
The Arabian physician Avicenna knew of its valuable medicinal qualities and called it *taraxacon*, edible, for the leaves and the roots have valuable health giving qualities. It takes its country name from the French *dent de lion*, because it was thought its bluntly-toothed leaves resembled lion's teeth. In France, its leaves have always been included in summer salads, containing vitamin C and in England, north country folk have for long made a beer from the roots, together with burdock, which acts as a tonic and blood purifier.
Description. Widespread everywhere, it is an unwanted weed of lawns and sports grounds and forms a long brown tap root making it difficult to eradicate. From the root at soil level, the leaves arise in rosette fashion so that every drop of moisture falling on them is directed to the root. From the root arises the flower stalk which is about 15 cm (6 in) long. The flowers are brilliant yellow, approx. 2.5 cm (1 in) diam., and from them, bees obtain pollen and nectar.
Culture. The plant is worthy of garden cultivation, the seed being sown in circles in the vegetable garden in April. Make the circles about 40 cm (16 in) in diameter, scattering the seed evenly. This will enable the plants in each circle to be covered by a large pot (a rhubarb pot is ideal) or deep box so that the leaves can be blanched when the plants are a year old. This will make them more tender and remove any bitterness. Always sow seed of a special broad leaf cultivated strain, the leaves being large and succulent and the richer the soil, the more tender will they be. The plants are covered soon after they begin to make leaf in April and in about ten days the leaves will be blanched. Then cover another circle and do not pull any further leaves that year from

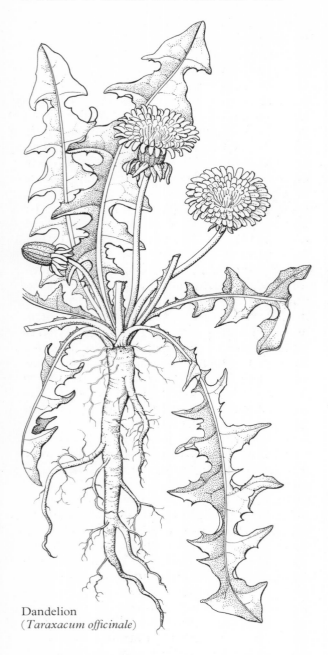

Dandelion
(*Taraxacum officinale*)

that the leaves will do when used in soups and stews. A tonic beer is made from the flowers, 5 litres (about 1 gallon) of water being poured over 5 litres of fresh flowers. Allow it to stand for three to four days stirring it frequently, then strain and boil for thirty minutes, together with 1.4 kg (3 lb) of sugar, a little ginger and the skin of two oranges. When quite cool, add 30 g (1 oz) of yeast and allow it to 'work' for two days then place in a cask for 2 months before bottling. Take a wineglassful daily when it will act as a tonic and blood purifier. As a substitute for coffee and without any of its adverse qualities, dandelion 'coffee' (mixed with chicory) is almost as pleasant to drink and acts as a tonic while stimulating the flow of urine. The roots of well-established plants are used, being lifted in September.

Wash the roots clean of soil and dry off by spreading them out on sacks. Then place in a low warm oven to dry completely. With roasting, the roots will be dark brown and when ground will have something of the coffee aroma. The roots of chicory can be treated in the same way and used with them. A decoction made from the roots affords relief for liver complaints and clears the kidneys. It is made by boiling 0.5 kg (1 lb) of the sliced roots (freshly dug and cleaned) with 4.5 litres (a gallon) of water for about half an hour. Strain and add a little honey before it goes cold. Take a wineglassful daily for several weeks. Dandelion is free of poisonous substances and though one of our most despised weeds, it is one of the most valuable of all health foods. Dandelion roots contain a bitter white juice which, if applied to warts on the skin will, in time, remove them.

Culinary uses. The young and blanched leaves make a tasty addition to an early summer salad and they may be included in sandwiches with cream cheese. They may also be simmered in a little water and served with spinach which has similar health-giving qualities. Those who have no garden can grow dandelions in large pots, in a soil containing some decayed manure and enjoy

those plants which have been blanched. Keep the plants well watered in dry weather and a mulch in autumn will encourage plenty of succulent new leaves in spring.

Medicinal uses. A small wineglassful of the water in which unblanched leaves were boiled will flush the kidneys in the same way the leaves by covering the plants with an inverted pot of the same size.

Dill (*Anethum graveolens*)

It takes its name from the Saxon *dilla*, to lull, for the water from the seed was rubbed on to women's breasts to lull babies to sleep after feeding. Dioscorides wrote of its carminative qualities and perhaps because of its tranquillizing effects, it was grown in every cottage garden as an antidote against witchcraft. The plant is mentioned in a 10th century manuscript of Aelfric, Archbishop of Canterbury and was probably introduced into northern Europe by the Romans.

Description. A hardy annual, to be found from the Iberian Peninsular to Albania and around the Black Sea and in these parts it is grown commercially. Growing 60–90 cm (2–3 ft) tall, it is of the Compositae order and has finely cut foliage, like fennel. In July and August it bears flat heads of pale yellow flowers followed by small light oval seeds which are bitter and pungent.

Culture. Grown commercially, an acre of dill will yield in an average year, about one third of a ton of seed which is cut when ripe and stacked into sheaves for threshing. Good quality seed will be obtained only in regions with a long hot summer but the plant is worth growing for its foliage which has culinary uses, seed being sown in shallow drills early in April, made 25 cm (10 in) apart. Ordinary soil is suitable but an open situation necessary.

Medicinal uses. It is used to ease flatulence and given to young children as gripe water, also to encourage sleep if taken at bedtime. To a tablespoonful of seeds, add half a litre (1 pint) of hot water, allow to cool and strain and add a little honey. For young children, give a teaspoonful of the water to ease wind and stomach pains. It is soothing and warming.

Culinary uses. The leaves have a spicy taste and so are included in soups and stews whilst they impart a pleasant spicy taste to fresh green peas and new potatoes if boiled with them. A sauce to serve with fish is also made from the leaves is also to be recommended.

Elecampane (*Inula helenium*)

It takes its name from the Greek *elenium*, a plant commemorating either Helen of Troy or the island of Helena where it grows in profusion. The roots candied and eaten, help the digestion and could be obtained from apothecaries' shops everywhere. In modern France, the root is used in the distillation of absinthe.

Description. It is probably native only in Asia but has long been naturalized in Europe and also in N. America where it is grown commercially. It is a perennial growing 1.2–1.5 m (4–5 ft) tall with a tuberous rootstock which Gerrard described as 'thick, as much as a man may grip but not long: blackish without, white within, sweet of smell, bitter of taste' which describes it well. The toothed leaves are 30 cm (12 in) long, deeply wrinkled and downy, the upper leaves clasping the stem. The flowers measure 8–10 cm (3–4 in) across and have spreading ray florets of bright golden-yellow. It blooms July and August and the flower stem is produced from a rosette of leaves.

Culture. It is best raised from seed sown in boxes or pans in a frame or greenhouse in spring. When large enough to handle, transplant the seedlings to small pots. Grow on until early autumn and plant out at the back of a sunny border 1 m (about 3 ft) apart. It may also be propagated from root cuttings. A plant is lifted in spring and pieces of root about 5 cm (2 in) long are removed before replanting. The pieces are planted in boxes horizontally and covered with 1–2 cm (about ½ in) of compost. Water them and place the box in a greenhouse or frame. They will root in a month or so and may then be planted out.

Medicinal uses. The roots contain helinin which resembles camphor, a starch, inulin, a volatile oil smelling like labdanum, and a trace of acetic acid. This is readily detected when the root is lifted. As it dries, the root develops the smell of ripe bananas which takes on the violet scent as it ages. It is the scent of violets which is released when a few small pieces of root are placed on a low fire, a perfume which resembles that of orris root. In his play *What You Will*, Marston says 'now are the lawn sheets fumed with violets', the reference being to the placing of bed linen around a fire to dry after their washing, when the violet scent from the elecampane would give them a lasting fragrance. Helinin contained in the roots is a powerful antiseptic and Korab has shown that 1 part in 10,000 is sufficient to kill the Tubercle bacillus. Since earliest times, the root has been used for all pulmonary diseases, to relieve asthma and bronchitis, either by eating the root after candying or by taking a decoction. This is made by cutting up the root and using 30 g (1 oz) to 1.1 litres (2 pints) of water. Bring to the boil and simmer for thirty minutes, then strain and drink a small wineglassful twice daily. It will also act as an excellent tonic and ease the stomach when troubled by colic or flatulence. Elecampane lozenges have for long been used in cases of whooping cough; or use 30 g (1 oz) of the dry and powdered root mixed with the same amount of honey. It also heals and relieves piles if applied to them. The same amount of root mixed with olive oil and applied to the face will relieve neuralgia and will also heal body sores and skin eruptions. For its antiseptic qualities and as a cure for so many simple ailments, elecampane should be grown in every garden. In addition, its stately beauty lends distinction to the border or herb garden.

Fennel (*Foeniculum vulgare* syn. *F. officinale*)

It may have been introduced by the Romans who used it to make chaplets and wreaths as an emblem of flattery. The Romans named it *foeniculum* because of its hay-like smell, though anethol is the principal constituent of its essential oil which accounts for the slight aniseed smell released when the leaves are handled. Milton refers to the pleasant smell of fennel in *Paradise Lost*:

A savoury odour blown,
Grateful to appetite, more pleased my sense
Than smell of sweetest fennel

Description. An erect perennial growing 1–1.5 m (4–5 ft) tall and suitable for the back of a border. Its three to four pinnate leaves are divided into numerous hair-like segments and in July and August its tiny yellow flowers are borne in large terminal umbels. These are followed by narrow ovoid fruits with eight longitudinal ribs. Long naturalized in most of the temperate world, it is probably a native of the mediterranean coastlands. All parts of the plant, except the flowers, are refreshingly scented.

Culture. Though perennial, it is not a hard-wooded plant and is readily raised from seed sown in boxes or in shallow drills in April, transplanted to a permanent place in the border before the end of summer. Or sow in gentle heat in a greenhouse or frame in February. It requires an open situation and it will transplant well. There is a bronze leaf variety which is a striking plant in the border. Fennel grows tall and bushy so plant 60 cm (2 ft) apart and it will need staking if it is not to be blown about by the winds. Some plants may be allowed to form seed each year, to sow themselves but others should have the flowers removed as soon as they form when the plants will retain their bushiness and produce more leaf.

Medicinal uses. It is, like caraway and dill, a carminative and a wineglassful taken in the evening should promote sound sleep. Pour a quarter of a litre ($\frac{1}{2}$ pint) of boiling water over a teaspoonful of crushed seed, strain and drink warm. With anise and dill, it will relieve flatulence in children and old people and was used to make 'gripe water', to be found in every cottage home, a teaspoonful to be given whenever necessary. Fennel 'tea', made as described was given to nursing women to promote the flow of milk. The crushed seed mixed with liquorice powder, acts as a natural and gentle laxative and warm fennel water will bring relief to tired and inflamed eyes after applying it

Alexanders *(Smyrnium olusatrum).* Although a native of the eastern Mediterranean coasts, this plant is nowadays found throughout Europe in hedgerows, on waste ground and by the sea. Both its fern-like leaves and the large black seeds which follow the flowers can be used to flavour soups, stews and salads.

RIGHT: Cotton Lavender *(Santolina chamaecyparissus,* syn. *S. Incana).* A hardy perennial shrub with small silvery-grey leaves, it is ideal for edging a border. The dried leaves, mixed with Rosemary or English Lavender and placed in small muslin bags act as a very efficient moth deterrent.

BELOW: Tansy *(Tanacetum haradjanii).* This hardy perennial was traditionally used to counteract the mustiness of damp rooms. The leaves and the small yellow flowers can be used to make Tansy tea, and the leaves can be used in omelettes or for seasoning sausages.

with lint, preferably at bed-time. It was thought to be good for cateract and Pliny said that 'it taketh away the film that dimmeth our eyes'. Poor people would eat the seed which relieved the pangs of hunger as mentioned by William Langland in *Piers Plowman*.

Culinary uses. Apart from its numerous medical virtues, fennel was used to make a sauce to serve with mackerel and eels which Henry VIII so much enjoyed and Falstaff before him. Chop a handful of the fresh leaves, boil slowly for twenty minutes then drain off the water. Melt 30 g (1 oz) of butter or margarine, stir in 22 g ($\frac{3}{4}$ oz) of flour and 0.25 litre ($\frac{1}{2}$ pint) of hot (but not boiling) water, season with salt, add the fennel and serve hot. The leaves can also be used instead of parsley to garnish fish while the stems, removed when young, add a spicy flavour to soups and stews. The stems when tender, may be served as a vegetable. Cut into pieces 10 cm (4 in) long, cover with butter and stew for twenty minutes. Serve with white sauce to accompany fish or game. The seeds can be used instead of dill, to make an aromatic vinegar and to add their distinctive flavour to pickled gherkins and cauliflower. It is a plant to use in the kitchen all the year round. The crushed seed will give a spicy taste to bread and cakes, and was used as a substitute for juniper to flavour gin when consumed by the gallon in the gin-houses of Hogarth's London.

Feverfew (*Chrysanthemum parthenium*)
Its country name is a corruption of febrifuge, a reference to its long-known value in treating fevers and agues for its essential oil contains camphor and acts on the nervous system.

Description. A much branched perennial growing 30–40 cm (12–16 in) tall with pale green leaves, the one to two narrow leaflets divided into lobed segments. The flowers are of the size of a thumbnail and are borne in terminal clusters, the ray florets white, the disc florets yellow. There is a double form known as batchelor's buttons which in Victorian times was a popular summer bedding plant. The plants have an aromatic pungent scent when handled. It blooms from June–September.

Culture. It is readily raised from seed sown in gentle heat in February, in a greenhouse or sunny window, transplanting the seedlings to boxes when large enough to handle. There is a strikingly beautiful golden leaf variety, 'Aureum' which associates well with scarlet geraniums in a tub or window box. The plants are set out in May. They are quite hardy and in light soils will sow themselves freely.

Medicinal uses. An infusion of the flowers and leaves, a handful to half a litre (1 pint) of water, will act as a tonic and lower the temperature when taken for a fever. Take a wineglassful twice daily. Its essential oil, two or three drops in water, will calm the nerves and give immediate relief to insect bites while a decoction of the leaves with a little honey will ease a tight chest and hard cough. The same will also remove freckles and skin blemishes if applied to the face with lint.

Culinary uses. The leaves will impart a pungency to soups and stews and if included in a frying pan will take away much of the greasiness from fried tomatoes and eggs and give them a pungent taste.

Other uses. The dried leaves placed among clothes will keep them free of moths. Mix them with those of wormwood and cotton lavender for greater efficiency.

Garlic (*Allium sativum*)
Native of central Asia, the Egyptians building the vast pyramids at Giza were sustained by garlic cloves as were farm labourers and pilgrims of mediaeval England. 'Well loved he garlecke, onyouns and the leeke' wrote Chaucer in *Canterbury Tales* and most pilgrims would carry with them a clove or two of garlic as protection against plague and to sustain them on their long journeys.

Description. A perennial with irregularly shaped bulbs, held together by a white

Garlic
(*Allium sativum*)

membrane and broad flat leaves tapering to a point. The flowers are white and borne in capitate heads during July and August. Probably introduced by the Romans to the lands they conquered, its cultivation has since spread throughout the temperate world.

Culture. To ripen correctly, it requires a light, sandy soil and an open, sunny situation. The cloves (as the offsets are called) are planted in October in mild climates and in March elsewhere and it is one of the few plants to enjoy a loose soil. Plant in drills made 5 cm (2 in) deep and 25 cm (10 in) apart, spacing the cloves 15 cm (6 in) apart in the rows. Water during dry weather and keep the hoe moving between the rows. Those planted in autumn will be ready to lift early August: those planted in March will be ripe by early October, when the leaves turn yellow. Lift on a dry day and place on trays in an open shed to dry. They are then strung up in fine mesh nets in a frost free airy room and used as required. The bulbs will ripen better and make a larger size if the flower stem is bent over as it forms.

Medicinal uses. Rich in alkaline salts and sulphur compounds, it acts as a tonic and blood purifier whilst if eaten regularly, it has the reputation of warding off colds and influenza. A tincture made from the cloves with spirits of wine is used for the relief of asthma and whooping cough. Take ten drops in a wineglassful of water. Garlic also makes a useful embrocation to use for sprains and rheumatic pains. Crush several cloves and add the juice to 230 g ($\frac{1}{2}$ lb) lard as it is softened in a saucepan over a low fire. Pour into ointment jars and allow to solidify. Then gently massage it into sprains, while a little applied to spots or a rash will give ease and aid healing. If rubbed on to the chest at bedtime it will give ease to a tight chest, loosening the phlegm.

Culinary uses. In recent years, garlic has become as widely used in cooking as it always has been in France and Italy. But it was first used to rub over meats when there was no refrigeration and its powerful (and to some, unpleasant) taste did much to hide the strong smell of the stale meat. When cooking, a clove can be inserted in a small cut made in the flesh, to improve the taste. The flavour may be imparted to a salad, stews and soups merely by rubbing the pan or bowl with a clove before the food is prepared. A small clove placed in a pan of fried tomatoes will add interest to the meal and the same may be said when making cheese sandwiches; just rub a clove on the cheese and add a few thin slices of tomato or cucumber. Garlic, however, does not appeal to all lovers of good food.

Good King Henry (*Chenopodium bonus-henricus*)
It is named after Henry IV of France who first drew attention to its edible qualities.
Description. Widespread on waste ground and naturalized in N. America and Europe, it is a perennial growing 60 cm (2 ft) tall with long-stemmed arrow-shaped leaves, waved at the edges. The greenish flowers are without petals and borne July-August in a leafless spike.

Culture. For its culinary value, it is worthy of vegetable garden culture, sowing the seed in spring in ordinary soil and in shallow drills made 30 cm (12 in) apart. Thin to 25 cm (10 in) in the rows and keep the plants watered in dry weather. Established plants can be divided in spring.

Culinary uses. The young shoots removed in spring when about 15 cm (6 in) long can be peeled and boiled and served with melted butter to accompany chicken and game. As the shoots grow, earth up and this will increase their tenderness. Later, the kale-like top growth and large basal leaves may be cooked like spinach, simmering until tender in a little water.

Ground ivy (*Glechoma hederacea* syn. *Nepeta glechoma*)

Like germander, it was used to clarify ale and grew in the garden of every wayside inn. It is a Labiate and is in no way connected with the common ivy though it resembles it in that it pulls itself over the ground, rooting at the nodes which are detached and replanted. It is a delightful plant for a hanging basket and window box, for it will trail down for several feet and is evergreen. It takes its old name from Nepet in Tuscany where it abounds and from the Greek *glechon*, mint, for its leaves when pressed give off a minty smell.

Description. A soft hairy perennial with creeping stems and with heart-shaped leaves of grey-green, which in the form 'Variegata' are marked with splashes of purple and white. The purple-blue flowers are borne in three's or four's at the axils of the leaves from April until August. It is a hardy plant of easy culture and being evergreen, its long elegant shoots were popular with countrymen to make into chaplets and garlands to give to their lady friends. It is present in damp woodlands and hedgerows throughout Europe and much of Asia and is frequently used by nurserymen to decorate hanging baskets in summer.

Culture. If two or three plants are allowed to trail over the ground, the numerous string-like stems which root at the leaf nodes, can be detached and replanted, either in the open ground or in small pots without lifting the parent plant; or it can be raised from seed sown in boxes or pans in spring, in a frame or sunny window. Transplant to small pots when large enough to handle.

Medicinal uses. It was used as a cure for lead colic and grew in the gardens of painters everywhere. It is also used as a diuretic and blood purifier as well as a tonic. Make an infusion of the leaves and stems, a handful to half a litre (1 pint) of water, and take a wineglassful daily all the year round. Taken hot and sweetened with a little honey, it will relieve a hard cough. The plant is also recommended by the French herbalist Maurice Messegue to relieve asthma, used with wild thyme and other herbs, in warm foot baths at bedtime, relying on external application only to bring relief. The dried leaves can be finely ground and taken as snuff to relieve a blocked nose.

Herb bennet (*Geum urbanum*)

It is also known as wood avens and clove root and it takes its name of holy herb or blessed herb from its old name *Herba benedicta* because it had so many useful qualities, whilst the trefoil leaf symbolizes the Holy Trinity; the five petals of the flowers represented the five wounds of Christ on the Cross.

Description. A slim, erect hairy perennial closely related to the potentilla and growing 30–40 cm (12–16 in) tall, the upper leaves composed of three narrow leaflets. The flowers, which measure 2 cm ($\frac{3}{4}$ in) across are golden-yellow and without scent. The rhizomatous root is the important part of the plant and when lifted has a distinct clove-like smell. The plant, which grows best in soil which does not dry up in summer, is found throughout Europe and Asia.

Culture. It is happy in the semi-shade of other plants and ordinary soil is suitable for its growth. Seed is sown *in situ* in spring, in boxes or in a frame and the young plants set out where they are to grow in July.

Propagation is also by root division in autumn or spring. Plant 30 cm (12 in) apart towards the front of a border.

Medicinal uses. From the roots, a drink is prepared by pouring 0.5 litre (1 pint) of boiling water on to 15 g ($\frac{1}{2}$ oz) of the dried and sliced root. Strain and sweeten with a little honey and take a wineglassful hot at night to induce sleep. It may also be taken cold as a tonic drink. With their clove-like smell, pieces of root were placed in ale and wine to impart its warm clove taste. In Germany, the roots are often placed in casks of beer for the same reason.

Culinary uses. The roots, either dry or preferably freshly dug and washed clean of soil, impart a clove taste to an apple tart, used instead of cloves.

Hop (*Humulus lupulus*)

Its fame lies in its value to the brewery trade; it was used in Europe in this way in the 9th century, but in Britain not until the 15th and 16th centuries. Before then, ale was made from malt and clarified by ground ivy. To improve the taste wormwood, germander and buckbean were used in its making. The word 'beer' did not come into the English language until hops were first used. Writing as late as 1670, John Evelyn said in his *Pomona*: 'Hops transmuted our wholesome ale into beer ... This one ingredient preserves the drink indeed but repays the pleasure with tormenting diseases and a shorter life'. The name hop is from the Anglo-Saxon *hoppan*, to climb, for this is how it grows.

Description. A hairy perennial climbing to a height of 4–5 m (about 15 ft), the dark green three to five lobed leaves being coarsely serrated and held on a long petiole. The flowers are yellowish-green, the males borne in a catkin-like inflorescence, the females in the axils of the leaves to form a cylindrical spike of overlapping bracts and on different plants. The bracteoles have glandular hairs which produce lupulin, a gold dust which is the important ingredient in brewing beer. Lupulin is a bitter principle with tonic properties and hop plantations consist mostly of female plants. The plant is present throughout Europe and western Asia.

Culture. It grows in hedgerows and open woodlands and may be used in the garden to cover a trellis or arbor. The stems will die back each winter when they are cut away at soil level and will arise from the roots in spring as in hop plantations. The roots are planted in autumn or spring 50 cm (20 in) apart and just below the soil surface. The plants can also be raised from seed sown in spring in boxes or in a frame and the plants set out in early autumn. Hops like a deep rich soil and appreciate a top dressing of humus in winter. They have many valuable uses and half a dozen plants growing against a trellis will provide flowers and leaves to make an excellent tonic drink.

Medicinal uses. The narcotic effect of hops is well known and George III is reputed to have always slept on a hop pillow. When dry, the flowers have a pleasant herby scent and are soft and downy when used to stuff pillows. Include with them the dried leaves of woodruff or agrimony as these too, are pleasantly narcotic and become more heavily scented the dryer they are. A hop pillow is soft and fragrant to sleep on. Hops together with other suitable herbs can be placed in large muslin bags and hung from the headboard of a bed when they will have a similar effect.

A quite excellent tonic drink is made from a handful of flowers infused in half a litre (1 pint) of boiling water. Take cold or hot after straining. It will aid the digestion and will induce sleep if taken warm at bedtime. The leaves can be dried in late summer, before they turn brown and fall, and used during winter in the same way. Hop 'tea' was recommended for those who suffer from heart trouble and from fits and all nervous disorders—presumably because of its sedative properties. It also cleanses the blood of impurities. Hop flowers, together with those of chamomile, act as a soothing poultice. Place in a muslin bag and immerse for a minute or two in boiling water. Press out the surplus moisture and apply as warm as possible to rheumatic joints and in cases of neuralgia.

Culinary uses. The young tops of the plants can be cut in spring and bundled like asparagus, and after boiling for twenty minutes served with melted butter to accompany meat or chicken. To make 'hop bitters' which, if taken a little each day (a tablespoonful before meals) will tone the system and stimulate the appetite, take a handful of hop flowers, and the same of angelica and holy thistle. Pour over them 2.3 litres (4 pints) of hot water, strain when cold and take as required. Meadowsweet and agrimony can be used instead of angelica and holy thistle.

Horseradish (*Armoracia rusticana*)

It is to be found in all parts of the temperate world and was so called to distinguish it from the more refined ordinary radish of salads and it should perhaps be called coarseradish. Pliny recommended its use medicinally and Parkinson tells of its roots being pounded and mixed with vinegar to accompany meats. At the time it was more commonly used in Germany and Poland than anywhere else. It is thought to be one of the bitter herbs that the Jews were ordered to eat during the Feast of the Passover.

Description. A perennial, growing 60 cm (2 ft) tall with large shiny dark green leaves and white flowers which appear in May and June. It forms a huge forked root which is used as a condiment and which is most difficult to eradicate from the garden once it takes hold. It will penetrate to a depth of several feet and the smallest piece broken off will grow. So confine it to an unused corner of the vegetable garden. The intense bitterness of the root which taken in quantity, causes the eyes to run, contains the same bitter principle as black mustard which is also used as a condiment with beef and other meats. They are an aid to its digestion and in olden times helped to camouflage meat that had 'gone off' when there was no refrigeration.

Culture. For the roots to grow large, it requires a rich soil and the thongs (as the roots are called) are planted in November, planting 45 cm (18 in) apart and with the top or crown of the root just below soil level. The thongs should be not less than 15 cm (6 in) long.

Medicinal uses. Always use the root freshly dug for it is then most potent, being rich in sulphur compounds so that it is useful for the relief of rheumatic complaints and sprains, whilst it is as good for the bladder and kidneys as asparagus and barley water. Make an infusion of 30 g (1 oz) of the chopped fresh root with 15 g ($\frac{1}{2}$ oz) of crushed mustard seed in 0.5 litre (1 pint) of hot water. Let it stand for an hour, then strain and take a small wineglassful once daily. It will also act as a gargle (used warm) and will relieve indigestion and may be given in cases of dropsy. The root macerated in wine vinegar and sweetened with honey will help children in times of whooping cough. To make an embrocation for sprains, slice the roots and crush out the juice, then mix with a little olive oil and put into bottles to use as required, gently massaging a little on to the injured parts. To clear blackheads and pimples, boil 230 g ($\frac{1}{2}$ lb) of the sliced root with a little milk. When cool, strain and bottle the liquid, and apply to the face with lint (gauze).

Culinary uses. To make a sauce to accompany beef, lift, clean and scrape the freshly dug roots, then grate about 30 g (1 oz) into a basin. Add a teaspoonful of sugar, a sprinkling of mustard and salt, a few drops of malt vinegar to moisten, then stir in a cupful of cream.

Hyssop (*Hyssopus officinalis* syn. *H. aristatus*)

It takes its name from the Hebrew *azob*, a holy plant, and it has always been known as the holy herb being mentioned so often in the Bible and used in the consecration of Westminster Cathedral. Michael Drayton wrote 'Hyssop is a herb most prime' and Parkinson began his *Paradisus* which he

Hyssop
(*Hyssopus officinalis* syn.
H. aristatus)

'knots' or to edge a border of herbs. It has linear leaves and bears its flowers which are white, pink or purple, in whorls from June until early October. Propagation is by sowing seed in boxes in a frame or sunny window in spring and transplanting to the border towards the end of summer, or by lifting and dividing the plants in spring. Plant 50 cm (20 in) apart, slightly closer if using it for a hedge or edging. It requires a well-drained soil and an open sunny position. The flowers are greatly loved by bees and butterflies which are attracted to the plants all summer. There is also an attractive golden leafed form.

Medicinal uses. Hyssop 'tea' made from the tops (leaves and flowers), a handful to half a litre (1 pint) of hot water, is an excellent tonic and aids the digestion. It will also ease an asthmatic condition and will help a rheumatic condition. The leaves are also used externally, placed in muslin bags and immersed in hot water before applying to a sprain or rheumatic joint. Countrymen would rub the juice from the stems on to cuts and sores for quick healing.

Culinary uses. The leaves and tops can be included in salads when chopped and in soups and stews in winter, to which they impart a 'sharp' taste. The flowers too, make a welcome addition to a salad.

Other uses. Include the dried leaves in pot-pourris and the fresh leaves in a moist pot-pourri and a handful in a warm bath will relieve a rheumatic condition or stiffness brought on by garden work or other physical activities. For greater effect, use with rosemary when the fragrance will be most pleasing. The dried leaves, together with those of lavender will, if placed in muslin bags, impart a pleasant scent to clothes and linen. It is a plant that has many uses all the year round.

Ladies' mantle (*Alchemilla vulgaris*)
Closely related to parsley piert, both of which belong to the Rose order. It was named in honour of Our Lady for the rough leaves, covered with small hairs, were

dedicated to Queen Henrietta Maria, in praise of the plant. Being evergreen, it could be used for strewing all the year and was included in pot-pourris. Native of the mediterranean region, it is naturalized further north, often on the walls of ruined castles and abbeys.

Description. An evergreen perennial growing about 45 cm (18 in) tall and bushy, it will stand clipping and was used to form likened to the cloth of the garments worn by Our Lady. The plant has always been associated with countrywomen.

Description. A perennial plant of extreme hardiness it is found as far north as the Arctic Circle in America and Europe and is abundant in Iceland and Greenland. It grows in damp grassy meadows, especially in mountainous areas, increasing by its creeping rootstock from which arise its hairy stems to a height of about 25 cm (10 in). The leaves have up to eleven lobes, 'like a star' wrote Culpeper and it bears greenish-white petal-less flowers in clusters from June to September.

Culture. Plant in front of a herb border, in an open sunny situation for the leaves are most attractive whilst its flowers are also green. Seed is sown in boxes or pans in April and the young plants set out in July about 25 cm (10 in) apart. They require well-drained soil.

Medicinal uses. An infusion of the leaves was used to restore feminine beauty after breast feeding. Cloths were saturated with the warm water in which a handful of leaves had been infused and placed on the breasts for twenty minutes at a time. In a fortnight or so, the breasts would be firm again. It was also used to apply to sprains and bruises and to stop the flow of blood caused by sword wounds or carpenters' tools so was much in demand by those who built the vast timber roofs of the great halls of England. Applied to wounds and sores with lint, it brought about rapid healing. The plant can be used fresh or when dried so that a regular supply was always on hand.

Ladies' smock (*Cardamine pratensis*)

Shakespeare often mentioned it and as it blooms at Lady-tide it is dedicated to Our Lady. It is also known as meadow cress or bittercress for it has the same bitter properties as watercress. It was named cardamine because it was thought to strengthen the heart and was also used in cases of epilepsy.

Description. An unbranched perennial growing about 38 cm (15 in) tall with dark green narrow leaves and it blooms April-July. The flowers are borne in clusters and are of an unusual silvery-mauve hue. At a distance they have the appearance of metallic silver. Native to temperate areas of the northern hemisphere, it is found by the banks of rivers and in water meadows.

Culture. It is propagated from seed sown in spring and by root division in autumn and it will reproduce itself from tiny plantlets which appear on the leaves. If detached and placed on top of a box of sterilized soil, they will soon grow into strong plants. In the border, they need a soil containing some humus for the plants require moisture at their roots in summer to keep them growing. Plant 25 cm (10 in) apart. There is a lovely double flowered form, 'Flore Plena' which Henry Phillips said should be in every garden.

Medicinal uses. For epilepsy, twelve grains of the powdered flowers were to be taken three times a day while the same was recommended for strengthening the heart.

Culinary uses. A plant (like watercress) of the Cruciferae family, its leaves contain vitamin C and should be included in all summer salads. They have the same bitter taste as watercress and act as an excellent tonic. Parkinson wrote that 'they are as effectual for scurvy as the water cresses' and no garden should be without the plants.

Lavender (*Lavandula angustifolia* syn. *L. spica*)

It takes its name from the Latin *lavare*, to wash, and in the 16th century, a laundress was known as a 'lavendre'. Writing of lavender in *The Garden of Health* (1579), William Lawson said 'boil it in water, wet thy shirt in it and dry it again' when it will retain the lavender scent for days. In Italy where it abounds, laundrywomen would hang their washing on rosemary and lavender bushes to dry, when they would impart their rich perfume to the clothes. It is native to the mediterranean region and probably came to the rest of Europe with the Romans. Nowhere does it grow better than in

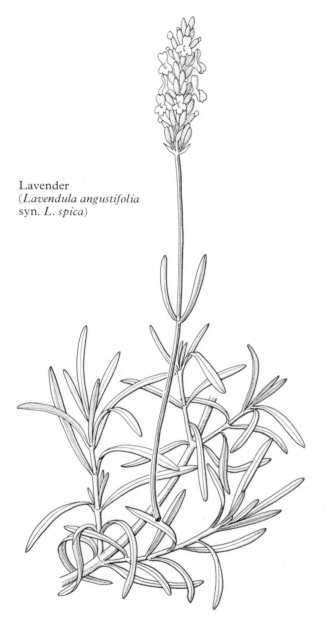

Lavender
(*Lavendula angustifolia*
syn. *L. spica*)

quality. After six years, the plants are taken up and burnt and a new plantation made.

Description. A shrubby perennial growing 60–120 cm (2–4 ft) tall with small lance-shaped leaves, downy on both sides which gives the plant a grey appearance. The flowers are borne July-September in whorls of six to twelve on an erect spike about 25 cm (10 in) long. Native of S. Europe, it has been a garden plant in the British Isles since early times.

Culture. It requires a well-drained soil, preferably of a calcareous nature and an open, sunny position. It will not grow well in shade. It will withstand the cold of winters down to −20° C (0° F) and enjoys a dry, sunny climate, where it can be harvested to best advantage and makes the finest otto. It requires no manure but the soil should contain a liberal amount of lime or mortar. It is also propagated from cuttings or pull-offs (shoots with a 'heel'). These are removed in July and August and inserted in pots or boxes or in a frame, in a sandy soil, planting them 2.5 cm (1 in) apart. Shade from the direct rays of the sun until they have rooted and plant out in spring. There are several species and varieties. Those of vigorous habit such as *L. angustifolia*, the Old English lavender and its variety 'Grappenhall' which bears spikes of deeper mauve are planted about 1 m (3–4 ft) apart. They will make a dense hedge 1 m (3–4 ft) tall and the same across. Plants may be used as a hedge and with their hardiness will protect the less hardy herbs. They may be used to surround a rose garden, associating well with modern hybrid teas and the old shrub roses or alongside a path. The flowers are visited by bees and butterflies all summer.

To make a smaller hedge of about 60 cm (2 ft) tall, plant *L.* 'Nana Compacta' or Miss Jekyll's 'Munstead Dwarf'. Plant about 50 cm (20 in) apart and they can be clipped into shape. This should be done in April but remember, the more the plants are clipped, the fewer flowering spikes they will produce. Where growing commercially, the plants are

England where the finest lavender water is still made, production starting in the 17th century and continuing to the present day. On average, 25 kg ($\frac{1}{2}$ cwt) of flowers will yield about 0.5 kg (1 lb) of essential oil. In the finest ottos, the stems are excluded and it is in their fourth and fifth years that the plants yield the most otto and of the highest never clipped. There is a white flowered form of *L.* 'Nana Compacta' whilst 'Hidcote Blue' bears flowers of deepest blue. With its dwarf habit and silvery foliage, 'Twickel Purple', the darkest flowered of all the lavenders, is a lovely variety, whilst 'Jean Davis' bears flowers of strawberry pink. For warm gardens French lavender, the dainty *L. stoechas*, which grows only 30 cm (12 in) high, is a beauty for its purple flowers have purple bracts, not green like the others but it is more tender, withstanding only a few degrees of frost. The same may be said of *L. dentata* which has soft feathery green foliage and has more of the scent of rosemary.

Medicinal uses. A few drops of spirit of lavender in a tablespoonful of water will relieve nervous palpitation and calm the nerves. Spirits of lavender is made by adding 1 part essential oil to 49 parts spirit of wine. To ease sprains and rheumatic pains, 1 part oil of lavender with 3 parts spirits of wine is an effective embrocation whilst oil of lavender is said to promote the growth of new hair if gently massaged into the scalp. A 'tea' made from lavender tops, a handful in half a litre (1 pint) of hot water and to which the skin of a lemon has been added, will revive those suffering from fatigue in warm weather. Strain and drink ice cold from the refrigerator with a sprig of borage in it.

Other uses. The dried flowers scattered over a carpet or rush matting will release a powerful smell of lavender when walked upon whilst the dry flowers, in small muslin bags will impart the delicious scent to bedding and clothes if placed with them in a drawer or airing cupboard (closet). The bags can be placed in cushions and will release their scent when sat upon or in pillows when the head is laid upon them. The dried stems dipped in saltpetre and dried off will, if lit with a match after fixing the base of the stems in sand, burn slowly for an hour or more and release an incense-like fragrance in a sick room. No pot-pourri will be really appreciated if lavender flowers are absent. The flowers should be harvested early September before they begin to part from the stems and whilst the weather is still dry and warm.

Lesser periwinkle (*Vinca minor*)
Its name is derived from *pervincere*, to overcome, for the plant was reputed to cure many illnesses. Its botanical name is from the Latin *vincio*, to bind, for its long stringy stems were bound into chaplets for those to wear at funerals on account of its dark green

Lesser periwinkle
(*Vinca minor*)

leaves and purple-blue flowers. Chaucer called it 'the fresh Perwinke, rich of Hew' and in France, it is the emblem of friendship.

Description. A prostrate perennial with thin wiry stems which reach out to a considerable distance from the plant, covering the ground and suppressing all weeds. The leaves are glossy and narrow, the flowers violet-blue and measuring 2.5 cm (1 in) across. The plant is evergreen and blooms almost the whole year. A plant of extreme hardiness, it grows in shady places and is common in deciduous woodlands. There is a variety with gold leaf variegations of great beauty, and a double flowered form.

Culture. Of easy culture, it roots at the leaf nodes like ground ivy and many plants can be obtained from a single stem simply by lifting and detaching them from the parent and replanting in pots or the open ground. This can be done at any time, except when the ground is frozen. Plants may also be raised from seed sown in spring in boxes in a frame or sunny window. Plant 45 cm (18 in) apart and they grow well in any soil.

Medicinal uses. If the leaves are crushed and applied to piles, they will give relief or an ointment made from the leaves will serve the same purpose. A decoction made from the fresh leaves after cutting them up will ease a sore throat if used as a gargle. A tincture made from the leaves with spirits of wine, if just two drops were taken three times daily in a tablespoonful of water, had a reputation for checking internal haemorrhages. It has binding characteristics medicinally. Being an evergreen plant, its leaves are always available.

Lily of the valley (*Convallaria majalis*)

Its name is from the Latin *convallis*, a valley, for it is to be found in leafy woodlands and valleys. Matthiolus called its distilled water *Aqua aurea*, for it was so valuable it was kept in vessels of pure gold. It is found wild across Europe into western Asia, and is naturalized in north-eastern N. America.

Description. One of the most beautiful of wild flowers, it is perennial with a creeping rootstock and bearing in May and June, greenish-white bells 15–30 cm (6–12 in) in a 15 cm (6 in) tall one-sided raceme. They have a delicious scent used synthetically as hydroxy-citronellal in Lanvin's famous Arpège perfume. The blooms are enhanced by the reflexed edge to the petals and they are backed by a pair of dark-green root leaves with a sheathing petiole.

Culture. It enjoys semi-shaded conditions and a moist leafy soil containing some lime. Before planting in autumn, dig in some leaf mould or decayed manure or a little of both or some used hops, give a dusting of lime or mortar and plant the crowns as the roots are called, about 2.5 cm (1 in) deep and 20 cm (8 in) apart. They grow well in a northerly position. To maintain the quality of the flower spikes (which always find a ready sale to florists to sell for corsages and evening wear), lift, divide and replant into prepared ground every four or five years and mulch each winter.

Medicinal uses. The plant acts on the heart like digitalis, from foxgloves. Unlike digitalis, it is quickly excreted from the blood stream as a poison and is therefore less likely to have toxic effects. For a weak heart, a tincture was made by immersing a cupful of flowers in spirits of wine and eight to ten drops taken in a tablespoonful of water twice daily. A dozen of the fresh or dried flowers infused in half a litre (1 pint) of boiling water was a favourite remedy to soothe a palpitating heart; a wineglassful was taken twice daily. The dried flowers and roots (which have a smell similar to that of the flowers) will clear the head if taken as snuff and act like a smelling bottle, clearing the mind in stuffy places; the ancients believed it was able to restore the memory.

Other uses. The water distilled from the fresh flowers and applied to the face with lint (gauze) after washing, tightens the skin and maintains its whiteness.

Liquorice (Licorice) (*Glycyrrhiza glabra*)

Since earliest times, large quantities of the root have been imported into northern

Europe, mostly from Spain where it has always been known as Spanish juice. But it may have been first imported by the Romans who ate it in large amounts for it was believed to increase one's stamina. It is grown commercially for its value as a gentle natural laxative and is included in cough mixtures, while large quantities are used in the British sweet trade to make Pontefract cakes and liquorice all-sorts. Chaucer knew of its many virtues and in *The Garden of Love* wrote that

> Ther was eke wexing many a spice
> As clove gillyflower and liquorice

Dioscorides named it glukorhiza from *geykys*, sweet, and *rhiza*, a root.

Description. In its native lands it grows in shady woodlands and is found from Spain, across S. Europe and N. Africa to the China coast, the dried roots being a valuable commercial crop but Spanish liquorice is in most demand. A perennial plant, it increases by underground stolons with the roots penetrating to about 1 m (3–4 ft), like those of horseradish and once established is difficult to eradicate. The plant grows 1 m (3–4 ft) tall with pinnate leaves and in June and July bears pale blue pea-like flowers (like the edible pea, it is a legume) in the leaf axils. They are followed by long smooth pods.

Culture. As long straight roots are required by the confectionery trade and the makers of cough mixtures and laxatives, a light deeply worked soil is necessary containing some humus and manure and being free from large stones. The roots are planted in October and November (which is also the time for lifting) or in March and are cut into pieces 8–10 cm (3–4 in) long, each piece having two 'eyes' or 'buds'. Plant 30 cm (12 in) apart and just below the surface. As they are left undisturbed to grow on for four years, clean ground is essential. The roots are lifted by digging down to a depth of at least 1 m (about 3 ft) and care must be taken that they do not break up. They are dried on shelves in an open shed, later being taken indoors to complete the drying. An acre will yield about five tons. Well-grown liquorice root is 60 cm (2 ft) long and about 2 cm ($\frac{3}{4}$ in) in diameter. The root is light brown when dug up and yellow when peeled, with the sweet earthy smell associated with the product. In Europe, the roots when partially dry are first crushed, then boiled in water, the evaporation being taken off into copper vessels and the black mass kept stirred. When as thick as tar it is rolled into the familiar liquorice sticks some 15 cm (6 in) long and dried, then tied into bundles to be exported. The product is generally known as liquorice juice, that from Spain as Spanish juice.

Medicinal uses. The juice is included in stout to increase its sweetness and blackness and to impart a special flavour, and in cough mixtures and laxative medicines. Mixed with a little linseed, the juice acts as a tonic and laxative, whilst a tonic beer, together with elecampane root and fennel water, is made from dried liquorice root. This was the drink John Josslyn made for the American Indians when they were 'off-colour' and it is pleasant and nourishing. Only when the roots are peeled and dried is the juice obtained clear and bright. A preparation of the juice is used by the medical profession to treat peptic ulcers and it has other valuable uses. In *The Daily Telegraph* of February 9th 1973 appeared the story told by two Leeds' doctors who reported in *The Lancet* how a local woman cured herself of Addison's disease by her craving for liquorice cakes, consuming 340 g ($\frac{3}{4}$ lb) daily for two years. Her body must have known exactly what it needed to restore it to full health. To ease a sore throat, boil 30 g (1 oz) of the crushed root with half a litre (1 pint) of water and use as a warm gargle night and morning.

Lovage (*Levisticum officinale* and *Ligusticum scoticum*)

There are two distinct plants called lovage, *L. officinale* from the Mediterranean, and *L. scoticum* which grows on rocky coasts in N.

W. Europe. *Levisticum officinale* may have been introduced to Northern Europe by the Romans for it grows in profusion in Liguria and along the Mediterranean coast where, since earliest times, it was appreciated for its medicinal and culinary qualities. Culpeper said of them that 'the whole plant smelleth strongly and aromatically, of a hot, sharp, biting taste'.

Description. *Levisticum officinale* is perennial, growing 1 m (3–4 ft) tall with erect hollow stems, its dark green leaves divided into narrow segments, like those of celery to which its taste may be likened. An umbellifer, it bears its small yellow flowers in stiff umbels during June and July and these are followed by pale brown elliptical fruits which are highly aromatic, as is the entire plant which is filled with an aromatic juice. The plant forms a fleshy tap root some 15 cm (6 in) long.

Ligusticum scoticum has white flowers in June and July and is not so tall-growing, reaching about half the height. It has glossy, bright green leaves with more broadly-toothed leaflets. The leaves and stems of both species were used to scent bath water.

Culture. With their highly polished foliage, both plants are attractive in the border. The foliage will die down in winter but comes again in spring. It requires a soil containing humus and a little decayed manure, also an open, sunny situation. Propagation is by root division in autumn or spring, pulling the roots apart and replanting before they dry out, or from seed sown in spring. The seed must be fresh. If growing it in the vegetable garden, sow in drills made 50 cm (20 in) apart and thin to 45 cm (18 in) in the rows.

Medicinal uses. Both plants have a warm taste, due to angelic acid, present also in angelica which they resemble in taste. An infusion of the leaves can be used as a gargle to ease a sore throat and the leaves when bruised and simmered in lard and placed on a boil will bring it to a head. Dr. Johnson said that a spoonful of a mixture of flour of sulphur and mustard washed down by a cupful of lovage water (an infusion of the root) was an excellent cure for rheumatism, whilst an infusion of the roots and seeds, taken hot, relieved stomach pains. From the leaves, a handful infused in half a litre (1 pint) of hot water, a tonic 'tea' is made; a cupful taken daily will relieve rheumatic pains. From the freshly dug roots, a tonic beer was made and sold in English north country inns, with dandelion and burdock.

Lungwort (*Pulmonaria officinalis*)
A native of Europe with cowslip-like flowers which are two-coloured, red and pale blue;

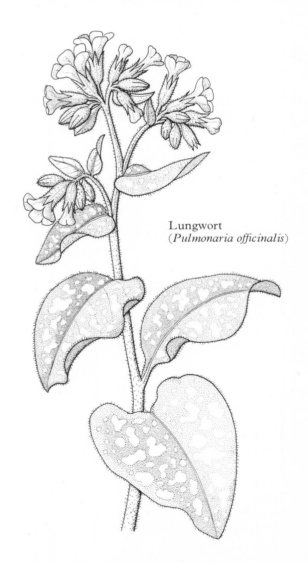

Lungwort
(*Pulmonaria officinalis*)

hence its country name of Adam and Eve for blue was associated with men, red or pink with women. It was also known as soldiers and sailors, the red for soldiers' tunics at Waterloo, the blue for Nelson's sailors' suits at Trafalgar.

Description. A delightful downy perennial growing about 25 cm (10 in) tall with plain green oval leaves terminating to a point and the lower or root leaves stalked, the upper leaves sessile. The flowers with their tubular calyx and funnel-shaped corolla bloom (with cowslips) from April–June. It is a plant of open woodlands and hedgerows.

Culture. It grows in semi-shade and in ordinary well-drained soil, bringing colour to the front of a border early in summer. Propagation is by root division in spring or from seed sown in boxes in spring in a frame or sunny window.

Medicinal uses. The leaves are mucilaginous and act as a demulcent if used when fresh, while when dried, a teaspoonful in a cupful of hot water, taken twice daily will soothe the throat which has been irritated by a hard cough.

Male fern (*Dryopteris filix-mas*)
One of the common ferns of the world found throughout Europe, Asia, Africa, N. and S. America and even some of the Pacific islands. The ancients used the roots to expel tapeworms in humans and animals whilst in times of food scarcity, the young fronds were boiled and eaten with stewed rabbits and provided a nourishing meal. It is so named because the roots resemble a man's hand and it was the custom on the Eve of St. Agnes to put a root in a girl's bed when the likeness of her future husband would appear to her in a dream.

Description. A perennial plant, the leaves arising from the rhizome-like roots which creep along the ground just beneath the surface. The fronds or leaves grow to a height of about 1 m (3–4 ft) and are lance-shaped with the stalks clothed in brown hairs, the leaves being pinnately lobed into leaflets.

Culture. It is propagated from pieces of rootstock planted in spring when the new fronds appear. It dies back in autumn.

Medicinal uses. When the foliage dies down, the cylindrical rhizomes are dug up and the scales and soil removed. The roots are cut lengthwise and into pieces about 10 cm (4 in) long and dried sufficiently for them to be ground to a powder. Only fresh roots are used. The root is then exhausted with ether and the extract used to expel tapeworms from humans and animals. Because of the high doses needed to expel tapeworms it is dangerous to use male fern except under medical supervision.

Culinary uses. The young fronds are cut in spring when about 15 cm (6 in) long and are tied into bundles like asparagus, then boiled until tender. Serve with melted butter to accompany chicken or game. They are pleasant to eat and nourishing.

Marigold (*Calendula officinalis*)
It takes its botanical name from the fact that it is in bloom on the calends (first day) of almost every month of the year and its country name because it blooms on each of the festivals of the Virgin Mary, the word 'gold' being a reference to the rays of gold seen around the head of the Virgin in medieval paintings. Lyte in his *Herbal* (1578) said 'The marygolde hath pleasant bright and shining yellow flowers which close at the setting downe of the sun and do spread again at the sun's rising'. Native of S. Europe, it has since spread over much of northern Europe and into N. America. It is called pot marigold in the United States where the term 'marigold' usually refers to the genus Tagetes.

Description. It is an annual which, though native of S. Europe, is a plant of great hardiness and since early times it was common in cottage gardens, usually seeding itself. Growing 30–40 cm (12–16 in) tall with oblong sessile leaves, the flowers (which last well in water and are most attractive in bowls and vases of smoky glass) have orange or yellow ray florets and black or brown disc

Marigold
(*Calendula officinalis*)

to mature, thinning to 20 cm (8 in) apart. It will transplant well. Plants from an early sowing will be ready to use a month before those sown in the open. With its bright green leaves and continuous flowering, this is a valuable plant for summer and autumn bedding and the two best varieties for all purposes are 'Radio', with its orange quilled petals and 'Golden Beam', its yellow counterpart.

Medicinal uses. Marigold water, made by pouring half a litre (1 pint) of hot water on-to a handful of flowers and straining, may be used lukewarm to ease tired and sore eyes and it may be taken as a 'tea' either warm or cold at bedtime, to induce sound sleep. Taken hot, it will cause one to perspire and reduce a temperature. The plant is reputed to assist in the healing of wounds and the juice from all parts was used by surgeons in the American Civil War to treat wounds and burns and leg ulcers. The juice rubbed on insect bites and wasp stings will give relief and marigold ointment will ease the pain of first degree burns. Its essence is used in modern face and hand creams as it is healing when the face has been exposed to cold winds or a hot sun and makes the skin soft and smooth.

Culinary uses. From earliest times, the flowers were dried and sold in grocers' shops from wooden drums, to include in soups and broths while the fresh flowers were used in the same way, hence its name, pot marigold. The fresh petals can be included in salads and in cream cheese sandwiches, after chopping small. To dry marigolds, remove the flowers when quite dry, spread out on sheets of paper in an airy room and as they dry, pull the petals from the centre disc. Spread them out on trays and leave for about ten days, turning them daily, until quite dry. Then place in strong paper bags or cardboard boxes and keep in a dry room to use in winter.

Marjoram (*Origanum vulgare*)
There are several species with valuable culinary uses while sweet marjoram (*O. mar-*

florets and measure about 5 cm (2 in) across. They appear in long succession from early summer until almost the year end if the weather is mild.

Culture. Seed is sown in boxes in a frame or sunny window early in March, the young plants being set out in April 20 cm (8 in) apart into ordinary soil. The plants require an open, sunny situation. Seed may also be sown broadcast in beds where the plants are *jorana*) has been grown since early times to use in sweet bags and pot pourris. *O. vulgare* is native of Europe and Asia where it is found in grassland. It takes its name from the Greek *oros*, a mountain, and *ganos*, joy, for its presence when in bloom in July and August, allegedly brought happiness to all who came upon it. It has been used since early times to make marjoram 'tea' and to flavour many foods.

Description. *O. vulgare* is a hardy perennial with woody stems, like those of thyme and small dark green opposite leaves covered in soft hairs. The flowers are rosy-purple or whitish with purple bracts and are borne in crowded terminal cymes on stems 25–30 cm (10–12 in) tall. As its stems are also purple, the whole plant has a smoky appearance. It shows a great preference for calcareous soils and is found especially in sunny, warm parts of Europe. *O. marjorana*, sweet marjoram, which exudes a more powerful balsamic perfume than other species, was also known as knotted marjoram for it was grown in the knot beds of Tudor gardens, interlaced with hyssop and upright thymes and used mostly to please the ladies, as Parkinson said 'to put in nosegays and to use in sweet powders, sweet bags and sweet washing waters'. Tusser included it in his herbs for strewing for it released a refreshing balsamic perfume when trodden on.

Sweet marjoram is native of Spain and Portugal where it is cultivated commercially, also of N. Africa. It is a perennial but is usually treated as an annual in countries where frosts are regular, only thriving as a perennial where winters are mild. The plant secretes an essential oil from the stems and leaves which yields a crystalline matter, stearoptene which has a camphor-like smell. The plant grows about 25 cm (10 in) tall and upright and the flowers first appear as tiny brown buds, like knots of string which some believe, gave the plant its name.

O. onites is the pot marjoram, a native of Sicily and other Mediterranean islands. It is of more vigorous habit than the others and is hardier than *O. marjorana*, surviving

moderate, but not severe, frosts. There is a handsome golden leaf variety, 'Aureum', which should be planted to the front of a border. All the marjorams are visited by bees and butterflies.

Culture. They require much the same culture and as they are slow to germinate from seed, are best propagated either by root division in spring or from cuttings or pulloffs, taken with a 'heel' of the half-ripened wood in July and August. Treat with hormone powder for quicker rooting and insert in boxes or around the side of an earthenware pot filled with sandy compost. They will have rooted by late autumn and should then be potted separately and kept under glass through winter, planting out in sandy soil in April, 25 cm (10 in) apart. If growing from seed, sow in early summer in boxes under glass and transplant to small pots. Grow on under glass during winter and plant out in April.

Medicinal uses. An infusion of the leaves and tops, a handful to half a litre (1 pint) of boiling water and after straining, taken a wineglassful at a time sweetened with a little honey, will relieve a nervous headache and taken at bedtime will induce sound sleep. The same may also be taken cold as a tonic drink when it will relieve depression. To relieve rheumatic joints and sprains, the shoots and leaves are placed in a muslin bag and warmed in a low oven before being held against the stiff and tender parts. The oil too, will bring quick relief if gently massaged into the scalp night and morning. It will also promote the growth of new hair. In a bath, marjoram and rosemary will relieve tired limbs.

Culinary uses. The marjorams are an important part of a bouquet garni, together with parsley, thyme and the leaf of the bay tree, tied together and used fresh to flavour soups and stews, or dried and placed in a muslin bag, to impart the flavour in a similar way. Marjoram (and the dried wild marjoram of S. Europe is known as origanum) makes the best stuffing for pork and veal and for a duck or goose, taking away any greasiness and, with sweet basil, is the herb to accompany tomato and egg dishes. Include it in a tomato or egg omelette to bring out the flavour and sprinkle the dried or fresh leaves, finely chopped, on to soups and scrambled eggs. Marjoram tops were once used to flavour ale, to impart its balsamic flavour and to clarify it and a sprig placed in a tonic wine will improve the taste. Like bay, a sprig in a glass of cold milk, or cooked in a milk pudding, will add interest.

Other uses. Sweet marjoram, dried and mixed with lavender is the principal ingredient of pot-pourris and sweet bags and from the fresh leaves and tops, a sweet washing water to apply to the face is made by immersing a handful of tops in a pint of boiling water, straining and bottling and applying it after washing. It is most refreshing and may be used by men as an 'after shave' lotion.

Marsh Mallow (*Althaea officinalis*)

One of the most beautiful of European wild plants and handsome in the border but as it seeds itself freely, and forms a long woody tap root, it is difficult to control in the garden. It takes its name from the Greek *malassein*, alluding to the demulcent qualities of the plant whilst Althaea is from *althos*, a remedy, for Pliny said 'whosoever shall take a spoonful of mallow shall that day be free from all diseases that may come to him'. The plant takes it popular name 'cheesecake plant' from the circular head of seeds and all parts are edible.

Description. *A. officinalis* is a hoary perennial growing 1 m (about 3 ft) tall with broad, undivided three to five-lobed leaves soft and downy to touch, the silky hairs giving the plant a greyish appearance. The large pale lilac/pink flowers are borne in axillary and terminal cymes during August and September. It is a plant of marshlands and ditches by the sea occurring in Europe, N. Africa, and N. America.

Culture. It grows in any kind of soil and comes readily from seed sown in drills in spring and transplanting to the back of the border when the seedlings are large enough to handle. Plant 60 cm (2 ft) apart. The flower stem dies down in winter but the tuft of basal leaves remains green. All parts of the plant contain mucilage. The common mallow, *Malva sylvestris*, is similar but more often found on dryer ground and it begins to bear its purple-blue flowers with dark veins before the end of June. It is not as mucilaginous as *Althaea officinalis* nor is it so valuable medicinally.

Medicinal uses. As a demulcent, marsh mallow has the same qualities as slippery elm and carrageen moss, the roots containing half their weight of saccharine viscous mucilage which soothes internally when taken for colic and diarrhoea. To 110 g ($\frac{1}{4}$ lb) of the dried and sliced root, add 2.3 litres (4 pints) of water. After boiling for twenty minutes strain and take a wineglassful warm or cold three times daily. It can also be prescribed for a hard cough. The syrup is given for whooping cough. Mallow water will remove soreness from the eyes if bathed with lint (gauze). A teaspoonful of the dried and ground root mixed with one of slippery elm and a little hot water will remove inflammation from a gash or sore if applied and left on for an hour.

Culinary uses. A pleasant 'tea' can be made by slicing 30 g (1 oz) of the clean and dried root and placing in a pan containing half a litre (1 pint) of water, allowing it to stand for several hours. Strain and add a little orange or lemon juice and a teaspoonful of honey; heat before drinking. If taken at bedtime it will relieve a cough and induce sleep. A 'tea' may be made in a similar way from the flowers. The leaves which should have been boiled, make a nourishing meal fried with sliced onions and served with a rasher of bacon. The young leaves may be used in salads.

Meadowsweet (*Filipendula ulmaria* syn. *Spiraea filipendula*)

The Dutch named it reinette, little queen and Ben Jonson knew it as meadow's queen, though its botanical name is from *ulmus*,

Hop *(Humulus lupulus)*. This
hardy perennial has been
used for making beer since
the 9th century. Its sedative
and narcotic effects (the dried
flowers have a pleasant scent
and are often used to stuff
pillows) are also well known.

Cowslip *(Primula veris)*, one
of the loveliest of wild
flowers. Cowslip wine or tea
can be made from the
flowers, and the leaves,
which resemble watercress,
are ideal for spring salads.

Elecampane *(Inula helenium)*. This tall (1.2–1.5 m; 4–5 ft) growing perennial is probably native only in Asia but has long been naturalized in Europe and N. America. The plant has powerful antiseptic properties and traditionally was used to relieve asthma and bronchitis.

elm, from the shape and appearance of its leaflets. Gerard said that 'the leaves far ex-cell all other herbs to strew in chambers, hall and banqueting houses in summertime' and Queen Elizabeth I liked to have it in her apartments above all other herbs, for its aromatic foliage is due to the presence of wintergreen. Parkinson said it had 'a pretty sharp scent'.

Description. A glabrous perennial growing about 1 m (3–4 ft) tall with wiry stems and pinnate leaves, smooth and dark green above, grey and rough on the underside and releasing a refreshing scent when pressed. The terminal leaflet is lobed while the leaflets have serrated edges. The creamy white flowers like those of the *Spiraea* appear from June to September and are borne in crowded cymes. They have an unpleasant smell, and are pollinated by insects. The plant is found in damp meadows and open woodlands and by rivers and streams, occurring now through all the north temperate zones.

Culture. It requires a soil containing some humus to retain summer moisture, or plant it by a pond. It is propagated by root division in autumn or spring or raised from seed sown in pots or boxes in April and growing on the young plants in small pots to plant out 45 cm (18 in) apart the following spring.

Medicinal uses. Like fennel, the distilled water of the leaves is used to bathe the eyes, to take away soreness and to strengthen them. It is astringent and can be given for diarrhoea. Infuse 30 g (1 oz) of the dried leaves in half a litre (1 pint) of boiling water, strain and sweeten with a little honey and give a small wineglassful twice daily. The same makes a pleasant tonic drink. A century ago, it was discovered that the salicylic acid and its derivatives present in meadow-sweet were valuable in easing all manner of pains and rheumatic complaints if taken internally. This in due course led to the synthesis of aspirin which became the world's most commonly used drug. The dried leaf of the plant can be taken instead of aspirin if a more natural remedy is preferred for synthetic aspirin does not suit everybody, often causing unpleasant side effects whereas meadowsweet does not.

Culinary uses. The leaves, used fresh or dry, impart a pleasant taste to soups and stews and to wine (especially a tonic wine) when the fresh leaf is placed in a glass for an hour before drinking. Parkinson said that 'a leaf or two in a cup of wine, will give as quick and fine a relish thereto as Burnet'.

Other uses. The leaves are an important ingredient in dry pot-pourris for they retain their strength for many months. The fresh leaves placed in a bath will give it a refreshing smell and ease tired limbs.

Mugwort (*Artemisia vulgaris*)

Dioscorides advised using the dried leaves to place amongst clothes and bedding to keep away moths and the plant does indeed take its name from the Saxon *moughte*, a moth. A sprig placed in a buttonhole will keep away flies in hot weather and a bunch of the dried plant, hung in a room will have the same effect. Perhaps for this reason it was one of the nine 'sacred herbs' of the ancients.

Description. It is an erect perennial growing about 1 m (3–4 ft) high with grooved stems and one to two pinnate leaves, the leaflets deeply toothed and pointed and downy on the underside. This gives the plant a grey appearance which distinguishes it from wormwood. The brownish-yellow flowers are borne in July and August, in loose spikes. It is a common plant of waste ground and hedgerows throughout the British Isles and across N. Europe and Asia to Japan, and also in N. America.

Culture. It is propagated from offsets, planted in spring about 50 cm (20 in) apart into ordinary soil, or from seed sown in pots or boxes in spring and planted in the border in July.

Medicinal uses. It is a nervine. Use 30 g (1 oz) of the fresh or dried leaves to half a litre (1 pint) of boiling water, and strain; a wine-glassful twice daily may be taken as a tonic drink, cold in summer or hot in winter. Prolonged use is not without danger and may be injurious to the nervous system. As mugwort contains tannin, the same may be used warm as a gargle to ease a sore throat. A handful of leaves used fresh in baths, together with rosemary or meadowsweet or bergamot will impart an aromatic odour and relieve a tired body whilst an infusion of the leaves, together with those of chamomile and agrimony can be used for bathing sprains. An ointment made from mugwort juice and lard gives relief when applied to sprains and rheumatic joints and will reduce glandular swellings. Fresh mugwort leaves when used in turkey and poultry foods, act as a tonic and keep them free from the usual poultry ailments. Sheep, too, remain healthy when feeding on mugwort.

Culinary uses. It contains the bitter principle absinthin and the dried leaves were once used in stuffings for the richer meats such as pork and also ducks and geese for it will take away much of the richness or grease and helps the digestion. A tonic beer is made from the herb. Collect 90 g (3 oz) of fresh leaves and tops and simmer for an hour with 9 litres (2 gallons) of water: strain and whilst still hot, stir in 0.5 kg (1 lb) of brown sugar. Pour into an earthenware jar or bowl and add a tablespoon of yeast. Allow to ferment for ten to twelve days, then strain into bottles and cork. Place in the dark and keep for a month or so before drinking, taking a wineglassful daily. Before the introduction of hops, mugwort was used to clarify ale, to which it gave an appetizing bitter taste.

Mullein (*Verbascum thapsus*)

Widespread in Europe and Asia it is also naturalized in N. America and is one of the most handsome of wild flowers. It takes its name from the French *molens*, or Anglo-Saxon *moleyn*, soft, for its leaves are like flannel when touched: its botanical name is from the Latin *barbascum*, bearded, for the whole plant, including the filaments of the flowers, is covered in white hairs. Cottagers would put the leaves into children's shoes to protect the feet when walking on the stony roads to school and many a man driving cattle for miles along the roads would put the thick comfortable leaves in his boots. Cottagers would also dry the stems and make into tallow and when lighted they would burn for hours with a brilliant glow, hence its country name of candlewick. The dried leaves are excellent for lighting fires.

Description. An unbranched biennial growing up to 2 m (6–7 ft) tall, hence its name, great mullein, with lanceolate leaves densely covered in thick hairs, almost like wool; these give the plant a grey appearance and prevent too rapid evaporation of moisture. One of the most handsome plants for the back of a border for in July and August, it bears dull orange-yellow flowers in a large and dense terminal spike. It will seed itself. The plant is widespread on waste ground and on railway embankments, liking dry conditions and an open sunny situation.

Culture. Sow seed in July where it is to mature but the seedlings, which form a rosette, will transplant; or sow in small groups, thinning to 40 cm (16 in) apart.

Medicinal uses. It is a carminative and induces sleep. Infuse a handful of fresh flowers in hot water, strain and drink a wineglassful at bedtime. Such an infusion used to be given to children, an hour before bedtime, to prevent bedwetting. It was also a great standby for the relief of earache. The fresh flowers are steeped in an earthenware jar of olive oil, adding more flowers and more oil every other day over a period of two to three weeks. This was left in a sunny window for another two weeks, strained and bottled. Two or three drops were placed in the ear twice daily. Particular importance was attached to giving two drops at bedtime and applying a warm flannel to the ear. The same may be rubbed on an aching tooth and on to piles when it will give relief.

Other uses. The water from the flowers was used by countrywomen to dye the hair yellow, which Lyte mentions in his *Herbal*.

Mustard, Black (*Brassica nigra*)

It is white mustard (*Sinapsis alba*) that is grown as 'mustard and cress'; the black is grown as the condiment and it also has other medicinal and culinary uses. It is a plant which is now found all over the world where the climate is suitable, having been taken about by man long before records were made. It takes its name from Anglo-Saxon *must*, grape juice, and *ardens*, hot, since in olden times, the crushed seed was mixed with grape juice. Mustard oil obtained from the seed is so little affected by frost that it was always used by watch and clock repairers. William Coles said (1656) that 'mustard balls are brought to London as being the best the world affords'. Parkinson said that 'with some vinegar added to make it liquid and running .... it was served as a sauce both for fish and flesh'.

Description. It is an annual growing 60 cm (2 ft) tall, the lower leaves pinnate and rounded, the upper narrow and pointed. The brilliant yellow flowers (seen from afar as a field of gold where the crop is cultivated) are followed by quadrangular seed pods. It is also a weed of the wayside.

Culture. White mustard is sown thickly in boxes of soil or on damp flannel and cut when 7.5 cm (3 in) high to enjoy in salads and sandwiches. If cress is also required, sow this 4 days earlier so that both are ready together. In a winter temperature of 9°C (48° F) they will be ready to cut in two to three weeks. Mega is a new cress, with thick leaves, like watercress. Black mustard is grown for its seed and if a bed of clean ground is sown thickly in spring, the seed will be ready in September. The home grower should dry the seed like those of other annuals, cutting away the pods on a dry day and spreading on trays in a sunny well ventilated room until the seeds leave the pods with the slightest pressure. After removing, place in boxes and to make mustard powder, crush them with pestle and mortar.

Medicinal uses. To draw out a cold, place a teaspoonful of mustard powder in a large bowl; put this on the floor and almost fill it with boiling water. When cool enough, put in both feet, adding more hot water as it cools and keep in the feet for at least half an hour. Dry the feet and pour away the contents. To ease a tight chest, mix to a paste a teaspoonful of mustard powder with a spoonful of honey and a little vinegar and take a teaspoonful every two to three hours. For obstinate hiccoughs, place a small teaspoonful of mustard in a cup, fill up with hot water and sip it. An ointment made from oil of mustard will relieve rheumatism if gently massaged into the painful area. Because of its strong irritant action it must be used with discrimination, as it may cause serious inflammation. Mustard is an antiseptic and a deodorizer and a little of the powder rubbed on to the hands will remove any unpleasant smell, likewise from a utensil. Put in a little mustard, pour on boiling water, swill round and empty, then wash it in the normal way when every trace of smell will have departed.

Culinary uses. Mustard to accompany most meats but especially beef, is made by mixing a teaspoonful of powder with a little vinegar, leaving it smooth but quite stiff. It quickens the appetite and helps the stomach to digest the meat but taken in excess, may cause watering of the eyes and an unpleasant sensation in the nose but this lasts for only seconds. The famous Dijon mustard is made from mustard powder, capers, a little cream and tarragon vinegar. It is used with meat and fish. To make a mayonnaise, place the yolk of an egg in a basin, add half a teaspoonful of mustard powder, and season with salt and black pepper. Then add 140 ml ($\frac{1}{4}$ pint) of olive oil, a few drops at a time, stirring well in, then a tablespoonful of tarragon vinegar. Add a teaspoonful of finely chopped parsley or chives and finally, a small cupful of cream.

Nasturtium (*Tropaeolum majus*)

Native to Chile and Peru, it reached Britain at the end of the 17th century and was named *tropaeolum*, a trophy, from the resemblance of its long stalked leaves to a

Nasturtium
(*Tropaeolum majus*)

seeds 2.5 cm (1 in) deep to the front of a border or on a wall early in April. Ordinary soil is suitable but the plants require an open, sunny position. They can also be grown against a trellis when they will climb to 2 m (6–7 ft) in one summer.

Medicinal uses. Like watercress, it contains iron and sulphur and vitamin C and was used by sailors at sea as an alternative to scurvy grass, the seeds being sown in boxes or pots of soil in a port-hole window.

Culinary uses. Used sparingly, both the leaves and flowers can be included as an alternative to watercress in salads, while the seeds make a suitable substitute for capers in pickles and sauces. To pickle, gather the seeds as they form in summer, whilst still green and place in a screw-top jar, not quite filling it. Then fill up with tarragon vinegar which has been boiled with 15 g ($\frac{1}{2}$ oz) salt and a few peppercorns and allowed to cool. Leave for 2 months before using and in a dark cupboard the seeds will retain their quality for a year or more. To make caper sauce, chop up a tablespoonful of the seeds, place in a pan with a little tarragon vinegar and a cupful of melted butter. Stir over a low flame and serve hot with fish. A delicious tartare sauce can be made by mixing together a teaspoonful of freshly chopped parsley, and one of nasturtium seeds, a gherkin and a small onion, together with a tablespoonful each of mayonnaise and double cream. Do not make it until shortly before required. It should be as fresh as possible.

Roman shield and the flowers to a centurion's helmet. It was used as food by South American tribes and was first called there: great Indian cress.

Description. It is a climbing annual with peltate round leaves, bearing brilliant flowers in red, orange, yellow and pink, the upper petal forming a long free spur. The fruit or seed is tri-lobed and fleshy.

Culture. It is used to decorate hanging baskets and window boxes, the seed being sown in pots or boxes under glass in March, and the plants set out late in spring for they are almost hardy. Alternatively plant the

Nettle (*Urtica dioica*)

An unwanted weed of gardens the world over it takes its name from the Anglo-Saxon *needl*, a needle, from the sharp stinging hairs which cover the plant. At one time the highlanders of Scotland wove the hairs into sheets and tablecloths and rubbed the leaves and stems on to wooden drinking vessels for the juice coagulates and fills up all small holes making them watertight.

Description. It is an unbranched perennial growing 60–90 cm (2–3 ft) tall with stems and leaves covered in stiff hairs which pen-

Nettle
(*Urtica dioica*)

leaves, add half a litre (1 pint) of boiling water. Leave until cool and strain and take a wineglassful twice daily. It is more palatable if kept in the refrigerator until required. The same nettle 'tea' will also purify the blood and improve the complexion. John Wesley, a keen herbalist, gave his treatment for sciatica which he said could be relied on: boil nettle tops for twenty minutes in a little water and place in a muslin bag, then apply as warm as possible as a poultice to the buttocks and thighs. Urtication or flogging with freshly cut nettles about the buttocks and thighs for two or three minutes was practised until the end of the 19th century as a cure for sciatica. It was performed daily for several weeks.

Culinary uses. Nettle tops, used when young and steamed in a little butter or margarine, make an excellent vegetable to serve with meats, having the taste of spinach. They clear the blood and act as a tonic. They are also fed to turkeys and serve a similar purpose. From the fresh tops an excellent tonic beer is made. Fill a large saucepan with them, add 0.5 kg (1 lb) of malt, 30 g (1 oz) of hops, 60 g (2 oz) of sarsaparilla and a small piece of ginger. Add 1.1 litres (2 pints) of water and boil for twenty minutes. Then place 0.5 kg (1 lb) of sugar in an earthenware pan and stir in the hot mixture. Finally add 15 g ($\frac{1}{2}$ oz) of yeast and leave to ferment for ten to twelve days. Then pour into bottles and use after two weeks.

Ox-eye daisy (*Chrysanthemum leucanthemum*)

It is also called the moon penny and marguerite or maudline, from St. Mary Magdalene and believed to be the flower of Chaucer's *Flower and the Leaf*. Gerard knew it as maudlinwort.

Description. An erect woody perennial growing 30–60 cm (1–2 ft) tall, the lower dark green leaves being toothed or lobed, the upper lanceolate. The 5 cm (2 in) flowers, borne in May and June, have twenty white rayed petals and as many as five

etrate the skin when touched, releasing formic acid, which causes intense irritation. Rubbing the affected area with the juice of a dock leaf will give immediate relief. The leaves are heart-shaped and toothed; the flowers are greenish-white and borne in clusters from the leaf axils. One of the most useful of all plants, it is one of the world's most common weeds, present on waste ground and in hedgerows and in farmyards everywhere, throughout the temperate world.

Culture. It is so common it is not cultivated.

Medicinal uses. A teaspoonful of the juice is given to stay nose bleeding from high blood pressure. To 110 g (4 oz) of dried hundred yellow disc florets where honey rises to a depth of 1 mm (0.04 in) making it accessible to short-tongued insects, attracted to it by the unpleasant smell. The plant is widespread in meadows and cornfields in Britain and Asia and is well naturalized in New Zealand and the Americas.

Culture. It is propagated by divisions which are planted 30 cm (1 ft) apart to the front of a border or from seed sown in pots or boxes in a frame in spring. Transplant to the border in July. Ordinary soil is suitable.

Medicinal uses. A 'tea' is made by immersing a small handful of flowers in half a litre (1 pint) of hot water and after straining sweetened with a little honey. Take a wineglassful daily as a tonic and blood purifier. To relieve a hard cough, make a similar infusion from the leaves and flowers or just with the leaves only when not in bloom and take warm at bedtime. It will cause sweating and bring down the temperature. Culpeper suggested using the leaves and those of agrimony as a poultice for sciatica. Boil together, place in a muslin bag and apply as warm as can be bearable. The leaves and flowers can also be used, like those of chamomile, when dried and the leaves may be included in a herbal smoking mixture as a help to those with asthma.

Culinary uses. The young leaves can be included sparingly in salads, to which they impart a balsamic flavour.

Parsley (*Petroselinum crispum*)

Found wild on cliffs, rocks and old walls in the mediterranean region, it has been cultivated since earliest times. It is mentioned in a 14th century manuscript by Master John, gardener, a copy of which is in Trinity College Library, Cambridge, England. Its taste was much appreciated by the royal heads of Europe. Charlemagne enjoyed cheese flavoured with parsley seed and Henry VIII believed it to make the best of all sauces to accompany fish. It is a source of vitamins A, C and E as well as iron. The Greeks held the plant to be sacred, crowning victors at the games with its leaves.

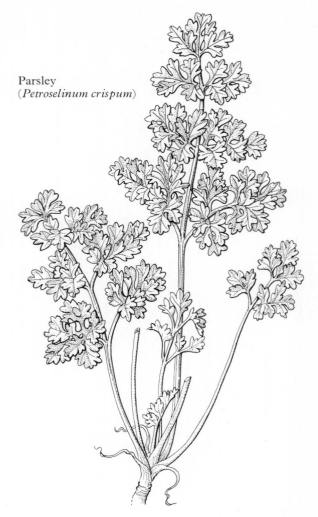

Parsley
(*Petroselinum crispum*)

Description. A bright green glabrous biennial growing 25–30 cm (10–12 in) tall and the same across, the tripinnate leaves being crisped and crimped to give them a fern-like appearance so that they are widely used for garnishing and by fishmongers to decorate their slabs. The tiny yellow flowers are borne in umbels but garden-grown plants should not be allowed to flower as they will do so at the expense of foliage. If they do not flower, the plants will remain green for a second year or more.

Culture. Seed is sown in spring in well-manured soil or in one in which plenty of humus is present, otherwise the plants tend to make flower too quickly. Use fresh seed which in any case, takes more than a month to germinate: old seed will not germinate at all. Sow in shallow drills 25 cm (10 in) apart and keep the seed moist to assist germination. Before the end of summer there will be some leaf to remove from many of the plants and they will continue to make leaf through a mild winter and throughout the following year.

Where severe frosts are regular, parsley must be sown annually or over-wintered under glass. The plants will benefit from an early summer mulch. To maintain a supply of fresh leaf, make a second sowing in July and repeat each year. Those who have no garden can sow in pots in a sunny window. 'Champion Moss Curled' with its densely crimped fronds of emerald green is one of the best varieties. With its compact habit, it can be used as an edging for a border. Also recommended is 'Green Velvet' which is handsomely curled and of deep emerald green. If the plants become coarse in late summer, clip back with shears when fresh growth will arise.

Medicinal uses. If a small piece of leaf is chewed after eating onions or garlic, it will take away the smell from the breath. Because of its vitamin content, a bowl of freshly chopped parsley should be on every table, to sprinkle over many savoury dishes. Parsley seed, 15 g ($\frac{1}{2}$ oz) infused in 1.1 litres (2 pints) of hot water and a wineglassful taken twice daily including once at bedtime, is an old remedy for a fever, lowering the temperature and if taken once a day, it will tone the system and aid the digestion. It is also given to expel wind. A decoction of the root, fresh or dried 230 g ($\frac{1}{2}$ lb) to 1.1 litres (2 pints) of water, stimulates the kidneys. From the root is obtained the principle apiin and a volatile oil, apiol. Gerard recommends that the seeds or roots boiled in ale will act as a tonic to the system. It is also a carminative.

Culinary uses. It is the best of all herbs for garnishing for it retains its 'crispness' and green hue for many hours (indeed, days) after it is cut and so is used in large amounts by hoteliers for garnishing and for sprinkling over soups. The leaves will freeze well. Blanch for 2 minutes in boiling water, allow to cool, then place in plastic bags before putting in the freezer. To make sure of fresh parsley through winter, cover a row of July sown plants with cloches from November until March; or grow some plants in pots in a sunny window.

To make parsley sauce to serve with fish, melt 15 g ($\frac{1}{2}$ oz) butter in a saucepan and stir in the same of flour. Then add 0.25 litre ($\frac{1}{2}$ pint) of fish stock, just bring to the boil and add a tablespoonful of freshly chopped parsley. Season and simmer for 10 minutes before serving.

Pennyroyal (*Mentha pulegium*)
Pliny named it *pulegium* because when strewn over floors, it was able to rid the house of *pulices* (fleas). John Pechey said that 'the fresh herb, wrapped in a cloth and laid in a bed, drives away fleas but it must be renewed weekly'. Later, the name became *puliall*, to which was added 'royal' because the plant was used to keep royal apartments clear of fleas. Gerard tells us that the plant was found 'at Mile End, near London' and was sold by women in the streets of London to sailors to take to sea, to add its minty taste to drinking water, often stale and also to rid their sleeping quarters of fleas. It was one of the plants taken to America by the Pilgrim Fathers.

Description. A prostrate, pubescent perennial with oval toothed leaves covered in glandular dots which release a strong minty smell when pressed but which is not so pleasant as that of other mints. The flowers are borne August and September, in tiny whorls and are reddish-pink, with the corolla hairy on the outside. It is found through much of Europe in ditches and by streams, also in water meadows, usually in sandy soil.

Culture. Like all the mints, it requires a soil that is well drained in winter but containing some humus to hold moisture in summer. It quickly spreads by underground stems and is grown from offsets or stems with pieces of root attached and planted 15–20 cm (6–8 in) apart. Make up a small bed in spring. It is also grown from seed sown in boxes in spring; the seedlings are planted out in July.

Medicinal uses. It acts as a carminative and a tonic if a wineglassful of the 'tea' is taken twice daily, once at bedtime. The 'tea' is made by pouring half a litre (1 pint) of boiling water on to a small handful of leaves and stems. Used warm as a gargle, it will ease a sore throat and Matthiolus said that when used slightly warm for bathing the eyes, it refreshed them. Oil of pennyroyal is used in embrocations instead of menthol and is warm and comforting. The oil will ease a toothache if gently massaged into the cheek.

Culinary uses. It was so often used in stuffings that it was known as 'pudding grass' and was once cultivated on a commercial scale for packeting the dried herb, like sage and thyme. Stuffings not only made the meat go further but when there was no refrigeration, the refreshing minty taste and smell of pennyroyal took away much of the strong taste. It may also be included in sausages and in sausage meats but must be used sparingly. A pinch of the dried or fresh herb finely chopped will add interest to all egg dishes as an alternative to chives.

Peppermint (*Mentha × piperita*)

A natural hybrid of *M. aquatica* and *M. spicata*, its striking smell and taste were early recognized. From the begining of the 18th century, it was and still is, grown commercially at Mitcham in England, to provide sweet makers with essence to flavour the celebrated Mitcham mint creams. It was also grown commercially, with lavender and other 'hot herbs' and can still be found nowadays in many old gardens or sometimes in hedgerows.

Description. It is a perennial, growing 30–40 cm (12–16 in) tall with stalked lanceolate leaves serrated at the edges. The

Peppermint (*Mentha × piperita*)

reddish-purple flowers are borne in a terminal inflorescence from July–Sept., when the entire plant takes on a purple appearance in dry weather. There are two forms, 'white' and 'black', the latter having dark purple-brown leaves which are more strongly scented and yield more essential oil.

Culture. Like all the mints, it requires a soil containing humus, including a little decayed manure and is happier in a position of semi-shade, where the roots do not dry out in hot weather. Plant small pieces of root in autumn, 15–20 cm (6–8 in) apart and 5 cm (2 in) deep. Mints should be planted in small beds to themselves for if in the border they will soon spread into other plants by means of their underground roots. Where there is no garden, plant in boxes 10 cm (4 in) deep and keep moist in summer.

Medicinal uses. Under commercial cultivation it will yield about 13.6 kg (30 lb) of essential oil per acre planted 60 cm (2 ft) apart. Harvesting for distillation begins early in August and continues until the end of September, the work proceeding by day and night. Oil of peppermint improves with age and retains its quality for up to fifteen years.

Since *The Lancet* drew attention to its qualities exactly a century ago, the oil when applied to the temples will relieve a headache, and tooth ache when rubbed into the gums. Peppermint water relieves indigestion and will take away the feeling of sickness or nausea when at sea or during pregnancy. It is made by pouring a pint of boiling water on the fresh tops or dried leaves and taking a small quantity when necessary. It will calm the nerves and induce sleep. A warming drink to take at night for a cold or for when one comes in from the cold in winter is made from peppermint essence, a teaspoonful to a large cup of hot water to which is added the juice of half a lemon and a teaspoonful of honey. For a hard cough or tight chest, add a small amount of horehound 'tea' or half a teaspoonful of ground ginger. 'Oil of peppermint is the best, safest and most agreeable of all antiseptics' said Dr. Braddon.

Other uses. Include the fresh stems and tops, with rosemary or balm in a hot bath to relieve stiff joints and to relax tired muscles. It will give the body a feeling of well-being during warm weather.

Primrose (*Primula vulgaris*)
It has been acclaimed by poets since earliest times on account of its earliness of bloom and because the pale fragile appearance of the flowers belies its extreme hardiness. Shakespeare often mentioned it in his plays and Gerard described the double white form, still obtainable, in his *Catalogue of Plantes*. Its early name was spelt prime-rose, from the Latin *primus*, first, for it is one of the first wild flowers to bloom.

Description. A hardy perennial from Europe with deeply wrinkled lanceolate leaves down which moisture can flow to the roots quickly and with little of it lost by evaporation. The flowers borne from March until June, appear on short peduncles, as if growing singly rather than in short umbels. They are pale yellow with a mossy perfume and there are various forms found growing naturally, such as the double flowered yellow and white; hose-in-hose was so named because one flower grows from another like the hose worn by 16th century gentlemen when one stocking was pulled to the thighs and another over it, and turned down just below the knee. There is also the Jack-in-the-green where the flower rests on a ruff of small emerald green leaves. All possess great charm. Primroses are found in open woodlands and hedgerows, also on railway embankments and in most meadows where rainfall is high. They cannot stand dryness at the roots coupled with a hot sun overhead.

Culture. Plants of easy culture, they are propagated by root division in July (after flowering) which is often a wet month, and at any time from November until April, even when in bloom. Plant them in semi-shade or in a northerly situation, 15 cm (6 in) apart with the crown of the plant from which arises the leaves and flowers, about

2.5 cm (1 in) below soil level. Keep them moist in dry weather. They are also readily raised from seed sown in boxes or pans in spring in a frame or cold greenhouse. Transplant to open ground beds or to boxes of compost in July and to a permanent position early in winter. Primroses require a humus-laden soil which will retain moisture in dry weather, hence they grow better in heavy soil than in light, sandy soil.

Medicinal uses. The juice of the flowers, stems and leaves is healing when applied to skin blemishes and sores. Culpeper said it was the best of all herbs to heal wounds. To make a healing salve, pound a handful of the flowers and stems in a small saucepan containing 230 g ($\frac{1}{2}$ lb) of lard. Heat it for 20 minutes over a low flame, strain and pour into screw-top ointment jars and allow to set. A little of the ointment on a piece of lint laid on a wound will bring about comfort and rapid healing. A soothing drink can be made by infusing a handful of flowers and stems in half a litre (1 pint) of hot water. Strain and drink a wineglassful in the evening and it will encourage sleep.

Culinary uses. The young leaves (one or two removed from each plant), finely chopped, make an unusual addition to a spring salad for they have the same bitterness as watercress and contain many of the same health-giving vitamins. The flowers may also be included for they have a sweet, honey-like taste. Mary Eales, confectioner to Queen Anne, has described how to candy the flowers for cake decoration. Steep gum arabic in water and wet the flowers with it. Then dip them in castor (finely granulated) sugar and place on trays in a warm, airy room to dry before placing in boxes on layers of tissue paper.

Rampion (*Campanula rapunculus*)
A native of Europe which takes both its common and botanical name from the Latin *rapa*, a turnip, because of its thick bulbous root. In earlier times it was cultivated as much as a vegetable as for its other qualities.

Description. A handsome plant, it is an unbranched perennial growing 60–90 cm (2–3 ft) tall, with broad ovate leaves and in June and July, it bears purple or white flowers in erect panicles. It is most striking when in bloom in the middle of a border. Its thick radish-like root, when cut, exudes a milky substance; once established, the plant is difficult to eradicate.

Culture. It associates well with the grey-leaved sages and artemisias; being difficult to propagate by root division it is best grown from seed sown in spring, preferably in boxes; the seedlings are transplanted to small pots to grow on. If allowed to form too large a root before moving, it will not easily move. Grow on in the pots and plant out in the following spring. If required for their roots, make up a bed in the vegetable garden, planting 25 cm (10 in) apart in ordinary but deeply cultivated soil. If growing in the border for their beauty and for their leaves, which have several uses, plant 40 cm (16 in) apart. They die back in autumn but new stems arise each year. The plants grow well in semi-shade.

Culinary uses. The young leaves can be included in an early summer salad, resembling watercress in their slight bitterness; they may also be steamed like (and with) spinach to serve with meats. In earlier times, the roots were boiled as soon as they reached a reasonable size and could be used all year round so that in times of food scarcity, they were a valuable standby of cottage gardens, being hardier than turnips. The roots were also used like winter radishes to grate raw into salads. Evelyn said they were more nourishing and with a similar 'pleasant nutty flavour'.

Other uses. The water in which the leaves have been boiled is excellent for the complexion, taking away any soreness or redness caused by cold winds or sun exposure.

Red rose (*Rosa gallica* or *R. officinalis*)
Perhaps the oldest of cultivated plants, it was used to adorn the shields of Persian warriors 1000 B.C. and is native to southern

and central Europe, extending to Belgium and central France. As it had so many uses in the ancient world and because the flowers retained their scent when dried, it became known as the apothecary's rose and may have been introduced into Britain from France (Gaul) (hence *R. gallica*) by the Romans who occupied that territory first. In the Middle Ages it was grown commercially around the walled towns of Provins in France, hence Shakespeare's reference in *Hamlet* to 'two Provincial roses' and in the *Sonnets* to its ability to retain its perfume when dry:

> The rose looks fair, but fairer we it deem
> For that sweet odour that doth in it live.

The red rose was taken as a symbol by the House of Lancaster in the wars of the Roses and it may be recalled that Edmund, brother of Edward I of England, was first Earl of Lancaster and also Count of Champagne, in whose territory was the town of Provins, the red rose being the emblem of his second wife Blanche, widow of Henry of Navarre. The red rose of Lancaster and the white rose of York, superimposed one over the other, is the emblem of British monarchy to this day.

Description. A deciduous shrub, it grows only 60–90 cm (2–3 ft) tall and compact, its habit being passed onto the modern hybrid tea rose. Thomas Rivers, in *The Rose Amateur's Guide* (1840) said that 'the semi-double rose was grown (with other herbs) at Mitcham in Surrey, England for the druggists', the dried petals being sold from wooden drums or chests, like marigolds; the rose petals were used in pot-pourris and sweet bags and to make rose water for washing.

Culture. Owing to its hardiness and ability to survive in poor soils, in which it grows wild in the mountainous ranges of Persia and Afghanistan, it has remained unchanged through the centuries. It is a plant for the shrub border or for the herb garden and is planted 60 cm (2 ft) apart at any time from November until mid-March, except when the soil is frozen. Make the hole large enough to enable the roots to be spread well out several inches deep, then replace the soil and tread in firmly. *R. gallica* and its numerous varieties grow well in sandy soils by the coast and they have no thorns in the accepted sense, but are covered in stiff hairs. It forms circular flowers of deepest red and is in bloom from July until September. It makes a lot of twiggy growth but requires little pruning, merely the cutting away of any dead wood.

Medicinal uses. An old remedy for lung ailments was to pound red rose petals with fine sugar or honey in a mortar and to take a teaspoonful three times daily. The same will also help in cases of diarrhoea. Rose water taken hot, will bring relief to those suffering from asthma or a tight chest and used slightly warm for bathing the eyes, it will remove soreness and tiredness. It is also applied to the face where it has a reputation for smoothing out wrinkles and improving the complexion. To make rose-water, infuse a handful of flowers or petals of the red rose or of any strongly scented red or pink roses such as 'Fragrant Cloud' or 'Wendy Cussons' in 0.25 litre ($\frac{1}{2}$ pint) of boiling water in a basin. Cover immediately with a plate and leave for an hour. Then strain into bottles and apply to the face with lint (or raw cotton), or use for other purposes when necessary. The petals can be used fresh or when dried.

Culinary uses. To crystallize rose petals, dip them into syrup of sugar, made by boiling 0.5 kg (1 lb) of sugar in 0.25 litre ($\frac{1}{2}$ pint) of water and simmering over a low flame. Dip in the petals, holding them singly with tweezers, then place on sheets of grease-proof paper in an airy room until dry. They can be placed on layers of greaseproof paper in a cardboard box and used to decorate cakes, trifles and ice creams.

Other uses. The petals after drying in an airy room on trays or sheets of paper, are one of the principal ingredients of dry pot-pourri and of sweet bags for placing among clothes and linen. They can be used on their own or with lavender and sweet marjoram.

Always gather the roses at their best (just fully open) when they will be most heavily scented and this perfume will be retained when they are dry. Cut the blooms just before noon when dry and complete their drying quickly otherwise they will become mildewed (as they often are in wet weather) and lose their sweet scent, becoming musty instead. The most fragrant roses correctly harvested and dried will retain their perfume for several years.

Rose root (*Rhodiola rosea*)

The previous name of the plant was *Sedum rosea* and it is still often listed as such. The leaves and stems are fleshy (succulent) and store up moisture so that the plants can survive long periods without rain, hence its name 'long life'. Even when pulled up with its roots and hung up in a room, the plant will remain fresh for a long time. It will keep a room free of flies and moths and all the time, the rose scent of the root will increase as it dries.

Description. A grey-green succulent perennial growing 30 cm (12 in) tall, with the broad flat leaves overlapping all the way up the erect stems. The obovate leaves are round at the base, toothed at the apex, while the greenish-yellow or reddish flowers (male and female on separate plants) are borne in a terminal inflorescence. They are scentless but the long rhizomatous root when dry, has a rose perfume which increases with age. It is present on cliffs and mountain rocks in northern Asia, in Europe and America and south to Mexico.

Culture. It requires an open sunny situation but is tolerant of dry, shallow soils. It is readily propagated by pulling away pieces of stem with roots attached. Plant in April 25 cm (10 in) apart.

Medicinal uses. The plant contains lime and sulphur and a decoction of the stems and leaves, a handful to half a litre (1 pint) of hot water, may be applied to running sores with lint to facilitate healing.

Other uses. The distilled water from the dried roots is used to apply to the face, to smooth out the wrinkles of tiredness and soothe soreness and was sprinkled over clothes when there was no dry cleaning. If sprinkled on rush matting which is an excellent cover for stone floors, it will impart its rose perfume to it and the fragrance is pleasantly increased if dried lavender flowers are also scattered over the matting.

Rosemary (*Rosmarinus officinalis*)

No garden plant has more uses and none is more steeped in history. It takes its name from *Ros marinus*, 'dew of the sea', for it is to be found growing on the islands of Corsica and Sardinia and about the mediterranean coastline usually close to the sea, where in the gentle breezes, it wafts its sweet balsamic perfume far from the shore. The plant may have been introduced into northern parts of Europe by the Romans who used it in their warm spring water baths, to relieve their tired limbs after a long march and to invigorate the body muscles.

In the Library of Trinity College, Cambridge, England is a manuscript sent by the Countess of Hainault to her daughter Philippa, wife of Edward III in which she describes the numerous virtues of rosemary. No plant so much enjoys the comfort and protection of a warm wall, against which it may be trained to a height of 2 m (6–7 ft) and the same in width. This is how it was grown in the 16th century and how it grew in the Chelsea garden of Sir Thomas More. 'As for rosemary', he wrote 'I let it run all over my garden walls, not only because my bees love it but because it is the herb sacred to love and remembrance, and therefore to friendship'. It was the 'herb of remembrance' because it was always 'green', always alive, not only when growing but also when cut, retaining its 'green' longer than any other herb; hence it was used at weddings for bride and groom to give each other as a token of their everlasting love (Ben Jonson said 'tied with ribbons'); it was used also at funerals, when sprigs of rosemary were dropped into the grave as the coffin was lowered, as a token of everlasting remembrance.

Rosemary (*Rosmarinus officinalis*)

Shakespeare refers to the custom in *Romeo and Juliet* when Friar Laurence tells the mourners to take the rosemary which was to have been used at Juliet's wedding and instead to place it on her dead body. Each year on Shakespeare's birthday, April 23rd, also St. Georges Day, those who walk in procession through his native town of Stratford-on-Avon, carry sprigs of rosemary to place on his grave in Holy Trinity church, in his remembrance. Hentzer in his Travels (1598) has told that at Hampton Court rosemary 'was so planted and nailed to the walls as to cover them entirely'. Anne of Cleves is said to have worn a head-dress of rosemary at her marriage to Henry VIII.

Description. An evergreen shrub, hardy except where temperatures of −18° C (0° F) are experienced. It has stalkless linear leaves, hoary on the underside. The essential oil is contained in microscopic goblet-shaped cells deep in the leaflets, hence the scent is retained for a long time when the stems are cut. The tiny linear leaves also ensure that the plant can survive long periods of intense heat and without moisture for there is little moisture evaporation. The flowers are borne in short axillary racemes and have a two-lipped calyx and corolla. Though they appear in March and in great profusion until June, they do so intermittently throughout the year. They are a valuable source of nectar for bees in spring.

Culture. Rosemary is grown in the shrub border and herb garden; at one time it was planted on either side of an entrance gate leading to the herb garden and on either side of a doorway entrance to the home so that those who entered would brush their long clothes against the bushes to which they imparted a delicious resinous smell, so much appreciated when there was no dry cleaning. Nowhere, however, does rosemary grow better than against a sunny wall, facing south or west. The strong woody shoots can readily be fastened to the wall and the plants remain evergreen and colourful when in bloom, the whole year. Where winters are severe, this is the only way to be sure of its survival. It can also be used fresh throughout the year.

Rosemary requires a dry well-drained soil containing some lime rubble or mortar but no manure. Plant in spring and allow 2 metres (about 6 ft) apart when growing against a wall, or about 1 m (3–4 ft) in a shrub border. The plants can be clipped into shape if desired. Propagation is from cuttings of the half-ripened wood, taken with a 'heel' in July; after treating with hormone powder for quicker rooting, insert into sandy soil in pots or boxes. When rooted, move to small pots and grow on during winter and under glass. Plants may also be raised from seed sown in pots or boxes in a frame or sunny window in spring and transplanted to small pots towards the end of summer. Grow on under glass over winter and plant out in April. During their first year, until established, the plants may suffer from cold winds and hard frost but rarely do so when growing against a wall. If the plants become very large and straggling, remove with the secateurs any unduly long shoots or those which have become thick and woody with age. If it can be obtained, the upright growing 'Miss Jessop's' variety is excellent for wall culture and bears lavender-blue flowers. *R. lavandulaceus* (*R. officinalis prostratus*) grows almost over the ground and will cover a sunny bank or may be used on top of a wall or on a rock garden. It bears flowers of brilliant blue, but is not as hardy.

Medicinal uses. A handful of shoots placed in a warm bath, firm the flesh and soothe tired nerves, in addition to releasing a refreshing resinous scent. Rosemary wine is carminative and stimulating to the kidneys. It is made by pouring $\frac{1}{2}$ bottle of white wine on to 230 g ($\frac{1}{2}$ lb) of rosemary tops. Allow to stand for a week, then strain back into the bottle and place in the refrigerator until required. It makes a delicious tonic drink in summer and prevents nervous fatigue.

Spirit of rosemary, made by treating the essential oil with spirits of wine is kept by most drug stores and is used as a hair tonic or restorer by gently massaging into the scalp each day. It will also give relief to rheumatic joints if gently massaged in. Oil of rosemary is obtained by treating 0.5 kg (1 lb) of tops with 4.5 litres (1 gallon) of proof spirit. After standing for a week, it is distilled and the oil collected. A handful of tops simmered for ten minutes in half a litre (1 pint) of water, makes an excellent hair rinse and the same may be taken ice cold in summer, a wineglassful at a time, when it will act as a tonic and sweeten the breath. At one time, jugs of rosemary water were found in every home. A delicious 'honey of rosemary' will calm the nerves and stimulate the appetite. It is made by placing 230 g ($\frac{1}{2}$ lb) of flowers in a jar containing 0.5 kg (1 lb) of honey. Place in the sun for three weeks then use as required, a teaspoonful daily or use it on toast or scones. The honey will have taken on the delicious scent of the rosemary.

Culinary uses. The flowers in spring make an appetizing addition to a salad and if powdered with twice their weight of sugar and allowed to set hard, make a pleasant sweetmeat for after a meal to aid the digestion. To impart its delicious scent to steak or roast beef, a sprig or two of fresh rosemary should be stuck into the meat before cooking. It is the best of all herbs to include with roast meats.

Other uses. Butlers and those waiting at table would drink rosemary water night and morning, to sweeten the breath and it may be used before an evening engagement. Take a tablespoonful an hour previously. Hungary water, for improving the complexion and eau-de-Cologne, used by Napoleon in large quantities on the battlefield, to pour over his neck and shoulders after washing to invigorate and refresh, both contain rosemary as the main ingredient. The finest French eau-de-Cologne is made from the ottos of rosemary and bergamot with grape-spirit.

In earlier times the plant was widely used to perfume the home and it was Queen Anne's favourite scent. Mary Eales, her Confectioner, in her *Book of Receipts* (1682), gives the method by which she perfumed the Queen's apartments. This was to take three teaspoonsful of dried and powdered rosemary and 'as much sugar as half a walnut' (a teaspoonful) beaten to a powder. Placed in a pan over hot embers (or today heated on the electric ring of a cooker (stove)) and carried to other rooms, filled the room with a refreshing scent. Both men and women would carry sprigs of fresh rosemary in the pocket, to smell during warm sultry weather, or when tired during a long journey to become invigorated. It was said to 'gladden the spirits'. Bancke, in his *Herbal* (1525) said 'smell it oft and it shall keep thee youngly' and he advised placing it under the pillow when it would 'deliver one from evil dreams'.

Rue (*Ruta graveolens*)

Shakespeare tells us that because of its bitterness, and it is the most bitter of all herbs, it was known as the herb of repentence or the herb of grace. Parkinson said that 'it is a most wholesome herb, although bitter and strong (smelling)'. The plant was used to strew the floors of prisons to rid them of fleas which were known to carry the dreaded 'gaol fever'. There is an old rhyme which says:

> Rue maketh chaste and eke preserveth sight;
> Infuseth wit, and putteth fleas to flight.

During an outbreak of gaol fever at Newgate Prison in London, in 1750, stems of rue were placed on the bench of the dock at the Assize Court, a custom which has been symbolically continued until this day. Rue is included in the collar of the English Order of the Thistle which dates from 1540.

Description. A glaucous evergreen growing 60 cm (2 ft) tall with leaves divided into obovate segments. The leaves are unlike those of any other plant and are of metallic-blue, a shade unique amongst herbs; when handled, they emit a bitter pungent scent, difficult to describe. The greenish yellow flowers appear in terminal panicles from May until September. In the wild it is a plant of S. Europe and quite uncommon; elsewhere it is a garden plant.

Culture. A handsome foliage plant for the middle of a border, it possesses extreme hardiness and is of easy culture, flourishing in ordinary well-drained soil and in calcareous soils. Plants are readily raised from seed sown in shallow drills in April or in boxes in a frame, transplanted to the border in July. Allow 40 cm (16 in) between the plants. Alternatively, propagate from cuttings taken in July which will root easily in sandy compost. Grow on in small pots and plant out in April. The best form is 'Jackman's Blue' which is even more 'blue' than the type and is propagated from cuttings.

Medicinal uses. Pliny mentions that rue was so effective in preserving the sight that writers and painters would eat it daily. In *Paradise Lost* Milton mentioned it with the plant eyebright which also reputedly restored sight. It was carried by travellers to guard them against witches for it was said to enable one to recognize witches before they could see the traveller and they could take evasive action in time. The crushed leaves and stems bound round the buttocks and thighs will ease the pains of sciatica, and on the temples will relieve a nervous headache. An infusion of the leaves, a small handful to half a litre (1 pint) of hot water, taken at bedtime will relieve those suffering from nervous exhaustion and nightmares and induce sound sleep. The same will also act as a tonic if a wineglassful is taken daily, for the plant is rich in iron and mineral salts.

Culinary uses. It is so bitter that if it is included in an omelette, use only sufficient of the finely chopped leaves, fresh or dry, to cover a thumbnail. The same may be included in a salad but must be mixed in thoroughly, and if used in tomato, egg or cream cheese sandwiches, use only a pinch.

Other uses. It is so bitter that it will drive away flies and fleas if scattered over a floor, and may be used for this purpose in poultry houses. The plant was also given to poultry to prevent outbreaks of croup: a little given daily will keep them in good health.

Sage (*Salvia officinalis*)

At one time, the common sage had almost as many uses as rosemary and like it, it is native of S. Europe. It takes its name from *salvia*, salvation, or *salvere*, to be saved, because as an Anglo-Saxon manuscript says 'why should man die whilst sage grows in his garden?'. The monk, Walfred Strabo, writing in the 9th century said: 'Amongst my herbs, sage holds place of honour, of good scent it is and full of virtue for many ills'. Gerard said '... it quickens the senses and memory; strengthens the sinews; restoreth health to those that have the palsy; and taketh away tremblings'. Pepys in his *Diary* mentions that once when near Southampton, he came across a village churchyard where all the graves were planted with sage, in the hope that the plants would ensure salvation of life after death.

Sage (*Salvia officinalis*)

Description. A shrubby perennial growing 45–50 cm (18–20 in) tall, with square stems covered in down and wrinkled oval grey-green leaves. The small purple flowers appear in whorls in the leaf axils July–September. Native to S. Europe especially Dalmatia, the plant is more pungently scented than the smaller *S. pratensis* of meadows and woodlands. There are a number of lovely forms of the common sage, including a golden variegated leaf variety 'Icterina', while *S. officinalis* 'Purpurascens' has a red stem and dark purple leaves. Both are admirable border plants of reasonable hardiness. These sages come true only when propagated from cuttings. Not as hardy is *S. rutilans*, the pineapple sage, the scent of its leaves having the true scent of ripe pineapples, the most refreshing of all herbal scents for which it is used in pot-pourris. It has handsome red flowers. The distinctive *S. horminum*, clary, is described under a separate heading, having different uses.

Culture. The sages are raised from cuttings taken in July and August, preferably with a 'heel' and rooted in boxes or pots of sandy compost. Winter under glass and plant out in spring 60 cm (2 ft) apart. It requires a well-drained sandy compost and an open, sunny situation. It is not completely hardy in severe weather, and where temperatures fall below −18° C (0° F) may be killed to the ground. Sage is a shallow rooting plant so to keep it healthy, give a mulch each autumn of finely sieved soil, if possible mixed with some decayed manure. Except for the ornamental sages plants are also raised from seed sown in shallow drills in April.

TOP: Fennel *(Foeniculum vulgare)*. A tall (1–1.5 m; 4–5 ft), bushy plant, it is easily grown from seed and is ideal for the back of a border. Both the stems and the leaves can be used in the kitchen; the stems add a spicy flavour to soups and stews and can even be served as a vegetable, while the leaves make an attractive garnish.

RIGHT: Feverfew *(Chrysanthemum parthenum)* gets its name from its traditional use in treating fevers and agues. Today it is more likely to be found in the kitchen, for its leaves have a pungent taste which add a pleasant flavour to soups, stews, tomato and egg dishes.

Sea Holly *(Eryngium maritimum).* As its name would suggest this 15–60 cm (6 in–2 ft) tall, very reliable perennial grows best in a well-drained sandy soil within a reasonable distance from the sea. It is the roots that are used; these are sweet and very nourishing and can be either gently boiled and served as a vegetable, or grated raw into salads.

Rose Root *(Rhodiola rosea)* grows best in a sunny, open situation, and can survive long periods without rain. Its roots have a strong rose-like scent which increases as they dry. Hung up in a room, it will keep it free of flies and moths for a very long time.

Keep the seed moist to encourage germination and late in summer, move to the border. A broad-leaf sage is best for drying to use in stuffings.

Medicinal uses. Use the leaves, together with those of marjoram, made hot in a little water, to place in muslin bags to apply to rheumatic joints and pains caused by sciatica. To make a tonic drink, make an infusion of the fresh leaves, a small handful to half a litre (1 pint) of hot water, and the rind of half a lemon and after straining, take hot in winter or ice cold in summer. Where the tops, including the flowers are used, the 'tea' will have a more pleasant balsamic taste. It will purify the blood, relieve indigestion and soothe nervous excitement. A small wineglassful should be taken daily. It is also excellent for a sore throat when used as a gargle and a mouth wash for ulcers or sore gums. A pleasant way to relieve a tight chest is to take sage cordial. This is made by boiling the tops or fresh leaves with the juice of a lemon and a little honey in a cupful of water and taking a dessertspoonful every two to three hours, preferably when hot. Sage is used with peppermint in tooth powders and if the fresh leaves are rubbed on the gums, it will strengthen them. Sage water made from an infusion of the leaves, a handful to a pint of hot water and used as a hair rinse, will darken the hair. The dried leaves can be smoked, with those of chamomile, to relieve asthmatic attacks.

Culinary uses. Sage is the most popular of herbs for stuffings, especially for veal and venison; and for ducks and geese. To make a stuffing, boil two small onions for ten minutes then drop in about a dozen sage leaves for a minute. Remove the onions and sage and chop finely: mix with them two or three chopped marjoram leaves and a pinch of dried thyme. Then mix in 110 g (4 oz) of breadcrumbs, 30 g (1 oz) of butter or margarine and the yolk of an egg. Season and work into a reasonable thickness. Russell in his *Boke of Nurture* said that sage fritters were always served at the end of medieval banquets to settle the digestion and take away any greasiness caused by the meats. The young leaves are dipped in batter and fried for a few minutes, then sprinkled with lemon juice before serving. In Europe, sage is used to flavour various cheeses and the chopped leaves may be included in cream cheese sandwiches.

Savory, summer (*Satureja hortensis*)
Gerard said that it was known as St. Julian's herb for it grew in abundance on cliffs known as St. Julian's rocks in Italy and is a native of the mediterranean countries. It was widely grown in the 16th century for stuffings to accompany veal and venison and for its powerful scent; Shakespeare included it with those other 'hot' herbs such as marjoram, mint and lavender in *A Winter's Tale*. It was one of the most useful plants introduced into America by the early settlers for it had medicinal and culinary uses.

Description. It is a half-hardy annual growing 20–25 cm (8–10 in) tall with branched hairy stems and downy oblong linear leaves. The white, pink or pale lilac flowers are borne in small clusters in July and August. It is usually grown in the vegetable garden or in small groups to the front of the border.

Culture. Seed is sown in boxes under glass in March, the seedlings being moved to small pots or boxes when large enough to handle and planted out 15 cm (6 in) apart early in May. Alternatively, in warmer climates where late frosts do not occur, sow in the open ground early in April. If the plants are cut back early July to within 2.5 cm (1 in) of soil level and the cuttings strung up in an airy room to dry and use over winter, the plants will grow again and they can be cut again in autumn. It may be grown in pots in the kitchen window, with sweet basil.

Medicinal uses. It is a carminative and aids the digestion; it also warms the stomach and gives ease to colic pains. Infuse a small handful of the dry or fresh plant in half a litre (1 pint) of hot water and after straining, take a wineglassful when necessary.

Culinary uses. A sprig or two should be cooked with broad (green) beans; as an alternative to parsley, make a sauce with the fresh leaves to serve with the beans. The fresh leaves finely chopped give distinction to a Welsh rarebit or to scrambled eggs if sprinkled on top; also to soups and stews. It is also a suitable alternative to marjoram, to season pork pies and sausages and to make stuffings for pork and veal. 'It is hotter and dryer than the winter kind' said Culpeper.

Savory, winter (*Satureja montana*)

The savories were believed to have associations with the Satyrs, hence their botanical name and all are herbs of the mountains and cliffs of S. Europe, especially Italy. In medieval times it was used for strewing as well as for medicinal and culinary uses. Thomas Hyll in *The Art of Gardening* (1568) said that in Britain the knots of Tudor gardens were usually made 'with Isope and Thyme or with winter savory and thyme for these endure all the winter through greene'.

Description. It is perennial, hardy where frosts are not too severe, growing 30 cm (12 in) tall, with spreading branches and oblong linear leaves which terminate in sharp points. The purple-pink flowers are borne in racemes July–September and are a valuable source of nectar.

Culture. Seed is slow to germinate and it is best propagated from cuttings taken in July and rooted in pots or boxes of sandy compost. Plant 25–30 cm (10–12 in) apart to the front of a border, or as a low hedge which can be cut back in autumn to 15 cm (6 in) high; the clippings are dried in an airy room.

Medicinal uses. An infusion of a handful of tops in half a litre (1 pint) of hot water, a wineglassful taken daily, will comfort the stomach during colic. The leaves when rubbed on wasp or bee stings will give relief.

Culinary uses. Michael Drayton suggested using the dried leaves with those of tansy to mix with breadcrumbs 'to bread meate, be it fish or flesh, to give it a quicker relish'. The finely chopped leaves mixed with parsley

Winter savory
(*Satureja montana*)

and scattered over fish dishes or made into sauces, impart a pleasing taste. In Italy, the savories are used with basil and mixed with sage or thyme for all stuffings. A delicious savory butter to serve with steak or grilled fish is made by beating 110 g (4 oz) of butter almost to a cream and adding seasoning and a teaspoonful of finely chopped savory, mixing well in. Place in the refrigerator for an hour before using.

Sea holly (*Eryngium maritimum*)

In Tudor times the roots were candied and eaten as sweetmeats to which Shakespeare referred in *Merry Wives of Windsor* when Falstaff, in Windsor Great Park, said: 'Let the sky rain potatoes: let it thunder to the tune of Green Sleeves; hail kissing-comfits, and snow eringoes....'. Shortly after Shakespeare's death, Robert Burton, a confectioner of Colchester, began to market his eringoe sweets on a national scale and became well known in consequence. They were supposed to be good for old people and to help those suffering from cramps.

Description. A short to medium, erect, herbaceous, very reliable perennial, growing 15–60 cm (6 in–2 ft) tall with long rhizomatous and brittle roots which extend deep into the ground. The blue-green leaves are spiny and thistle-like, with white veins. The flowers are borne 20–30 to a stem during July and August and are bluish, with blue bracts and are covered in short bristles. It is the roots that are used, being sweet and nourishing. Sea holly is widespread about the coasts of Europe from Scandinavia to the Black Sea.

Culture. A handsome border plant, it is propagated from root cuttings removed in spring and cut into pieces about 5 cm (2 in) long. Plant in pots of sandy compost with the top of the root just below compost level. Keep moist and move to the border planting 90 cm (3 ft) apart in autumn. They require a well-drained sandy soil and a sunny position and can withstand long periods of drought but make larger roots when in reach of the sea.

Medicinal uses. The root is diuretic. It is also restorative and has a reputation as an aphrodisiac when eaten as sweetmeats or when boiled. Culpeper also advised drinking the distilled water from the roots and stems as a restorative.

Culinary uses. The roots, which are obtained from plants at least two years old, can be cut into pieces about 15 cm (6 in) long and boiled, to serve with white sauce to accompany meats and are sweet and succulent, like parsnips. The water in which the roots are boiled should be used to make the sauce. They may also be grated raw into salads and Linnaeus said that the young shoots can be cut when about 15 cm (6 in)

long in early summer and boiled or simmered in a little water; served with a little melted butter they are eaten like asparagus and are tender and nourishing.

Shepherd's purse (*Capsella bursa-pastoris*)
It takes its name from the Latin *capsella*, little box, from the flattened seed-pods and its country name, pick purse, was given it

Shepherd's purse
(*Capsella bursa-pastoris*)

because it took the goodness (and value) from the land, though the plant was valued by farmers in that its ointment cleared up skin troubles of horses. It also had many medicinal uses.

Description. It is an annual of cultivated and waste ground all over the world, growing from 10–45 cm (4–18 in) tall depending on the type of soil in which it grows. The root-leaves form a rosette, the stem leaves being arrow-shaped. In bloom throughout the year, the tiny white flowers are borne in terminal cymes.

Culture. Common everywhere but if required in the garden, it grows readily from seed sown in circles to the front of a border or in shallow drills 30 cm (12 in) apart in April. It requires an open situation.

Medicinal uses. It had a reputation for arresting excessive menstruating as an infusion prepared from a handful of fresh or dry leaves in half a litre (1 pint) of boiling water, strained and taken (a dessertspoonful) twice daily. The same was also given for dropsy and for diarrhoea. The juice of the leaves and stems applied to cuts and bruises will heal them and the whole plant put into a warm bath will take away body bruises and relax the muscles.

Culinary uses. A few leaves can be used in a salad, to which they impart a bitterness resembling watercress. Indeed it is of the same Cruciferae order, the plants containing iron and sulphur. Countrymen would collect the leaves in spring and boil them to serve with meats.

Sorrel (*Rumex acetosa*)

A common plant of the British Isles and N. Europe, especially Scandinavia, with *R. scutatus*, the French sorrel, distributed through C. Europe. It is closely related to the dock family and not to the wood sorrel, also an important herb.

Description. *R. acetosa* is a tufted perennial growing 20–40 cm (8–16 in) tall with arrow-shaped leaves, the lower shortly stalked, the upper stem-clasping. The reddish-green flowers (like those of the docks) are borne in terminal spikes June-August. It is widespread in grassland over much of Europe, Asia and N. America and if cultivated, it should be confined to the vegetable garden.

Culture. Seed is sown in spring in ordinary soil in shallow drills made 25 cm (10 in) apart, the plants thinned to 15 cm (6 in) in the rows. Where there is no garden, grow it in deep boxes or pots as it has many uses.

Medicinal uses. Long famed for their healing powers, the leaves and stems were crushed and bound over open wounds and sores, to bring about healing. An infusion of the leaves, a small handful to half a litre (1 pint) of boiling water, makes a useful gargle for a sore throat if used warm and the same is taken to allay a fever at bedtime. Michael Drayton alluded to this in the *Muses Elysium:* 'the ... curling sorrel, that again we use in hot diseases'. It will also flush out the kidneys and purify the blood.

Culinary uses. John Evelyn said that the leaves 'sharpened the appetite, strengthened the heart, and gave so great a quickness (sharpness) to a salad, ... that it should never be omitted'. The young leaves which contain vitamins A and C, may be included in omelettes and sprinkled over scrambled eggs, while they impart a pleasant sharpness to soups and stews. They can accompany spinach to serve with meats but first partly boil and pour away the water, adding a little fresh water to complete the boiling. This will remove much of the bitterness. In France, sorrel was always served in soupe des herbes at most country inns, to those arriving exhausted after a long journey, as a restorative. With its sharpness, sorrel sauce is served with duck and goose and is the ideal complement for most fish dishes. It is called green sauce and is made by pouring a little malt vinegar over the leaves, beating to a fine consistency, then adding a small teaspoonful of fine sugar. It also adds piquancy to cold meats.

Southernwood (*Artemisia abrotanum*)

It was called southernwood as it came from 'the south', from the warmer climes of the

Mediterranean and it may have come with the Romans. It was one of the earliest plants introduced into America and is listed in John Gent's *New England's Rarities Discovered* (1672). It is also known as Lad's Love and is found in many cottage gardens. The French know it as citronelle, on account of the deliciously pungent lemony smell it releases when the leaves are pressed.

Description. A shrubby perennial of upright habit growing 90 cm (3 ft) tall, the grey-green leaves are twice pinnately dissected and the flowers are borne in a panicle. In S. Europe and in similar climates with a good hot summer and mild winter it is evergreen, but in areas of more severe winters it will lose its leaves, leaving the brown stems bare — unless temperatures have been well below −18° C (0° F), it will come again in spring. It is used (with cotton lavender) to place amongst clothes and linen, to impart a refreshing scent and to keep away moths.

Culture. It requires a well-drained sandy soil and an open, sunny situation. It is propagated from cuttings taken with a 'heel' in July or in spring; after a hard winter it is advisable to cut back the stems to three buds from the base and the prunings can be rooted, planted 7.5 cm (3 in) apart in trenches of sandy soil. In the shrubbery or border, plant 90 cm (3 ft) apart.

Medicinal uses. It is antiseptic and healing. Carpenters who were often injured by their tools, would bind the leaves over their wounds. It is also a tonic. A handful of leaves or tops infused in half a litre (1 pint) of boiling water (kept covered to retain the steam) and when cool, taken daily, a wine-glassful at a time, will tone up the system. The drink is more pleasant if a piece of lemon rind is included in the infusion and it is sweetened with a little honey. Drink cold from the refrigerator. The same infusion will, if massaged into the scalp night and morning, prevent falling hair. If possible, use with rosemary and if hot cloths wrung out of rosemary and southernwood water are applied to the head, this will stimulate the hair glands and cause new hair to appear. It should be done in the evening. Southernwood was one of the ingredients of a famous Devonshire salve made by an English lady which brought her a national reputation for its powers of healing. It was made by taking a handful each of the leaves of southernwood, greater plantain, black-currant, elderflower buds, angelica and parsley, mixing them together and chopping finely before simmering in butter or lard for 20–30 mins. It was then poured into ointment jars to cool.

Other uses. The fresh leaves are used in moist pot-pourris and placed beneath a pillow; sound sleep will follow. The bags can be placed amongst clothes to keep away moths.

Spearmint (*Mentha spicata*)

The plant derives its name, *mentha*, from Mintha, daughter of Cocytus, who was transformed into the plant. Parkinson said that 'where docks are not handy, bruised mint leaves laid on any place stung by wasps and bees, is to good purpose'. Bees are attracted to mint, especially spearmint and will never desert a hive if it is first rubbed with the leaves.

Description. It is an almost hairless perennial growing 30–90 cm (12–36 in) tall with lanceolate leaves, serrate and brilliant green, and lilac flowers borne in a spire-like inflorescence; hence its name used to be spire-mint. In bloom August-September, it is native to central Europe but is naturalized in many hedgerows and damp places.

Culture. Like all the mints, it is happier in semi-shade and in a moist soil containing some humus. Plant pieces of the underground roots any time between November and April when the soil is free of frost, setting them 5 cm (2 in) deep and 30 cm (12 in) apart. To propagate, dig up the roots and pull them apart, replanting before they dry out.

Medicinal uses. Spearmint, which has a sharp, hot smell like peppermint, is used to make crème de menthe, a green liqueur

Spearmint (*Mentha spicata*)

($\frac{1}{2}$ lb) sugar and when dissolved, add a cupful of the fresh mints mixed together. Leave for at least two hours, strain and add a tablespoonful of gin so that the cordial will keep through winter. If no fresh mint is available, use 2 tablespoonsful of mint essence which can also be used to make the cordial in winter.

Culinary uses. Spearmint is the best mint to accompany spring lamb but it will be further improved if used with applemint which has a unique delicate flavour. To make a mint sauce, gather the fresh young leaves and chop finely. To a dessert spoonful each of spearmint and apple mint, add one of fine sugar and a small cupful each of white wine and best malt vinegar. First boil the sugar, wine and vinegar until the sugar has dissolved, then remove from the heat and stir in the mints. Leave until cold and pour into screw top jars to use as required. The sauce will keep a year or more. Mint vinegar is made by filling a large glass jar with various mints and pouring malt vinegar over them. Leave for four weeks, shaking it occasionally, then strain off the minty vinegar and store in bottles in a dark place.

A sprig or two of spearmint placed in new potatoes and garden peas while cooking, will improve the flavour, and especially so when serving with lamb. Other delicious mints to make sauce are the hairy leaved *M. × rotundifolia*, the round-leaf mint, also known as the apple mint or Bowles mint. It is highly resistant to rust disease which often appears on *M. × rotundifolia* as orange spores, attacking the stems and leaves but not the roots. 'Bowles' variety has the mild scent of ripe apples and is readily available from specialist growers. Other valuable culinary mints are *M. × cordifolia* with large heart-shaped leaves which have much of the spearmint flavour and *M. longifolia*, the horse mint which is found in damp soil by roadsides and in waste places. All parts of the plant of the last are covered in silvery hairs. It makes a most handsome border plant to accompany *Stachys lanata*.

which will settle a rich meal better than anything else. An infusion of the leaves will be warming on a cold day if taken hot, and taken warm, it will relieve indigestion and bad hiccoughs. Served with a few drops of lemon juice, it may be taken hot in winter or ice cold in summer instead of ordinary tea and is most invigorating. To make a delicious mint cordial for cold days, use it with the American apple mint, *M. × gentilis*. To 0.5 litre (1 pint) of boiling water, add 230 g

St. John's wort (*Hypericum perforatum*)

The common St. John's wort takes its name from St. John the Baptist for it is usually in bloom on the feast day of the saint (June 24th). Its botanical name signifies that the leaves are perforated with resinous glands which also appear on the petals of the flowers. In France it is called mille-pertuis, a thousand perforations, the cells being filled with caproic acid which gives off the unpleasant smell of wet fur when the plant is handled.

Description. It is a handsome evergreen perennial growing 60 cm (2 ft) tall with small elliptic leaves and bright yellow flowers borne in terminal corymbs. They appear from the end of June until early September. The sepals and petals are covered with tiny black dots. It is a quite common plant of hedgerows and open woodlands throughout Europe, W. Asia and N. Africa, and has been naturalized in N. America.

Culture. It is propagated from cuttings removed from the plant in July and rooted in sandy compost in pots or boxes. When rooted, move to small pots and grow on under glass, planting out in spring 60 cm (2 ft) apart. Ordinary soil is suitable and the plant grows well in semi-shade. It is also grown from seed sown in boxes of light sandy compost in spring. When large enough to handle, move to small pots and grow on until the following spring.

Medicinal uses. Gerard said that the oil had antiseptic properties and was applied to open wounds caused by tools or in battle. An ointment made from the flowers and leaves is used for bed sores. Countrymen knew it as St. John's wort salve and it is made by taking a handful of tops (flowers and leaves) and crushing them before covering with half a litre (1 pint) of olive oil and leaving for three to four days. Add a large cupful of white wine and place over a low flame for several hours; strain and make a second infusion of the flowers and repeat the process. Add 60 g (2 oz) of turpentine, bring to the boil and cool off, before pouring into ointment jars to set. An infusion of the leaves, a handful to half a litre (1 pint) of hot water, is excellent for coughs. A small wine-glassful given an hour before bedtime is said to prevent children from wetting the bed.

Sweet cicely (*Myrrhis odorata*)

It takes its name from the Greek *murrha*, myrrh, for the whole plant when handled gives off a warm, myrrh-like smell, whilst the leaves taste as if they have been steeped in sugar, hence its name sweet cicely. In medieval times, the seeds which measure nearly 2 cm (about 1 in) long, were crushed and rubbed with cloths on to oak furniture to which was imparted a beautiful gloss and myrrh-like smell.

Description. It is an erect pubescent perennial growing about 1.5 m (4–5 ft) tall with

Sweet cicely (*Myrrhis odorata*)

a hollow stem and large pale green pinnate fern-like leaves, downy on the underside. The tiny white flowers are borne in terminal corymbs in May and June, to be followed by dark brown fruits which are sharply ridged and which have a slight smell of cloves. It is the commonest umbellifer of mountain districts in Europe, often naturalized in hedgerows and woods.

Culture. It is a slow growing plant; seed is sown in small pots in spring under glass, the plants being set out at the back of the border towards the end of summer. Plant 60 cm (2 ft) apart for it grows upright rather than bushy. Ordinary soil is suitable but should contain some humus to hold moisture in summer, and unlike most herbs sweet cicely prefers a cool climate. The plants will die down in winter but will come again in spring while it will seed itself in the border.

Culinary uses. At one time the roots were candied like those of the sea holly and sold by chemists as sweets. They are also grated raw into salads and served with a little olive oil, vinegar and seasoning. The roots may also be boiled and served with white sauce to accompany meats, while the young leaves can be included in a salad to which they add their sweet myrrh-like taste.

Tansy (*Tanacetum vulgare*)

Its name is a corruption of the Greek *athanaton*, immortal, for it remained long in bloom and those who drank of its 'tea' were expected to live to a very old age. Tansy leaves, finely shredded and beaten into eggs to fry as tansy-cakes, were eaten during Lent, in remembrance of the bitter herbs eaten at the Passover and to counteract the large amounts of salted fish consumed. Gerard described the cakes as 'pleasant to taste'. Today, the leaves are included in omelettes.

Description. A hardy perennial growing 60–90 cm (2–3 ft) tall with branched stems and dark green aromatic leaves divided into numerous pairs of deeply pinnatifid leaflets with serrated edges. An essential oil smelling of camphor, is stored in the leaves in minute glandular cells. The small button-like flowers, borne July and August, have yellow disc-florets and appear in flattish terminal heads. As a native plant it is distributed across Europe where it is found in hedgerows and on waste ground, preferring to have its roots in some moisture. It has been naturalized in parts of N. America.

Culture. It is readily propagated in autumn or spring, by dividing the creeping roots and planting the offsets 60 cm (2 ft) apart in soil containing some humus; alternatively use pulloffs, removed in July and rooted in pots or boxes of sandy soil. Plant out in autumn or spring. The best garden form is *T. v.* 'Crispum' which has fern-like leaves of emerald green.

Medicinal uses. Tansy 'tea', made by infusing a handful of flowers and leaves in half a litre (1 pint) of hot water and taken a wineglassful daily when cold, is a valuable tonic; a more appetising drink, however, is obtained if the juice of half an orange and a teaspoonful of honey are also included. Keep in the refrigerator until required. Warm tansy water can be used as a gargle for it contains tannin. An infusion of the flowers and leaves in hot water and applied as a poultice to sprains and rheumatic joints will give pleasing relief. *This is a potentially dangerous herb when taken internally. It must never be taken during pregnancy.*

Culinary uses. It may be used fresh or dried in stuffings to accompany turkey and pork and for seasoning sausages. It also makes a delicious butter. Finely chop a fresh young leaf and one of sage and several of mint and beat to a creamy consistency 230 g ($\frac{1}{2}$ lb) of butter. Then mix in the herbs and use as a spreading for egg or cheese sandwiches. A young leaf or two may also be used in soups and stews.

Other uses. Tansy was one of Tusser's strewing herbs for besides releasing a pleasant camphor smell to freshen the mustiness of those rooms which had no damp course, it kept away fleas and lice. For the same reason its dried leaves were placed in muslin bags to put in beds and among clothes and linen. The fresh leaves were rubbed on meat before cooking, to take away the strong taste in warm weather. Coles, in his *Art of Simpling*, advised soaking a few leaves in buttermilk for ten days, then applying to the face, 'when it would make the complexion very fair'. It makes a soothing complexion milk especially when the skin has become sore by strong winds or by long exposure to sunlight.

Tarragon (*Artemisia dracunculus*)

Its botanical name is derived from its serpent-like roots (a little dragon) and its country name from the French translation, *esdragon*, of the same meaning. There are two forms, the French and the Russian, both of which grow naturally in Russia and Central Asia. The French is the better form. It is known as French tarragon for it is that used on the Continent to make tarragon vinegar but it is not as hardy as Russian tarragon which should be grown in colder regions.

Description. French tarragon grows about 60 cm (2 ft) tall and has branching stems and pointed lance-shaped leaves of darkest green. Russian tarragon grows 90 cm (3 ft) tall and has pale green leaves which are slightly rough to the touch. The flowers are white and drooping, with tubular disc-florets and are borne in July and August. French tarragon needs winter protection, such as ashes or sand placed over and around the base of the plants.

Culture. Propagation is from cuttings taken in July and rooted in boxes/pots filled with sandy soil. When rooted, move to small pots and plant out in spring 60 cm (2 ft) apart. Tarragon requires a well-drained soil for it to be long-lasting in the border and an open, sunny situation. Propagation is also by root division in spring or from seed sown in boxes in spring, in a frame or sunny window. When large enough to transplant, grow on in small pots and plant out in April.

Culinary uses. It has no medicinal uses but it is grown commercially in France to make tarragon vinegar which is the most important ingredient of mayonnaise and tartare sauce. It is also included in the best Dijon mustards. To make it, collect 230 g ($\frac{1}{2}$ lb) of young leaves and place in a wide-topped glass jar. Fill up with a pint of white wine and a pint of malt vinegar and allow to stand for twelve to fourteen days. Then strain into bottles and store in a dark place to use as required. A few tarragon leaves should be included in pickles. Tarragon can be dried and used in winter, the stems cut away in September and strung up in an airy room; or it can be cut in summer and after blanching for a few minutes, placed in plastic bags and in the deep freeze unit. It will keep as fresh as parsley. The leaves may also be frozen in ice cubes in the refrigerator to use in summer drinks, to which the tarragon will impart a pleasant balsamic flavour. A pinch of tarragon improves the taste of omelettes and soups.

Thyme (*Thymus vulgaris*)

The common or garden thyme and its closely related species and varieties is native of S. Europe and of the islands of Corsica and Sardinia, also N. Africa; it was introduced into England during Tudor times. Parkinson described eleven species, including the lemon-scented, with 'the smell of Pome-citron' and the gilded thyme *T.* × *citriodorus* 'Aureus' with its scent of balm and golden leaf markings. He added 'we preserve them with all the care we can in our gardens for the sweet and pleasant scents they yield'. Virgil suggested it for fumigating buildings and for the Greeks, 'to smell of thyme' was the highest praise a person could bestow upon another. Bees delight in visiting the flowers and thyme honey of mount Hymettus in Greece has been appreciated for at least 2000 years.

Description. A hardy perennial shrublet growing from 7.5–25 cm (3–10 in) depending upon species and variety, with slender wiry stems and tiny elliptical leaves set in pairs along the stems, dark green above, grey on the underside. The purple flowers are borne in conical clusters from June until September.

The thymes grow well in sandy soil with a high lime content. There are a number of species and varieties: 'Silver Posie' has rose tinted stems and leaves which are splashed with silver, while 'Aureum' is a golden-leaf form of the lemon-scented thyme, *T. × citriodorus*. Of the other thymes, *T. caespitatus* releases the scent of pine trees when the leaves are pressed, *T. carnosus* that of camphor, *T. odoratissimus* of apples, and *T. fragrantissimus* of oranges. *T. herba-barona*, to use in cooking baron of beef and steaks, has a unique caraway scent and pretty fern-like leaves. These thymes grow about 15 cm (6 in) tall and remain green all year. They should be planted to the front of a border or preferably between paving stones over which they will spread in a delightful way. The fruit-scented thymes are used in pot-pourris and sweet bags to place among clothes, mixed with rosemary and lavender and red rose petals.

Culture. As for most woody plants, propagation is from cuttings, removed in July, with a 'heel' attached and rooted in pots or boxes of sandy soil in a frame or sunny window. Plants of the common thyme may also be raised from seed sown in spring in boxes of sandy compost in a frame. Grow on the seedlings in small pots and plant out in the following spring. Plant about 25 cm (10 in) apart and in an open sunny position. No amount of sunshine and drought will harm the plants. They require a well-drained soil containing some mortar (lime rubble) or lime and may be damaged in severe winters. To harvest the thymes, cut the plants well back in July and again in autumn. This will keep them free of old wood and bushy. Tie into bunches and string up in an airy room to dry, then rub down the leaves.

Medicinal uses. Thymol, present in the essential oil, is a valuable antiseptic. It is also highly agreeable to use. A few drops of oil of thyme (thymol) in a jugful of boiling water will give relief to a stuffed up nose or head cold if inhaled for ten minutes. It will also ease a sore throat if inhaled through the mouth. As a healing and cleansing lotion, to use on skin sores and pimples, dissolve five grains of thymol in 28 g (1 oz) spirits of wine and 28 g (1 oz) of glycerine. Pour into a bottle and add a small cupful of water. Shake up well before applying to the sores with lint. Thyme and rosemary together make an excellent hair rinse and if massaged into the scalp will keep the hair healthy and free from dandruff. The pounded leaves mixed with a little honey and given a teaspoonful two or three times daily, will give relief to whooping cough. Leaves or tops (or the dried herb) (30 g (1 oz)) infused in 0.5 litre (1 pint) of boiling water and sweetened with a little honey, is excellent to relieve a hard cough or tight chest if taken hot at bedtime. It is also a carminative and if taken cold in summer, is an excellent restorative during hot weather. Thyme 'tea' taken warm will relieve indigestion and warm the stomach during colic brought on by cold weather. Thyme provides more simple remedies than any other herb.

Culinary uses. It is used to give piquancy to pickled gherkins and in Spain and Italy, to pickled olives. It is one of the chief ingredients of all stuffings though for this purpose, the lemon thyme is preferable, with its distinctive lemon flavour. The leaves and tops may also be used to flavour soups and stews and one or two leaves of orange or lemon thyme finely chopped and scattered in a salad will add a delicious taste.

Valerian (*Valeriana officinalis*)
Chaucer called it setwall for it is seen growing on the walls of old buildings though this may in fact have been *Centranthus ruber*, the red valerian. Its name is derived from the Latin *valeo*, to be well, for it has so many medicinal qualities. Native to Europe and temperate Asia, it is grown commercially for its roots which have a most unpleasant smell which resembles that of stale perspiration. This is because, when exposed to air upon lifting, the essential oil becomes oxidized to form the unpleasant smelling valeric acid.

Description. A glabrous perennial growing 60–90 cm (2–3 ft) tall with pinnate leaves and lanceolate leaflets, mostly toothed. The pale pink flowers are borne in a terminal cyme, each floret having a long tube and they are visited in daytime by butterflies. In bloom July–September, *V. officinalis* is found mostly in damp places, in woodlands, hedgerows and by the sides of streams.

Culture. It is propagated from offsets removed with a piece of root and planted into ordinary soil containing some humus. Plant in autumn or spring 60 cm (2 ft) apart for it grows as wide as it grows tall. It is also readily raised from seed sown in spring in pots or boxes; it is transplanted to small pots and grown on for setting out in autumn.

Medicinal uses. A decoction of the roots is given in times of stress or for nervous exhaustion and as a carminative. The juice of the root is given for insomnia and is also a useful remedy for colic. A decoction of the roots will relieve a nervous headache and the leaves, boiled in 230 g ($\frac{1}{2}$ lb) of lard and cooled, make a reliable healing ointment. It now has no culinary uses.

Vervain (*Verbena officinalis*)

It is not the lemon-scented verbena of the perfumers but since earliest times has been revered for its medicinal qualities. The plant has long been known for its mystic qualities, the Druids holding it in the same veneration reserved for mistletoe, dedicating it to Isis, goddess of birth. Later, its mystic powers caused it to be used in love potions, maidens smearing their body with the juice in the hope that it would grant their wish in the choice of a husband. The Druids sent the dried plant to Rome for use in making healing salves and ointments so that in Italy, it has always been known as *Planta britannica*. In Germany, until the end of the 19th century, a hat made from the long wiry stems of the plant was given to newly married women to put them under the protection of Venus. The plant was used in sacrificial rites by witches to make their spells.

Description. A hairy perennial with thin square stems growing to 60 cm (2 ft) tall, with unstalked opposite leaves and bearing pale mauve flowers in elegant spikes. It is present in damp places but usually in limestone soils, is found from the British Isles across Central Europe to the China coast, and has been naturalized in N. America.

Culture. Though most frequently found in limestone districts, it is a charming plant for the herb border and is raised from seed sown in spring in shallow drills, or in pots or boxes in a frame or sunny window. Set out the plants towards the end of summer 45 cm (18 in) apart in a well-drained soil and sunny position. It is also increased by division of the roots in spring.

Medicinal uses. An infusion of the leaves and tops makes a pleasant 'tea' with a few drops of lemon juice added and sweetened with a little honey; if taken at bedtime it will encourage sound sleep. It is also used for tired eyes. Make an infusion of the leaves and tops and when still lukewarm, bathe the eyes with lint, preferably at bedtime. If bathed daily for several weeks, the eyes will be refreshed and will have sparkle. Pasteur advised using the same infusion to massage into the scalp, preferably with rosemary and the two together make an excellent tonic rinse for the hair. They will promote the growth of new hair and give the head a lustre. A decoction of the tops, a handful to a pint of hot water, and taken hot, a wineglassful daily, will help colic pains while the same may be used to bathe piles. It has no culinary uses.

Wall germander (*Teucrium chamaedrys*)

A labiate native to central and southern Europe and naturalized southwards as far as England and Wales. Tusser included it with his herbs for strewing, Sir Hugh Platt, in the 16th century, suggested growing it in pots in dark rooms; as Parkinson said 'it was pretty and sweet, with a refreshing lemony scent', like that of balm and lemon thyme for which reason the dried leaves were included in pot-pourris.

Description. It is a shrubby perennial growing 15–25 cm (6–10 in) tall and the same across. If kept under control by constantly cutting and using the shoots, Parkinson said it was excellent for making 'knot' beds. The small ovate leaves, hairy on the underside, and coarsely serrate are like small oak leaves hence its name, ground oak. The quite large rosy-purple flowers are borne in a one-sided raceme during June and July.

Culture. It is increased by cuttings of the half-ripened wood which are removed in July and inserted 2.5 cm (1 in) apart in sandy compost in a frame; or from seed sown in boxes or pots in a frame in April. Plant at the front of a border or in small beds 30 cm (12 in) apart and keep it under control by regular clipping. The plant can also be grown in pots or on a wall for it can survive long periods without much moisture. The whole herb is used, the stems, leaves and flowers.

Medicinal uses. It contains a bitter principle; this acts as a tonic which is made by cutting a handful of the leafy shoots and immersing for several minutes in half a litre (1 pint) of boiling water. Strain and drink when cool, a wineglassful each day. The same, taken each day for two months, is said to have completely cured the Emperor Charles V of his troublesome gout. A decoction of the herb, sweetened with a little honey and taken hot, will break up a hard cough. It will also clear the kidneys of impurities.

Other uses. The dried leaves mixed with rosemary and placed in a muslin bag were carried about during warm weather and inhaled at frequent intervals to 'lift the spirits' or refresh when tired. The leaves were also used in dry pot-pourris.

Watercress (*Nasturtium officinale* syn. *Rorippa nasturtium-aquaticum*)

For its mineral salts, it has been appreciated since earliest times. Culpeper said 'they that will live in health may eat watercress if they please: and if they do not, I cannot help it'.

Watercress
(*Nasturtium officinale*
syn. *Rorippa nasturtium-
aquaticum*)

It is of the Cruciferae family, the plants of which are rich in mineral salts, including iron and sulphur, phosphates and potash. So rich in iron is it that if the cut leaves and stems are left in the sun, they will turn brownish-purple, due to the oxidization of the iron salts. The American dietician Mr. Gaylord Hauser, believes it to be, with parsley, the most valuable of all plants for promoting good health and advises putting a bunch through the electric mixer each day and drinking the juice. The taste is improved if mixed with a few drops of lemon juice. It will tone the system and help to keep the complexion free from blemishes.

Description. An aquatic perennial with hollow stems and evergreen pinnate leaves. It bears small white flowers during July and August and increases by underground stems. The plant grows in marshlands and streams. Although native only to Europe and Asia it is naturalized in many parts of the world, but is also grown commercially to supply the all year demand from hotels and greengrocers, usually in warm sites where it can continue growing through the winter.

Culture. The plants need running water and beds are made in streams which do not dry up in summer. The beds are made 2 m (about 6 ft) wide with several inches of soil and manure at the base and the rooted cuttings or offsets are planted 7.5 cm (3 in) apart and so that there is about 10 cm (4 in) of water above the roots. If set out early in summer, the beds will be established before winter. If the winter is cold, place frames made of wood and plastic sheeting over the beds. The shoots are cut when about 15 cm (6 in) high and are made into bunches of a size that will go between the finger and thumb.

Medicinal uses. It is a blood purifier. It should be eaten fresh and every day, with an omelette or scrambled eggs, with steak or chops, or in a salad with other herbs. It may be used, like betony to apply to the temples after soaking the leaves in warm water, to relieve a headache, preferably when lying down for an hour in a darkened room. A bunch of watercress put through a mixer and the juice taken daily, will clear the skin of blemishes, as noted above.

Culinary uses. Parkinson said that 'Dutchmen eat cress with bread and butter' and because it is bitter, it is delicious in a salad, with oranges or in a sandwich, with cream cheese. He suggested including it in a salad, with lettuce and purslane, served with a sprinkling of tarragon vinegar. It is a pleasing accompaniment to cold chicken, served either cold or hot, after dipping a bunch in hot vegetable oil and serving with tarragon vinegar and new potatoes, sprinkled with finely chopped parsley.

Water mint (*Mentha aquatica*)
It is also known as wild mint, whilst *M. longifolia* is the horse or garden mint. Of the former, Gerard wrote that its savour or smell '... rejoiceth the heart of man for which cause they strew it in chambers and banqueting halls'. The garden mint is perhaps a cultivated form of the horse mint and is used in the same way as spearmint.

Description. *M. aquatica* is a perennial growing 30–90 cm (1–3 ft) tall with stalked ovate leaves, usually hairy on both sides. They release a pungent scent when pressed. The reddish-purple flowers are borne in axillary and terminal whorls, the upper ones forming a head, July-September. The variety 'Crispa' has curled leaves and is one of the main sources of oil of spearmint for the crude oil consists of a terpene and also carvol which has exactly the same odour as that of spearmint. It is found by streams and on river banks, also in marshy ground throughout temperate Europe, S.W. Asia and temperate parts of Africa.

Culture. It requires a bed to itself or near other mints as it increases rapidly by underground roots. It is propagated from roots planted 5 cm (2 in) deep and 25 cm (10 in) apart in rich humus-laden soil in autumn or spring; they will grow well in partial shade.

Medicinal uses. A handful of leaves or tops when in bloom, placed in a warm bath will bring relief to tired and aching limbs and tone the body. Preferably, use it with rosemary or balm. The dried leaves or fresh tops 30 g (1 oz) infused in 0.5 litre (1 pint) of hot water and sweetened with a little honey, make a capital tonic drink, taken when hot or cold; it can also relieve flatulence and help in cases of diarrhoea when taken hot.

White horehound (*Marrubium vulgare*)
It is found in S. Europe, the Near East, N. Africa and the Atlantic islands. It takes its name from the Hebrew *marrob*, bitter juice, as it was one of the five bitter herbs of the Mishna which the Jews were ordered to take during the Feast of the Passover.

155

Description. It is a perennial, growing about 60 cm (2 ft) tall, its square stems covered in woolly down like hoar frost, whilst the oval, bluntly-toothed leaves are deeply grooved. It is a labiate and the white flowers are borne June-September, in dense whorls from the leafy bracts, much visited by bees. It is found by the roadside and on waste ground, on railway embankments and in hedgerows though it is never common. It is a handsome plant in the herb garden for it retains its grey-green foliage all winter. When warmed by the sun, it emits a delicious musky or honey scent and before the introduction of hops, a tonic beer was brewed from the leaves which were sold in the streets of London.

Culture. A hardy plant, it grows best in poor, well-drained soil and likes a sunny situation. It is propagated by root division in autumn, planted 40 cm (16 in) apart; or from seed sown in spring in shallow drills and thinned to 30 cm (12 in) apart.

Medicinal uses. To make horehound 'tea' which is an excellent tonic and appetiser, especially in spring and early summer after winter illness, pour half a litre (1 pint) of boiling water on to a handful of leaves. Strain when cold and take a wineglassful daily before lunch. For colds, strain and drink when hot, twice daily. Since medieval times it has been considered the best of herbal remedies for coughs and lung disorders, also for asthmatic complaints. Fresh horehound, hyssop and rue, 14 g ($\frac{1}{2}$ oz) each item, together with the same quantity of marshmallow and liquorice root boiled in 1.1 litre (2 pints) of water will ease a hard cough and tight chest and will act as a gentle laxative. For children, syrup of horehound, made by boiling the leaves with honey in a little water, is pleasant to take as is candied horehound. Boil a panful of leaves and stems in a very little water and when most of the juice has been extracted, add half a pound of sugar and boil slowly until dissolved. Pour into a shallow dish, cool and cut into 2.5 cm (1 in) squares. Keep in a closed tin and give a piece when-ever a cough is troublesome. The leaves lose their fragrance when dry but as in all but the coldest climates the plant remains green all the year, it can be used fresh at any time and is more effective when freshly gathered.

Wood betony (*Betonica officinalis*)

There is an old Italian proverb which says 'sell your coat and buy betony' for it has so many virtues. 'He (or she) has as many virtues as betony' is also an Italian saying and during the heyday of the Roman Empire, Antonius Musa, physician to the Emperor Augustus, wrote a treatise entirely about the medicinal qualities of the plant. Later, Parkinson said that the leaves 'by their sweet and spicy taste, are comfortable both in meat and medicine'. Culpeper wrote 'this is a precious herb, well worth keeping in your house'.

Description. It is a hairy perennial growing to 50 cm (20 in) tall with a slender stem and oblong deeply crenate leaves, the lower stalked, the upper sessile. The purple-red flowers are borne in a terminal spike in July and August and are much visited by bees. It is present in damp woodlands and hedgerows throughout most of Europe, though not in the extreme south.

Culture. It enjoys semi-shade and soil containing humus to retain summer moisture but which is well-drained in winter, when it will prove a handsome border plant with its elegant flower spikes and dark green leaves. Plant 60 cm (2 ft) apart in autumn or spring. It is propagated by root division or from seeds sown in boxes or pots in a frame; or, cover with glass or plastic to hasten germination. Transplant when large enough to handle and move to the border in autumn or spring.

Medicinal uses. To relieve head pains brought about by a stuffy atmosphere, a pinch of the dried leaves taken as snuff will bring quick relief. It will also unblock the mucous membranes of the nose during a head cold. The warm damp leaves placed on the temples when one is lying down and held in place by a cloth wrapped round the head, will ease the most stubborn headache and from the fresh or dry leaves a 'tea' is made which will bring relief to a nervous headache. To a handful of fresh leaves or a teaspoonful of dried leaves, add half a litre (1 pint) of hot water and take a wineglassful as required. It was for the relief of head pains that betony reigned supreme and which also earned it a reputation as being good against 'fearful visions'. Indeed, the plant takes its name from Celtic words *bew*, head, and *ton*, good, or 'good for the head' which it is. The best time to use the fresh leaves and also to dry them is July and August. It is also carminative.

Wood germander (*Teucrium scorodonia*)

It differs from wall germander in that its leaves are larger, like those of sage, hence its other name of wood sage but it takes its botanical name from an ancient king of Troy named Teucer who is said to have made many cures with the plant.

Description. It is a hairy perennial with a creeping rootstock; it grows about 30 cm (12 in) tall with grey-green oblong leaves, coarsely toothed and deeply grooved, like those of sage. The yellow and purple flowers are smaller than those of wall germander and are borne from July-September in dense spikes. It is a plant of open woodlands, confined largely to the countries of western Europe.

Culture. It is propagated from seed or by root division in spring, the plants set out 30 cm (12 in) apart; it prefers a well-drained sandy soil. Alternatively, grow it from seed sown in boxes in a frame in spring, growing on the young plants in small pots and planting out the following spring.

Medicinal uses. It contains a bitter principle which gives it a special value for a tonic drink. Immerse a handful of the tops in half a litre (1 pint) of water and simmer for 30 mins. Strain and take a wineglassful daily. It will tone up the whole system. At one time it was used in brewing ale which it clarifies and to which it imparts its appetising bitter taste, like that of hops.

Wood sorrel (*Oxalis acetosella*)

It is a woodland plant found in all parts of temperate Europe and across Asia to Japan. The plant takes its name from the Greek *oxys*, acid, for oxalic acid (as in lemons) is present in its stems and leaves; also present is oxalate of potash, a restorative. It was known as wood sour and with its ternate leaves was associated with the Trinity, the Italian masters depicting it in their religious paintings.

Description. It is a dainty perennial which sends up its trifoliate leaves on long stalks

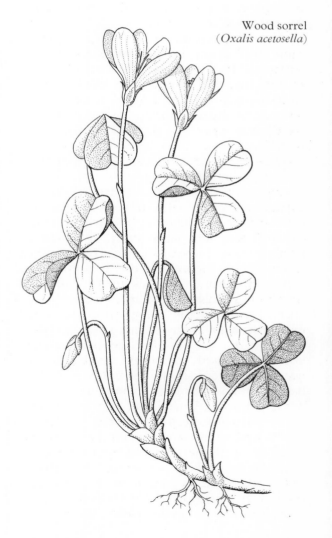

Wood sorrel
(*Oxalis acetosella*)

directly from the rootstock. The leaves are bright green above, purple on the underside and they fold up at night or in dull weather. The flowers which appear in April and May are of a delicate paper white, veined with purple and are borne on long slender stalks.

Culture. The creeping roots should be planted in semi-shade and in a soil containing some humus. Plant them in autumn, just below the surface and at the front of a border or on a rockery. Propagation is by root division.

Medicinal uses. No longer used in cooking, it is a blood purifier and an antiscorbutic which will quench the thirst during fever as well as reducing the temperature. An infusion of a small handful of leaves, fresh or dried, in half a litre (1 pint) of hot water or milk and taken a wineglassful twice daily, will purify the blood. With its potash content it acts as a tonic drink but because it contains oxalic acid, it should be avoided by those suffering from rheumatism or kidney complaints.

Woodruff (*Asperula odorata*, now more correctly *Galium odoratum*)

A native of Europe and parts of Asia, it takes its country name from its habitat and from the Anglo-Saxon *rofe*, a wheel, hence woodrof and then woodruff, this being an allusion to the wheel-like formation of its leaves. From the same word is derived the ruff worn around the neck in the 16th century and similarly wheel-like in shape.

Description. It is a prostrate perennial with erect four-angled stems growing 15–20 cm (6–8 in) tall, the dark green lanceolate leaves produced in whorls at regular intervals along the stem. The leaves have stiff hairs at the margins. The tiny flowers, which appear April–June, are white and borne in loose terminal heads. Like the leaves and stem, they smell of coumarin when dry so that all parts of the plant can be used. It will retain its fragrance for several years and can be included in dry potpourris. Widespread in open woodlands and hedgerows, it is a shade lover.

Culture. It is a charming plant where used to edge a shady path or to grow at the front of the herb border. Seed is sown in spring in ordinary soil, the plants being thinned to 15 cm (6 in) apart.

Medicinal uses. It makes a pleasant tonic drink and is a blood purifier. Take a handful of the fresh stems and infuse in half a litre (1 pint) of boiling water, keeping a lid on to prevent the steam escaping. When cool, take a wineglassful daily in summer.

Other uses. The plant was used to hang up in musty rooms to scent the air for, as it dries, it releases the pleasant smell of newly-mown hay. This is because it contains the sweetly scented principle, coumarin, which is also present in the sweet vernal grass of hay; the drier it becomes the more scent does it release. Water distilled from the fresh plant was applied to the complexion and took away any soreness caused by long exposure to winds and sunlight. It is also a moth deterrent and was put into muslin bags to place amongst clothes to which it imparted its refreshing smell. The dried leaves were also put into pillows and mattresses which when slept upon and warmed by the body would release a pleasing scent. It was included with hops to bring about sound sleep. In the 18th century, the whorls of eight or nine leaves were cut from the stem just above and below each whorl and were placed in the back of gold pocket watches so that in a stuffy atmosphere or where there were unpleasant smells, the back of the watch was opened and the refreshing smell inhaled. The dried and powdered leaves were also used to flavour snuffs, wines and liqueurs.

Wormwood (*Artemisia absinthium*)

It is present throughout the temperate regions of the world where it has been spread by man. In medieval times it was famed for its tonic qualities and ability to keep houses free of fleas, moths and lice. Tusser asks 'What saver is better (if physic be true) for places infected, than wormwood and rue.' With rue, it is the most bitter herb and was

Lady's Smock *(Cardamine pratensis)*. About 38 cm (15 in) tall, this attractive perennial is also known as meadow cress or bitter cress. It has a similar taste to watercress, to which it is related, and can be used in salads.

Marjoram *(Origanum vulgare)*. There are several species of Marjoram with valuable culinary uses while sweet Marjoram *(O. marjorama)* has long been used in sweet bags and pot-pourris. Chief culinary uses are as an ingredient of a 'bouquet garni' and, in its dried form, as a stuffing for pork and veal.

Rue *(Ruta graviolens)*. A glaucous evergreen growing to a height of 60 cm (2 ft), with distinctively-coloured leaves which, when handled, emit a pungent scent. The scent is so strong that when, for example, the herb is scattered over the floor of poultry houses, flies and fleas are said to be driven away. If used very sparingly the herb can be used to flavour omelettes and salads.

used in the making of ale before hops were introduced.

Description. It is a handsome grey-green perennial growing up to 60 cm (2 ft) tall and bushy, with angled stems and leaves divided into blunt segments or lobes. The dull yellow flowers, like those of mimosa are borne in panicles during July and August. It is common on waste land and by roadsides.

Culture. It retains its leaves through winter and is a most handsome border plant to accompany rue and sage whose purple flowers are an ideal complement. It is propagated by root division in autumn or spring, planted 60 cm (2 ft) apart and into well-drained soil. It is tolerant of sunshine or shade.

Medicinal uses. It makes a tonic drink or 'tea'. This is made by infusing a handful of leaves or tops in half a litre (1 pint) of boiling water, covering it to retain the steam. Sweeten with a little honey and when cool (and preferably iced), take a wineglassful daily, but not too frequently, and never during pregnancy. It is a remedy for stomach disorders. The herb is used to make the liqueur, absinthe and provides the bitter principle in vermouth, which means 'preserver of the mind', a drink with powers of invigoration. A few drops of essential oil together with that of rosemary or bay rum massaged daily into the scalp will prevent falling hair and give the hair a shine. The leaves and tops placed in hot water can be used as a poultice. After draining, place in a muslin bag and apply to bruises and rheumatic parts, as warm as possible, when it will be most soothing.

Other uses. The dried leaves, placed among clothes and furs, will keep them free from moths and if a bunch of fresh stems is hung up in a room, it will keep it free from flies in summer. It will also keep the air cool.

Yarrow (*Achillea millefolium*)

The botanical name is from the Greek warrior, Achilles who is said to have been told of its healing qualities by the centaur,

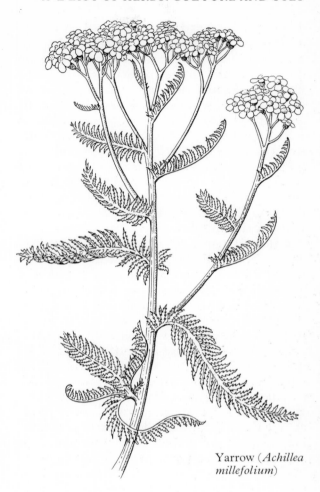

Yarrow (*Achillea millefolium*)

Chiron and so cured the wounds of his soldiers with the leaves. The name yarrow is derived from the Greek *hiera*, a holy herb, for it had so many virtues; it was also the most important plant of witches' spells and was the favourite of lovesick maidens who would pluck the flowers and put them on their pillow, chanting as they got into bed: '... In a dream this night, I hope my true love will appear'.

Description. It is perennial growing 30 cm (20 in) tall with erect downy stems and bipinnate leaves, the dark green leaflets cut into hair-like segments. Eucalyptol is present and gives the plant its herby smell. The flowers, borne June until mid-September, are usually palest lilac and are also scented.

They yield a dark blue volatile oil. A native of Europe and Asia, it has been taken to most of the temperate world where it grows by waysides and in pastures.

Culture. It increases by its creeping rootstock and is propagated by root division in autumn or spring. It is happy in ordinary well-drained soil but requires an open, sunny situation. Plant 60 cm (2 ft) apart and for the border, the varieties 'Cerise Queen' and 'Fire King' are most striking. The flower stems can be cut and hung up in an airy room to dry, to use for indoor decoration with everlasting flowers.

Medicinal uses. In France, the plant has always been called herbe aux carpentiers for it was grown in the gardens of carpenters everywhere, who used the leaves to bind over cuts made by their tools which it would soon heal, as the leaves are styptic,. An infusion of the leaves will help to sweat out a cold or a fever. Infuse a handful of leaves in half a litre (1 pint) of hot water, add a little lemon juice and a teaspoonful of honey; take a wineglassful twice daily, including once late evening. The same infusion is used as a gargle to ease a sore throat and as a hair wash (preferably with rosemary) to stimulate the hair and prevent falling hair. To relieve piles, the leaves macerated in warm lard and allowed to cool, may be used whenever necessary and especially at bedtime.

Yellow gentian (*Gentiana lutea*)

Named in honour of the Illyrian king, Gentius, it is found in the Alpine regions of central and S. Europe from the Pyrenees to the Balkans and in Corsica and Sardinia. Elsewhere it is a garden plant and before the introduction of hops was cultivated to use in the brewing of ale to which it imparted a bitter principle which stimulated the appetite. In Germany it is still used to make a tonic beer 'gentian bitters'.

Description. It is a perennial growing about 1.5 m (4–5 ft) tall with oblong ovate leaves, with prominent veins on the underside. The flowers are yellow, spotted with black and appear in whorls from the upper part of the stems in July and August. Gerard described it as a handsome border plant.

Culture. It is the roots that are used to make tonic bitters and where required for this purpose, it is grown in the vegetable garden, from seed sown in spring in shallow drills made 60 cm (2 ft) apart. Thin to about 40 cm (16 in) in the rows and support the plants as they grow tall by strong twine taken along the rows. The foliage will die back in winter but comes again in spring. The plants are allowed to grow for two years before the roots are lifted and used. This is done in autumn when the plants begin to die back, the small pieces of root (offsets) being replanted to grow on for two more years; they may also be planted at the back of the border. It requires a deeply worked soil. The roots are cleaned and dried before using.

Medicinal uses. The roots are yellow when lifted but become dark brown when dry. Gentian bitters is an excellent tonic for those suffering from debility after illness; it eases the stomach during periods of colic and stimulates the appetite. To make a 'pick-me-up' drink, place 30 g (1 oz) of the crushed root and 30 g (1 oz) of orange peel, together with 15 g ($\frac{1}{2}$ oz) crushed coriander seed in a jug and pour over, two large cupfuls of white wine. Leave for several hours, strain and take a sherry-glassful each day. Culpeper said that when steeped in white wine and taken (a small wineglassful) daily, 'it would refresh those such as be weary with travel, and grown lame in their joints either by cold or evil lodgings'; Parkinson said that although so bitter 'the wonderful wholesomeness of gentian cannot be easily known to us by reason that our daintie tastes refuse to take thereof, for the bitterness sake, otherwise it would undoubtedly work admirable cures'.

APPENDICES

Medicinal herbs

Culinary herbs

Herbs for miscellaneous uses

Medicinal herbs

Antiscorbutics

Bogbean
Brooklime
Dandelion
Ladies' smock
Nasturtium
Scurvy grass
Shepherd's purse
Sorrel
Watercress

Antiseptics

Agrimony
Balm
Mustard
Peppermint
Rue
Sorrel
Southernwood
St. John's wort
Thyme
Wormwood

To ease asthma

Anise
Coltsfoot
Elecampane
Feverfew
Garlic
Ground ivy
Mullein
Red rose

Blood purifiers

Bogbean
Brooklime
Burdock

Agrimony, common
Dandelion
Garlic
Ground ivy
Hops
Ladies' smock
Mugwort
Nasturtium
Watercress
Wormwood

For bronchitis and tight chest (expectorants)

Angelica
Anise
Coltsfoot
Elecampane
Feverfew
Garlic
Ground ivy
Horehound
Mustard
Peppermint
Red rose
Sage
Thyme

For bruises

Hyssop
Shepherd's purse

For coughs (expectorants)

Coltsfoot
Elecampane
Horehound
Liquorice
Peppermint

Demulcents

Bistort
Comfrey
Lesser periwinkle
Lungwort
Marshmallow
Shepherd's purse
Vervain

For diarrhoea (astringent)

Burnet
Chamomile
Comfrey
Meadowsweet
Mint
Red rose
Savory (summer & winter)
Shepherd's purse
Vervain

Embrocations

Cumin
Garlic
Horseradish
Lavender
Pennyroyal

External healing herbs

Balm
Burnet, great
Garlic
Ground ivy
Hyssop
Lady's mantle
Lesser periwinkle
Marigold
Primrose
St. John's wort
Shepherd's purse
Sorrel
Southernwood
Thyme
Vervain
Wormwood

To bathe the eyes

Agrimony, common
Chicory (succory)

Clary
Fennel
Marigold
Pennyroyal
Vervain

For flatulence and indigestion

Angelica
Anise
Calamint
Centaury
Chamomile
Coriander
Dill
Elecampane
Fennel
Hyssop
Mustard
Sage
Summer savory
Thyme
Wormwood

For foot baths

Bay
Bergamot
Cotton lavender
Ground ivy
Marjoram
Mustard (black)
Rosemary
Thyme

To relieve giddiness

Cowslip
Parsley
Rue
Spearmint
Tansy

To ease haemorrhoids

Elecampane
Lesser periwinkle
Mullein
Yarrow

To ease a headache

Lavender
Marjoram

Parsley
Pennyroyal
Rosemary
Rue
Sage
Tansy
Wood betony

To heal and cleanse the skin

Centaury
Chicory
Cowslip
Feverfew
Horseradish
Lily of the valley
Marigold
Red rose
Shepherd's purse
Tansy
Watercress

Healing ointments

Costmary
Garlic
Horseradish
Lovage
Marigold
Marjoram
Marshmallow
Mullein
Pennyroyal
Primrose
St. John's wort
Southernwood
Valerian
Yarrow

To strengthen the heart

Lily of the valley
Marigold

For hiccups

Anise
Caraway
Dill
Mustard (black)
Spearmint

For a hot fomentation

Chamomile
Marshmallow
Mustard (black)
Nettle

Laxatives

Chervil
Dandelion
Fennel
Hyssop
Liquorice
Sage
Succory

For a mouth wash

Chamomile
Sage

For palpitation

Lavender
Nettle

Restoratives (invigorators)

Alkanet
Balm
Borage
Lavender
Liquorice
Marjoram
Rosemary
Sorrel
Southernwood
Tansy
Thyme
Watercress
Wormwood

For rheumatism and sciatica

Angelica
Calamint
Cumin
Garlic
Horseradish
Hyssop
Marjoram
Nettle
Rue
Sage
Yarrow

Sleep inducing herbs

Anise
Coriander
Cowslip
Herb bennet
Hops
Marigold
Pennyroyal
Southernwood
Valerian
Vervain
Woodruff

As a gargle for a sore throat

Coltsfoot
Horseradish
Liquorice
Pennyroyal
Sage
Tansy
Thyme
Yarrow

For sunburn

Centaury
Marigold
Marshmallow
St. John's wort

To reduce a temperature

Chamomile
Feverfew
Marigold
Ox-eye daisy
Peppermint
Red rose
Sorrel
Vervain
Yarrow

For tonic beers

Angelica
Dandelion
Hops
Liquorice
Mugwort
Wormwood

For tonic drinks

Alkanet
Balm
Bergamot
Bogbean
Burdock
Burnet, great
Calamint
Dandelion
Feverfew
Ground ivy
Holy thistle
Hops
Hyssop
Lavender
Lovage
Marigold
Marjoram
Mint
Ox-eye daisy
Pennyroyal
Peppermint
Sage
Tansy
Wall germander
Wood germander
Yellow gentian

Tranquillizers and carminatives

Angelica
Balm
Bergamot
Catmint
Centaury
Chamomile
Coriander
Cowslip
Cumin
Dill
Feverfew
Fennel
Hops
Mugwort
Mullein
Parsley
Pennyroyal
Rosemary

Rue
Sage
Thyme
Valerian
Winter savory
Wood betony

For wasp and bee stings

Feverfew
Marigold
Savory (summer and winter)
Spearmint

For whooping cough

Clover
Coltsfoot
Garlic
Horseradish
Thyme

Culinary herbs

Herbs to clarify ale

Balm
Costmary
Ground ivy
Hops
Mugwort
Wood germander
Wormwood

To make a conserve

Cowslip
Primrose
Red rose

Herbs with edible flowers

Alkanet
Borage
Cowslip
Lavender
Marigold
Nasturtium
Primrose
Red rose
Rosemary
Sage

Herbs with edible roots

Alexanders
Caraway
Chicory (tops)
Eryngium (sea holly)
Rampion
Sweet cicely

To flavour drinks

Alkanet
Balm
Bergamot

Borage
Burnet, salad
Marjoram
Meadowsweet
Rosemary

To flavour soups and stews

Alexanders
Basil
Costmary
Dandelion
English mace
Feverfew
Fennel
Hyssop
Lovage
Marigold
Marjoram
Parsley
Savory, summer
Sorrel
Sweet cicely
Tansy

For pickling (seeds)

Dill
Nasturtium

Salad herbs

Agrimony, common
Balm
Bogbean
Borage
Burnet, salad
Chervil
Chicory
Chives
Cowslip

Dandelion
Ladies' smock
Lovage
Marigold
Nasturtium
Primrose
Rampion
Shepherd's purse
Sorrel
Watercress

Herbs for sauces

Chervil
Dill
Fennel
Horseradish
Mint(s)
Mustard (black)
Nasturtium
Parsley
Sorrel
Tarragon

For seasonings and stuffings

Bistort
Curry plant
English mace
Marjoram
Mugwort
Pennyroyal
Sage

Savory (summer & winter)
Tansy
Thyme

Seeds for flavouring

Alexanders
Anise
Caraway
Coriander
Cumin
Dill
Fennel
Lovage
Parsley

Herbs as vegetables

Bistort
Corn salad (lamb's lettuce)
Fennel
Good King Henry
Hops (shoots)
Lovage (shoots)
Sorrel
Chicory (succory)

To make a wine (flowers)

Agrimony, common
Cowslip
Dandelion
Hops
Primrose

Herbs for miscellaneous uses

Deodorants

Horseradish
Mustard (black)

Fly deterrents

Anise
Basil
Chamomile
Mugwort
Pennyroyal
Peppermint
Rue
Tansy

Herbs to freshen the air indoors

Balm
Bay
Germander
Hyssop
Lavender
Peppermint
Rosemary
Thyme
Wormwood

Hair tonics and restoratives

Chamomile
Rosemary
Sage (for darkening)
Southernwood
Thyme
Vervain
Wormwood

Moth deterrents

Calamint
Cotton lavender

Feverfew
Mugwort
Pennyroyal
Rue
Southernwood
Tansy
Woodruff
Wormwood

Herbs for pot-pourris and sweet jars

Agrimony, fragrant
Balm
Bay
Bergamot
Costmary
Hyssop
Marjoram, sweet
Meadowsweet
Rose
Rosemary
Sage (pineapple-scented)
Southernwood
Woodruff

Herbs to scent a bath

Agrimony, fragrant
Bay
Bergamot
Chamomile
Germander
Lavender
Marjoram, sweet
Mugwort
Pennyroyal
Peppermint
Rosemary
Watermint

To scent (fumigate) a room

Angelica
Bay
Lavender
Rosemary
Thyme

For a smoker's mixture

Bergamot
Chamomile
Coltsfoot
Cotton lavender
Ox-eye daisy
Sage
Thyme
Wood betony

For snuffs

Basil
Chamomile
Clary
Ground ivy
Wood betony
Woodruff

For sweet bags and sachets

Cotton lavender
Hyssop
Lavender
Marjoram, sweet
Meadowsweet
Red Rose
Rosemary
Southernwood
Thyme (orange-scented)
Woodruff

Index